Engineering A Financial Bloodbath

HOW SUB-PRIME SECURITIZATION DESTROYED THE LEGITIMACY OF FINANCIAL CAPITALISM

Engineering A Financial Bloodbath

HOW SUB-PRIME SECURITIZATION DESTROYED THE LEGITIMACY OF FINANCIAL CAPITALISM

Justin O'Brien

Queensland University of Technology in Brisbane, University of Glasgow, UK and Centre for Applied Philosophy and Public Ethics, Australian National University, Canberra

Imperial College Press

ICP

Published by

Imperial College Press
57 Shelton Street
Covent Garden
London WC2H 9HE

Distributed by

World Scientific Publishing Co. Pte. Ltd.
5 Toh Tuck Link, Singapore 596224
USA office: 27 Warren Street, Suite 401-402, Hackensack, NJ 07601
UK office: 57 Shelton Street, Covent Garden, London WC2H 9HE

British Library Cataloguing-in-Publication Data
A catalogue record for this book is available from the British Library.

ENGINEERING A FINANCIAL BLOODBATH
How Sub-Prime Securitization Destroyed the Legitimacy of Financial Capitalism

ISBN-13 978-1-84816-216-7
ISBN-10 1-84816-216-2

Printed by FuIsland Offset Printing (S) Pte Ptd. Singapore

For Jennifer

When all that story's finished, what's the news?
In luck or out the toil has left its mark:
That old perplexity an empty purse,
Or the day's vanity, the night's remorse.

W.B. Yeats

Preface

Every day brings further evidence of how dysfunctional capital markets have become across the world. The global financial crisis is the latest, if most catastrophic, in a series of boom-bust-regulate-deregulate-boom-bust cycles. As the impact moves progressively and decisively from Wall Street to Main Street, the enormous political, conceptual, and socio-economic costs associated with a failure to address the question of the role of the corporation and markets more generally in society comes into clear view. The President of the United States, Barack Obama, has promised to fundamentally review the structure of financial regulation following what he termed "the winter of our hardship." Obama maintained the need to inculcate a new spirit of political and corporate ethics informed by the old virtues of "honesty and hard work, courage and fair play, tolerance and curiosity, loyalty and patriotism....What is required of us now is a new era of responsibility—a recognition on the part of every American, that we have duties to ourselves, our nation, and the world, duties that we not grudgingly accept but rather seize gladly, firm in the knowledge that there is nothing so satisfying to the spirit, so defining of our character that giving our all to a difficult task."[1] Rhetoric alone, however, will be insufficient to deal with the enormity of the conceptual and practical challenges facing the incoming administration in fashioning a coherent response to a scandal of monumental proportions.

---

[1] Inaugural Address (Washington DC, 19 January 2009).

The elevation of innovation over security generated a flawed risk paradigm. Legitimated by influential policymakers, such as the former chairman of the Federal Reserve, Alan Greenspan, a new model of financial capitalism was exported across the globe. The implosion of that model and the regulatory framework on which it operated, across rules-based and enabling systems of oversight, has created what the chair of ANZ bank, Mike Smith, has termed a "financial services bloodbath."

This book tracks how and why that process developed. It derives from a program of research, funded by the Economic and Social Research Council (RES 156-22-0033) and GOVNET, an Australian Research Council funded network. I am grateful for the continuing support of the Director of the World Economy and Finance Program at the ESRC, John Driffil, and the Convener of GOVNET, Charles Sampford. Sally Wheeler at Queen's in Belfast has been a constant source of encouragement, as has my good friend Mel Dubnick, along with his wife Randi who proofread and indexed the manuscript. I benefited enormously from Visiting Professorships at the University of Glasgow and the University of New Hampshire. The Center for Study of Law and Society at the University of California at Berkeley proved to be a perfect location to complete the final edit of the manuscript and I am grateful to its director, Lauren Edelmen, for being such a gracious host. Fredrik Galtung at TIRI provided encouragement during frequent visits to Tel Aviv, while Michael Scallon provided friendship in Paris. Peter Murtagh commissioned major pieces for the *Irish Times*. The *Australian Financial Review* provided an excellent forum to explore initially some of the themes developed in this book. The Centre for Applied Philosophy and Public Ethics provided an intellectually rich environment and I wish to acknowledge, in particular, Christian Barry, Tom Campbell, and Seumas Miller. I would also like to thank John Braithwaite, Kevin Davis, Martin Fahy, Greg Golding, Pamela Hanrahan, Ian Harper, Ian Ramsay, Malcolm Rodgers, and Warren Scott. Writing a book on the financial crisis as it unfolded was an exceptionally rewarding, if at times frustrating, experience. It would not have been finished but for the strength of my children, Elise, Jack and Justin, the unstinting support of my brothers, Brian, Kieran and TJ, Barney and Angela Devlin, Kevin and Joan Gilmartin, and, most of all, Jennifer Henry, whose love and friendship provided sustenance for body and soul.

Justin O'Brien
Berkeley, May 2009

Contents

Chapter 1

A Capital Battle

After a week of wrangling on Capitol Hill, Congressional leaders presented the *Emergency Economic Stabilization Act* (2008) to a deeply skeptical legislature. Providing the US Treasury with a line of credit to buy up to $700 billion in impaired securities represented the largest single government intervention in capital market governance since the New Deal regulatory architecture was designed and implemented in 1933–34. In announcing its "frozen" provisions, including enhanced regulatory oversight, mechanisms for the partial nationalization of an array of complex financial institutions and concomitant caps on executive pay within those that avail of the rescue, the Speaker of the House of Representatives, Nancy Pelosi, said the package was designed to send a clear message to Wall Street: "The party is over."[1]

The proposed scale of the intervention was indicative of the continued—and worsening—dislocation in global capital markets. Despite warnings from President Bush that a failure to ratify would unleash catastrophe, House Republicans (and a sizeable Democrat minority) struck down the measure.[2] The decision reflected deep-seated ideational, practical and strategic reservations. It inevitably threw global markets into a tailspin. The Dow Jones Industrial Index immediately lost 7%, with $1.2 trillion wiped off capitalization values. Taking their lead from New York, Asian and then European markets fell and continued to fall heavily throughout October.[3] Across the world, political and

---

[1] "US Law Makers Publish Rescue Plan." *BBC News*, 28 September 2008.

[2] The vote was defeated 228 to 205, with 133 Republicans and 95 Democrats voting against. Passage was secured in the Senate on Wednesday following adornments, including $112 billion of unrelated tax breaks. Two days later, the bill returned to the House, where it was approved.

[3] By the end of the month, US and European markets had lost 25%. The S&P 500 Index was down 42% on the year; see M. MacKensie, N. Bullock, and D. Brewster, "Investors

regulatory leaders expressed anger and puzzlement at Congress. The Chinese securities regulator bluntly described US lending practices as "ridiculous," "dangerous," and "indefensible."[4] Europe's then trade commissioner intoned that it was necessary to reshape the global financial architecture. US politicians had, Peter Mandelson claimed, "taken leave of their senses."[5] The Australian Prime Minister, Kevin Rudd, appealed to Congress to put global security above partisan self-interest. Rudd explained subsequently that concerted intervention was needed to nullify the effects of "extreme capitalism."[6] It was far from clear, however, that the plan put forward and eventually agreed by the United States Congress was either workable or desirable. Notwithstanding international endorsement, there was something deeply unsettling about one arm of the US federal government offering to buy products from institutions under investigation by another for violating criminal law.[7] Moreover, the emphasis on providing emergency relief to the financial sector rather than immediate help to embattled homeowners or to industrial corporations who found access to credit curtailed, while perhaps understandable, risked undermining the legitimacy of the political system. In so doing, it called into question the efficacy of an underpinning social contract.

Reel From Punishing Month," *Financial Times*, 1 November 2008, 1. By the end of the year, global markets were decimated. Reykjavik had lost a staggering 94.4%; Moscow 72.5%, Dubai 72.4%, Bucharest 70.5%; Dublin 66.2%; Hanoi 65.9%; Shanghai 65.4%; Athens 65.3%; Vienna 61.2%; Lima 59.9%; Karachi 58.3%; Riyadh 56.3%; Cairo 56.4%; Brussels 53.3%; Oslo 52.8%; Mumbai 52.5%; Amsterdam 52.3%; Istanbul 51.6%. In the United States, the S&P 500 closed the year with a loss of 38%, the biggest loss since 1931, with bell-weather stocks such as Citigroup shredding 78% of its value and General Motors losing 87%, the biggest single decline.

[4] D. Gow, "Mandelson Calls for IMF Reform and a Voice for New Champions," *The Guardian*, 29 September 2008 (Online Edition).

[5] Ibid; see also P. Wilson, "Europe Wants US Power Shift," *The Australian*, 1 October 2008, 36.

[6] The crisis, he proclaimed, could be traced to the celebration in financial centers of the cultural values denigrated in the influential Oliver Stone movie, *Wall Street* (1987), see K. Rudd, "The Children of Gordon Gekko," *The Australian*, 6 October 2008, 12.

[7] M. Philip, "Remarks Announcing Results of Operation Malicious Mortgage" (Press Conference, Department of Justice, Washington DC, 19 June 2008); for UK, see J. Hughes, "Mortgage Fraud Crackdown on Brokers," *Financial Times*, 19 July 2008, 1. For background on lending practices, see G. Dell'Ariccia, D. Igan, and L. Laeven, "Credit Booms and Lending Standards: Evidence from the Sub-Prime Mortgage Market" (International Monetary Fund, Washington, DC, WP/08/06, April 2008).

For the contemporary industrialized state, this requires the provision of a functioning legal and regulatory framework that is informed by the interaction of rules, principles and norms. Within this framework, the banking system plays an integral part, both in driving wider economic activity and as a barometer for gauging whether trust is in fact warranted. As such, it is an example of a public good (i.e. a policy prescription that cannot be delivered solely by the market). Effective supervision is necessary to guard against the material and reputational costs associated with negative externalities. In this context, the global financial crisis is a scandal of monumental proportions. Effective and efficient capital markets depend on confidence in the integrity of financial institutions, in the regulatory apparatus and, ultimately, trust between market participants and financial intermediaries. Self-evidently, trust like solvency is now in very short supply, and confidence has evaporated. The collapse of Bear Stearns and Lehman Brothers, Washington Mutual, and Wachovia, along with twenty-one other banks in the United States alone, and dubious, if not criminal, underwriting practices exacerbate a wider metastasizing problem that cuts across the global banking firmament. In the process it highlights profound difficulties with financialization (i.e. the process by which the productive economy has been displaced politically, culturally, economically, and ideationally by a reliance on financial alchemy).

The former CEO of Commonwealth Bank of Australia and now head of the Future Fund, the country's own Sovereign Wealth Fund, David Murray, has reflected that "everybody got carried away by the concept of a "millionaires factory" which was not culturally good. Where you don't want your brightest, or at least too many of them, is in jobs which spend time interpreting or arbitraging rules. This is not really effective work and a lot of investment banking is that type of deal structuring, which is not very constructive. It produces over-engineered stuff that is the first to break when anything goes wrong."[8] Asymmetric information flow, variable capacity—or willingness—to use internal management systems, market mechanisms or regulatory enforcement tools, led to a profound misunderstanding of national and international risks associated with the rapid expansion of structured finance products such as securitization. Deepening market integration ensured that risk, while diversified geographically, remained undiluted. As the Nobel

---

[8] E. Connors, "Future Fund Chief Sees Day Of Reckoning For Banks," *Australian Financial Review*, 14 January 2008, 1, 38.

Laureate Joseph Stigliz put it in excoriating testimony to Congress, "securitization was based on the premise that a fool was born every minute. Globalization meant that there was a global landscape on which they could search for these fools—and they found them everywhere."[9] From northern Norway to rural New South Wales, local councils bought securitized products on the basis of misplaced trust in the efficacy of internal controls, the strength of independent directors to hold management to account, the attestation provided by external auditors, legal due diligence, the assurances of those providing corporate advisory services, including inherently conflicted rating agencies and, ultimately, the robustness of the overarching regulatory system at either national or international levels.

The seizing of credit markets also demonstrates the failure of piecemeal attempts to broker a regulatory solution. Until the Troubled Assets Relief Program (TARP) was proposed, economic policymakers in the United States and elsewhere had adopted a largely reactive approach. In the face of declining confidence, central banks enhanced the collateral accepted in return for short-term financing. In the case of the Federal Reserve, the range of institutional actors availing of its discount-lending window was stretched to—and arguably surpassed —formal legal power.[10] Each intervention was designed to provide reassurance about the resilience of individual banks, their capacity to deliver on counter-party obligations and the integrity of the overarching system. Paradoxically, the injection of liquidity reinforced rational fears that counter-party obligations could not be delivered on. Banks, fearful

---

[9] Evidence to House Committee on Financial Services, "Regulatory Restructuring and the Reform of the Financial System," Washington DC, 21 October 2008 (J. Stiglitz). For discussion of "an ideological agenda [which] has pushed excessive reliance" on capital adequacy standards," see J. Stiglitz, "Principles of Financial Regulation: A Dynamic Portfolio Approach" (2001) 16 *World Bank Research Observer* 1 (arguing that "despite its long history, financial market regulation is poorly understood" and suggesting the need for strong regulation to address "failures in the banking system [which] have strong spillovers, or externalities, that reach well beyond the individuals and firms directly involved": at 2).

[10] P. Volcker (Speech delivered at 101st Meeting of Economic Club of New York, New York City, 10 April 2008). Volcker, a former chair of the Federal Reserve, argued that the erosion of trust and replacement of relational with transactional imperatives created a crisis of such magnitude that "the Federal Reserve judged it necessary to take actions that extend to the very edge of its lawful and implied powers, transcending certain long embedded central banking principles and practices": at 2.

of even overnight exposure, refused to lend to each other. The problem thus transmogrified from a liquidity crisis to a systemic solvency one.

The precipitous decline in real estate prices was exacerbated by "mark to market" accounting rules. These required institutions to value portfolios that were trading, if at all, far below rational levels. A market price, of a sort, was found with the decision by Merrill Lynch to off-load a large proportion of its asset-backed securities to Lone Star at 22 cents on the dollar. When combined with advantageous lending terms needed to secure the transaction, the effect was to further depress broader mark to market values. A similar dynamic was apparent in the spike of foreclosures. This pushed prices on a downward trajectory. It made it exceptionally difficult for borrowers with even large equity stakes in their properties to find refinancing. Not surprisingly, as the level of mortgage default soared so too did the London Inter-Bank Offered Rate (LIBOR). Those institutions that required short-term financing found it impossible to survive, never mind compete. By the end of September, the contagion had spread to the multi-trillion dollar commercial paper market, necessitating further government intervention. The situation reached such critical proportions that the International Monetary Fund warned that the world was on the verge of a "systemic meltdown."[11]

The crisis has already cost $3 trillion dollars and is estimated to cost a further $1 trillion by the end of 2010. Market capitalization of financial stock across the world has dropped dramatically. Data compiled by Thomson Reuters is exceptionally sobering. In March 2007, Bank of America was valued at $225.3 billion. By late January 2009, this had fallen to S36.7 billion. JP Morgan Chase fell to $74.8 billion from $170.9 billion. Goldman Sachs had dropped to $25.4 billion from $82.1 billion, and Citigroup had fallen to $17.2 billion from $250.4 billion. Major international banks have seen similar drops within the same timeframe. HSBC has declined from $200.5 billion to $86 billion, while UBS has fallen to $32.8 billion from $123.9 billion.[12] These dramatic falls have had a profound impact on the banking sector's capacity to lend. Capacity is likely to be further stretched as short-term commercial debt becomes due throughout 2009. With many countries already in recession, banks are exercising even more caution despite interest rates approaching zero

---

[11] D. Strauss-Kahn (Press Conference, International Monetary Fund, Washington DC, 11 October 2008).
[12] K. Guha and A. Beattie, "Pressure Builds For Action On Bank Crisis," *Financial Times*, 22 January 2009, 3.

in the United States and 1% in the United Kingdom, the lowest in history. In many jurisdictions these cuts have not been passed through to consumers. In the United Kingdom and Australia, for example, low rates are only available if considerable equity stakes are pledged as collateral. While de-leveraging is necessary, the short-term consequences are severe and getting worse.

In many ways the situation we face across regulatory regimes was inevitable and avoidable. The influential investor Warren Buffet has pointed out that the current crisis has exposed a huge amount of "financial folly...You only learn who has been swimming naked when the tide goes out—and what we are witnessing at some of our largest financial institutions is an ugly sight."[13] It is an appalling vista that Buffet had warned about openly in his influential annual Berkshire Hathaway newsletter. Buffet had caused a major stir in 2003 with this public rebuke to regulators for their unwillingness to tackle the systemic risk associated with financial engineering.

> The derivatives genie is now well out of the bottle, and these instruments will almost certainly multiply in variety and number until some event makes their toxicity clear.... Central banks and governments have so far found no effective way to control, or even monitor, the risks posed by these contracts... In our view...derivatives are financial weapons of mass destruction, carrying dangers that, while now latent, are potentially lethal.[14]

The continuing chaos on global markets reflects the collateral damage from the detonation of these weapons. The first overt sign of contamination came in July 2007 when the US investment bank Bear Stearns announced that two of its hedge funds, which had been valued at $1.5 billion at the end of 2006, had become worthless. The more aggressive of the two, High Grade Structured Credit Enhanced Leverage Fund, had no capital. The more conservative High Grade Structured Credit Strategies Fund had lost a staggering 91%.[15] As analysts from BNP Paribas noted on August 8, 2007, in unself-conscious deference to Buffet's metaphor, the securitization market simply vaporized. The

---

[13] *Berkshire Hathaway Annual Report* (2008) 3.
[14] Berkshire Hathaway, *Letter to Shareholders* (2003) 14.
[15] For background analysis of the failure, see G. Morgenson, "Bear Stearns Says Battered Hedge Funds Are Worth Little," *New York Times*, 18 July 2007, A1.

Paris-based bank suspended withdrawals from three of its own asset-backed hedge funds because of a "complete evaporation of liquidity in certain market segments of the US securitization market."[16] This, the bank claimed, made it "impossible to value assets fairly, regardless of their quality or credit rating."[17] The note marked the moment the crisis turned global. Institutional investors retreated en masse from esoteric debt instruments and those most closely associated with their provision, marketing, insurance and rating.

Just weeks later, a leading and particularly aggressive United Kingdom mortgage specialist, Northern Rock, failed. Scenes of customers queuing to withdraw deposits fuelled fears of a banking run not seen in the United Kingdom since the collapse of Overend Gurney & Co in 1866. Overend's reliance on an emaciated deposit base and its excessive concentration on wholesale funding prompted Walter Bagehot to observe that its business strategy was "so reckless and so foolish, that one would think a child who had lent money to the City of London would have lent it better."[18] A damning Treasury Select Committee report into "The Run of the Rock" one hundred and forty one years later found market actors remained oblivious to the danger of recklessness derived from self-deception.[19] According to the Treasury Select Committee, the "absence of sufficient insurance and a failure to arrange standby facility or cover that risk, meant that [Northern Rock] was unable to cope with the liquidity pressures placed upon it by the freezing of international capital markets in August 2007."[20] The fact that the

---

[16] Cited in F. Norris, "A New Kind of Bank Run Tests Old Safeguards," *New York Times*, 10 August 2007 (Online Edition).

[17] Ibid.

[18] Cited in "The Run on the Rock" (Treasury Select Committee, London, 24 January 2008) 7.

[19] Ibid, 3. A similar reliance on wholesale markets has the primary cause of the failure of HBOS, a much larger bank in the aftermath of the Lehman Brothers bankruptcy in September 2008. In a joint statement to the Treasury Select Committee, the former CEO and chairman said they were "profoundly sorry" but claimed that "unprecedented global circumstances affected virtually all the top banks in the world and HBOS specifically. " They claimed that HBOS did not invest in sub-prime but in "highly rated AAA asset backed securities," a defense that was designed to offload responsibility to the credit rating agencies; see A Hornby and Lord Stevenson, "Memo to Treasury Select Committee," Westminster, 10 February 2009, 38.

[20] "The Run on the Rock," above n 18, 19 (Furthermore, the report found that the business model was clearly stated. As such, the shareholders were either greedy or gullible in not challenging the strategy. The report notes that "in a market environment

Financial Services Authority acknowledged ignoring red flags is described as a "substantial failure of regulation."[21] In a statement to the Treasury Select Committee, Lloyds Banking Group, which took over the failed HBOS, articulated the scale of the organizational and regulatory accountability failure.

> At a global level, risk was mis-priced and the sophistication of the new instruments out-paced the ability to manage and understand their long term implications particularly in a less benign economic environment. However, this lack of understanding was not just an issue for the banks. Regulators and Central Banks around the world did not always grasp the inter-dependencies in the financial system and the true nature and scale of the risk being taken by some banks. There was also a general lack of understanding of the dependency of the major economies on non-bank financing. To be fair this was always going to be difficult due to the sheer complexity of the system.[22]

In March 2008, the financial services contagion crossed the Atlantic. A $22 billion hedge fund controlled by the Carlyle Group, which was registered in Guernsey, listed in Amsterdam, but administered in New York, collapsed. The calamitous failure of Bear Stearns underscored the growing severity of the crisis. Bear Stearns, the fifth

---

shareholders as a whole must be viewed as taking a risk from which they sought a reward and for which they are paying a price": at 20).

[21] Ibid, 24 (The report concludes "the FSA did not supervise Northern Rock properly. It did not allocate sufficient resources or time to monitoring a bank whose business model was so clearly an outlier; its procedures were inadequate to supervise a bank whose business grew so rapidly. We are concerned about the lack of resources within the Financial Services Authority solely charged to the direct supervision of Northern Rock. … In the case of Northern Rock, the FSA appears to have systematically failed in its duty as a regulator to ensure Northern Rock would not pose such a systemic risk, and this failure contributed significantly to the difficulties, and risks to the public purse, that have followed": at 34). In a stunning mea culpa, the FSA acknowledged that it had failed to regulate Northern Rock appropriately; see FSA, *Annual Report* (2007/8). It argued, rather unconvincingly, that this did not invalidate the principles of risk-based regulation, but was rather a failure to apply it. The chief executive, Hector Sants, argued that he was "determined that the FSA will not be defined by the Northern Rock incident, but rather by our response to it. We have demonstrated our willingness to examine ourselves critically and to learn lessons from our mistakes—a quality we believe is central to giving the financial services industry and consumers confidence in the FSA. Like any thoughtful organization, we cannot and do not claim infallibility": at 9: at 42).

[22] Memorandum from Lloyds Banking Group, Treasury Select Committee, Westminster, 10 February 2009.

biggest investment bank on Wall Street, required emergency funding from the Federal Reserve of New York through a loan facility offered to and through JP Morgan Chase. Bear Stearns, which had a debt to equity ratio of 33:1 had attempted to quell "baseless speculation" by insisting that its "balance sheet, liquidity and capital remain strong".[23] In the event it was insufficient. By Friday 14 March, such an approach could no longer be sustained. The chief executive officer, Alan Schwartz, was forced to issue a press release revealing the emergency capital injection: "We have tried to confront and dispel these rumors and parse fact from fiction....Nevertheless, amidst this market chatter, our liquidity position in the last 24 hours had significantly deteriorated. We took this important step to restore confidence in us in the marketplace, strengthen our liquidity and allow us to continue normal operations." Ominously, the press release continued: "The company can make no assurance that any strategic alternatives will be successfully completed."[24] The directors of Bear Stearns agreed for the bank to be sold in a deal that initially valued the institution at just \$2 per share. This represented a 90% discount on its closing price the previous Friday and was substantially less than the (rapidly declining) retail value of its corporate headquarters on Madison Avenue.[25]

Policymakers and banks consistently sought to underplay the extent of the crisis, claiming erroneously that it was both contained and containable. It is not surprising that while many leading banks were initially able to raise money through rights issues or capital injections from Sovereign Wealth Funds, the visual revelation of contamination

---

[23] K. Kelly, S. Ng, and J. Strasburg, "In Dealing With Bear Stearns Wall Street Plays Guardedly," *Wall Street Journal*, 13 March 2008, C1.

[24] Bear Stearns (Press Release, New York, 14 March 2008). Headlines the following day in the two leading global business newspapers demonstrate a revealing emphasis in tone and significance; see F. Guerrera, B. White, and K. Guha, "Wall Street Rescues Bear Stearns," *Financial Times*, 15 March 2008, 1; G. Kelly, G. Ip, and R. Sidel, "Fed Races to Save Bear Stearns In Bid to Steady Financial System," *Wall Street Journal*, 15 March 2008, A1.

[25] JP Morgan subsequently quadrupled its offer price, and agreed to subsume up to \$1 billion in potential losses. The revised deal had the full support of the Bear Stearns board, a calculation designed to stave off potential legal action from disgruntled shareholders; see JP Morgan and Bear Stearns, "Revised JPM-BSC Deal" (Press Release, New York City, 2 March 2008).

made each form exceptionally problematic.[26] As a direct consequence of this failure, we are witnessing what the chief executive of the ANZ, Mike Smith, famously described as "a financial services bloodbath."[27] It was, however, largely self-inflicted.

The incapacity of institutional actors to exercise restraint was neatly encapsulated in a now infamous interview given in July 2007 by the then chief executive of Citigroup. Charles "Chuck" Prince swept aside concerns that excessive leverage created potential systemic solvency risks. "When the music stops, in terms of liquidity, things will be complicated. But as long as the music is playing, you've got to get up and dance. We are still dancing."[28] The now disgraced banking executive justified his confidence in modeling systems that had diversified risk. As Prince explained it, "the depth of the pools of liquidity is so much larger than it used to be that a disruptive event now needs to be much more disruptive than it used to be. At some point, the disruptive event will be so significant that instead of liquidity filling in, the liquidity will go the other way. I don't think we're at that point."[29]

The rash of banking failures and forced resignations (including his own) since Prince's interview reflects the deleterious combination of boardroom hubris, defective operational risk management systems and uninformed regulatory confidence.[30] This was, as noted above, an engineered crisis rather than the result of merely incompetent managerial or regulatory practice. It could not have happened but for the inculcation of an essentially ideological worldview that privileged innovation over

---

[26] See, for example, R. Wachman, "HBOS 4bn Rights Issue is Massive Flop," *The Observer*, 20 July 2008, B1; P. Thal Larsen, C. Hughes, and D. Shellock, "Banks' Cash Calls Shunned," *Financial Times*, 19 July 2008, 1.

[27] A. Cornell, "Smith Calm as Others Lose Heads," *Australian Financial Review*, 19 February 2008, 52.

[28] M. Nakamoto and D. Wighton, "Bullish Citigroup is Still Dancing' to the Beat of the Private Equity Boom,' *Financial Times*, 10 July 2007, 1; see also Stiglitz, "Principles of Financial Regulation," above n 8 (arguing that reliance on capital adequacy standards lowers franchise value and "actually induce banks to engage in riskier behavior": at 4).

[29] Nakamoto and Wighton, above n 26.

[30] For global overviews, see Financial Stability Forum, "Observations on Risk Management Practices During the Recent Market Turbulence" (Basel, 6 March 2008); Financial Stability Forum, *Report of Financial Stability Forum on Enhancing Market and Institutional Resilience* (Basel, 12 April 2008); J. Lipsky, "Dealing with the Financial Turmoil: Contingent Risks, Policy Challenges and the Role of the IMF" (Speech delivered to the Peterson Institute, Washington DC, 12 March 2008); President's Working Group on Financial Markets, *Policy Statement on Financial Market Developments* (Washington DC, March 2008).

security. Crucially, it retained cogency despite the increasing empirical evidence that undermined the practical and normative value of such an approach. This generated, in turn, a new (but defective) risk paradigm informed by naivety and ignorance. While most extreme in the United States, its rationale was inculcated across the globe. In large part the misguided insouciance could be traced directly to the now questionable policy choices adopted by Alan Greenspan. As chairman of the Federal Reserve, Greenspan presided over a flight from reality. He noted "irrational exuberance" in the stock market in the 1990s but after the dot com crash at the turn of the millennium, his subsequent interest rate reduction strategy inflated an even larger bubble that encompassed residential and commercial property markets, credit card and auto loan sectors. It also provided the financing for the emergence of private equity as a dominant global force in the mergers and acquisitions market. Greenspan held that securitization and derivative contracts allowed for the quantification of risk. Financial innovation, he proclaimed, had generated a "new paradigm of active credit management." For Greenspan, "the present health of banking is a dramatic testament to both the management skills of bankers and the ability of regulators and legislators to adapt, albeit slowly, to change."[31]

The initial housing collapse in the United States placed the world on collective notice of the potential costs associated with this suspension of disbelief. It also highlighted the interconnections within global capital markets, which, in turn, explains why the toxin could spread with such ease. The decision by US authorities to allow Lehman Brothers to collapse in September 2008 triggered the explosion of this much more serious problem. The current chairman of the Federal Reserve, Ben Bernanke, now maintains that "there was no mechanism, there was no option, there was no set of rules, there was no funding to allow us to address that situation."[32] The US Treasury and Federal Reserve performed a stunning volte-face, however, the day after the investment

---

[31] A. Greenspan, "Banking" (Speech delivered at American Bankers Association, New York City, 5 October 2004).

[32] B. Bernanke, "Stabilizing the Financial Markets and the Economy" (Speech delivered at the Economic Club of New York, New York City, 15 October 2008); see also J. Cassidy, "Anatomy of a Meltdown," *New Yorker*, 1 December 2008, 49 (citing an interview with Ben Bernanke in which he states "with Bear Stearns, with all the others, there was a point when someone said, 'Mr. Chairman, are we going to do this deal or not?' With Lehman, we were never anywhere near that point. There wasn't a decision to be made": at 62).

bank was forced to file the largest bankruptcy in history. The decision to rescue the insurance company American International Group through an initial injection of $85 billion, which has since mushroomed to $150 billion, but not Lehman Brothers was based on the fear that the collapse of the former would hasten enormous capital outflows from the remaining investment banks.[33] Even this rescue was not enough to quell growing fears that despite policymakers attempt at mollification, the governance of the global financial sector was hopelessly compromised. It is this realization that has animated decisions by the United States and other jurisdictions to engage in the most sweeping overhaul of financial regulation ever seen.

Despite criticism of the United States model in many European capitals—and discernible schadenfreude—in truth the continent has fared little better. The forced nationalization of Northern Rock, Bradford & Bingley, along with the implosion of Royal Bank of Scotland and HBOS demonstrates the hollowness of superiority claims about the risk-based principles-driven model of banking regulation exported by the United Kingdom.[34] Ostensibly more cautious oversight on the continental mainland has proved equally defective. As the negotiations on Capitol Hill continued over the weekend of September 26–28, the Dutch, Belgian, and Luxemburg governments attempted to nationalize large components of Fortis, a flagship European financial services

---

[33] For an examination of the critical role played by AIG in the financial architecture, see G. Morgensen, "Behind Insurers Crisis, Blind Eye to a Web of Risk," *New York Times*, 27 September 2008, B1; J. Nocera, "Diary of a Monumental Nightmare," *Australian Financial Review*, 3 October 2007, 64–65.

[34] The FSA CEO remains wedded to his conception of what constitutes or should constitute effective regulation, see FSA above n 19 ("I believe the events of last year, including Northern Rock, support principles-based regulation; they highlight how important it is that firms' management and the FSA focus on delivery of outcomes rather than just focusing mechanically on compliance with the rules. We therefore remain committed to pursuing more principles-based regulation and focusing on the outcomes that matter. We continue to believe that a successful financial marketplace requires innovation, the capacity for risk-taking, and competition — an approach which has served the UK economy and its financial markets well. A consequence of this philosophy is that we cannot guarantee there will not be failures. The inherent certainty that there will be failures within our framework results not just from this requirement to recognize that risks are unavoidable, but also that outcome-based judgments are essentially predictive and thus our judgments necessarily reflect the inherent uncertainty of forecasts": at 10).

conglomerate.[35] An emergency line of credit ensured the temporary survival of Germany's second largest commercial lender, Hypo Real Estate. German saving banks have been particularly vulnerable to the dislocation on the credit derivatives market. Through trading operations in Dublin, which has emerged as a vibrant and freewheeling financial center, two banks have collapsed. The Irish Financial Services Regulatory Authority relied upon a "passport" system which off-loaded oversight responsibility to its German counterpart. The Dublin authorities proved equally deficient in regulating their own charges.

In the end it was perhaps fitting that the demise of the Celtic Tiger came as workers at Waterford Crystal, Ireland's premier luxury good exporter, occupied the now closed visitor center. Outside, they hoisted the "Starry Plough," the symbol of the Irish trade union movement, on the corporate flagpole. While providing the muscle for a revolutionary tradition, the Left never quite managed to exert a role on the economic trajectory of post-independence Ireland. The country now is coming to terms with a markedly changed global landscape in which the traditional safety valves of easy emigration and international goodwill have been closed. In part this could be attributed to the global dimensions of the crisis; no region has emerged unscathed. In part, it derives from schadenfraude across the world at the demise of a freewheeling and misgoverned market, where hubris trumped prudence and the country's reputation with the new United States administration has descended to that of an offshore tax haven that facilitates deception.

The scale of the calamity now facing Ireland far exceeds situations faced by any of its European partners. Throughout the boom, the population was encouraged to engage in an act of stunning self-deception. The swagger of the Celtic Tiger has wilted in the face of

---

[35] Fortis was part of a consortium (along with Royal Bank of Scotland) that acquired ABN Amro in 2007. At the time the takeover was the largest banking consolidation ever. The Dutch government was obliged to take sole control of the bank's operations in the Netherlands, while the Belgian and Luxemburg components were to be sold to BNP Paribas for $15 billion. A court in Belgium has temporarily blocked the sale in advance of shareholder ratification and threatened the government with a $6.75 billion fine if it sought to disregard the ruling, see D. Jolly, "Belgium to Fight Ruling on Plan to Sell Fortis," *International Herald Tribune*, 17 December 2008, 11. The Supreme Court found that the Belgian Justice Minister and the Prime Minister's chief of staff had attempted to sway the initial decision by improperly telephoning the husband of the judge hearing the case at first instance, see J. Miller, "Belgium's Government Offers to Resign Over Fortis," *Wall Street Journal*, 20 December 2008, A8. The government subsequently resigned on 22 December 2008.

staggering regulatory, corporate, and political incompetence. Unsustainable property valuations created not just a speculative commercial and residential bubble but also a speculative economy. As the crisis intensified last September, Ireland took the unprecedented decision to provide an unlimited guarantee of all banking deposits. The move prompted large capital outflows from the rest of Europe, particularly the United Kingdom. It was designed to protect an increasingly strained domestic banking sector whose reckless lending has been instrumental in intensifying the scale of the crisis here. It is a criticism that can equally be applied to the regulatory and political authorities, which determined that it was necessary to retain consumer confidence, even when that confidence was, and remains, illusory. In essence the country degenerated into a crooked casino. Industry players set the rules of the game, unburdened by a political and regulatory elite mesmerized by financial alchemy. In a rare admission of failure, the Taoiseach, Brian Cowen, accepted "arrogance" played a role in transforming the country from "unknown prosperity to suddenly [facing] survival stakes."[36]

The International Financial Services Centre became the symbol for some of the worst excesses of financialization. The staggering losses made by a leading businessman on the esoteric Contract for Difference market encapsulate just what wrong and why confidence in the probity of the Irish market is so low and the cost of serving external debt so high. Sean Quinn, a reclusive billionaire, was forced to admit he lost $1.27 billion in the recently nationalized Anglo Irish Bank. It emerged that the entrepreneur's family had amassed a 25% indirect interest in the bank through Contract for Difference options. The holding was reduced to 15% and converted to shares, with a consortium of business people taking a 10% stake in increments that did not surpass the 3% limit that forces disclosure to the Irish Stock Exchange. The nationalization of the bank in January 2009 crystallized the loss. The financing for these transactions came from the bank itself through non-recourse loans.[37] Quinn mused "we all got carried away a little" during the boom. He broke his silence after allegations arose that implicated him in the share support scheme. Quinn claimed the investment was made on behalf of

---

[36] Brian Cowen (Speech delivered at the Chamber of Commerce Annual Dinner, Dublin, 5 February 2009), excerpted in H. McGee, "Cowen Says Recession to Cut Living Standards By Over 10%," *Irish Times*, 6 February 2009, 1.
[37] *Anglo Irish Bank Annual Report 2008* (20 February 2009).

his wife and children. He conceded involvement in the transaction but insisted that there "was no impropriety in anything we've one in that bank...." Any money we put into shares was money we could afford to be without; in hindsight, we were too greedy." The entrepreneur portrayed himself as a victim.[38] While there is merit in the argument that a disorderly public unwinding could have exacerbated the situation and caused panic earlier, the critical issue remains how the regulatory authorities allowed such a large problem to develop in the first place.

Crucially, the Irish government has accepted that it was aware as early as March 2008 of the size of the holding and the threats this posed to the stability of the bank and to the banking sector in general, as was the Financial Regulator. Both were involved in facilitating the transition, which not only involved the non-recourse loans advanced to prominent businessmen but also a series of circular transactions involving largest mortgage provider in the country, Irish Life & Permanent.[39] The decision by three directors of IL&P to step down on 13 February 2009 capped an extraordinary week for corporate Ireland. What made the resignations even more remarkable is that the chairman of the IL&P, Gillian Bowler, claimed the problem was not the transactions that led to their departure but the manner in which it was done. The only motivation in facilitating Anglo Irish Bank, she claimed, was to follow "a policy objective of both the Central Bank and the Financial Regulator that Irish financial institutions would work to support each other in the face of an unprecedented threat to the stability of the Irish financial system arising from the international credit crisis."[40]

---

[38] The interview was broadcast by RTE, the national broadcaster. All quotations come from J. Brennan, "Quinn Admits He Was Too Greedy as Losses Hit Euro 1 billion," *Irish Independent*, 31 January 2009, 2; C. Madden, "Quinn Admits His Family Lost 1 Billion in Anglo, " *Irish Times*, 31 January 2009, 19; N. Brennnan, "Quinn Says He Did No Wrong in Anglo Share Deal. For the Moment I Am Sceptical," *Irish Independent*, 31 January 2009, 25. Quinn was not alone in using CFD instruments to engage in speculative activity. One report suggests that the mechanism accounted for "almost half of the activity of the Irish stock market just two years ago"; see E. Quinn, "Developers Lost E6 Billion Gambling on Stocks with Controversial Wagers," *Sunday Tribune* (Dublin), 1 February 2009, B1; see also E. Quinn, "The Power of One, " *Sunday Tribune*, 1 February 2009, B5.

[39] The regulator claims now that it was misled, see C. Kenna, "Financial Regulator Believes It Was Misled By Anglo," *Irish Times*, 20 February 2009, 1.

[40] "Statement by Chairman of Irish Life & Permanent," (Press Release, Dublin, 13 February 2009). Regulatory and political authorities reject this interpretation; see Kenna, above n 39.

The finance director, Peter Fitzpatrick, and head of treasury, David Gantly, departed to salve the board's "strong disapproval of and disappointment with some of the specific measures used to support Anglo Irish Bank during 2008 and the fact that the board itself was not informed of the specific manner in which such support had been afforded".[41] In the early hours of 12 February, the board initially refused an offer by the chief executive, Denis Casey, to resign with his colleagues. He insisted later in the day, "having reflected on the situation with his wife and family overnight" and so the board relented. Bowler, accepting Casey's resignation with the "utmost regret", said it had been prompted by his "dedication and loyalty to the company".[42] The board changes followed the intervention of Minister for Finance who had publicly called on the board of IL&P to "face up to its responsibilities" after an emergency meeting with senior executives.

It is hard to know who has less credibility: the Minister, who admitted to the Irish parliament that he had failed to even read a report he had commissioned into the risks posed by Anglo Irish Bank; or the chairman and now outgoing chief executive of IL&P who were not informed of unilateral decisions that have irretrievably marred the reputation of their organization. The board statement describes Fitzpatrick and Gantly as men of "utmost integrity" and professionalism. It would appear they were victims of a misguided belief that supporting a corporate neighbor trumped any concern that the transaction seriously misled the investing public.

The controversy centers on a series of circular transactions in March and September, which were characterized as deposits rather than bank loans. The effect was to flatter the books of Anglo Irish Bank, which was hemorrhaging customer deposits in both March and by late September was at risk of immediate failure. The explanation provided by both Anglo Irish and IL&P lacks sufficient detail. We still do not know who made the decision and why. Furthermore, it is unclear whether the representatives at Irish Life Assurance (the IL&P subsidiary used to effect the transaction) knew the purpose and, if not, why not? The fact that neither the Financial Regulator nor the Department of Finance appear to have questioned the March transactions may have provided support for a misguided belief that saving corporate Ireland was more important than transparency and accountability. The conceit is staggering

---

[41] Ibid.
[42] Ibid.

and demonstrates a complete lack of understanding of international regulatory developments either within IL&P or within the Financial Regulator, a member of the International Organization of Securities Commissions.

Late on the night of 20 February 2009 the Irish government authorized a highly edited release of the confidential report into the stability of the Irish banking system. The 43-page extract focuses only on Anglo Irish Bank and covers three separate presentations (27 September, 27 November and 17 December). It discloses that in the week prior to the announcement of the Irish government blanket guarantee, Anglo Irish Bank experienced a $6.9 billion run on deposits. The report also found that the bank had a concerted exposure of more that $640 million with just 15 key account holders. According to the report

> From a review of the loan files it is evident that personal guarantees and net asset statements are obtained from borrowers. While these show the borrowers' net worth in a favorable position it must be noted that collateral valuations, in particular property, in the current environment may be significantly lower and realizing some of these collateral assets may be difficult. However, given the satisfactory performance of the book to end of August 2008 it is not anticipated by Anglo management that forced 'fire sales' of collateral will occur.[43]

The presentation to government on 27 September showed that it was clear that the bank's available for sale financial assets, totaling $2.43 billion, were in fact "difficult to value and probably illiquid."[44] The revelation may have provided the impetus for the rushed decision to provide the guarantee. By the end of November the difficulties associated with the Anglo Irish trading model became painfully apparent. PriceWaterhouseCoopers note

> Anglo has built up strong relationships with its key customers. Management state that this strategy of developing deep relationships with what it deems to be the strongest operators is deliberate. From our review of the larger loans in the portfolio it is evident that a small number of key customers are involved in a large number of transactions and represent a significant proportion of the loan portfolio. Anglo considers itself able to attain a thorough

---

[43] "Project Atlas–Anglo Irish Bank" (Report Prepared for Irish Financial Services Regulatory Authority, 20 February 2009) 18.
[44] Ibid, 19.

understanding of its client's business, finances and relevant risks, which are continually reassessed in face-to-face client meetings often held weekly. There are a number of customers which are not currently on the Bank's watch, notable or impairment lists all of whom exhibit potentially serious short-term liquidity issues.[45]

The third phase of the reporting, which was presented on 17 December highlighted a broader systemic problem.

There is currently a large over-hang of unsold higher density residential units in these areas accounting for a number of years supply and on top of this there are sites without planning permission in relation to which developers are hoping applications will be processed when local authority infrastructure and planning issues are resolved. Successful disposal of the current and 'pipeline' stock will take many years and appear unlikely to occur at current unit price levels. There are likely to be significant losses for individual developers.[46]

The situation has become even more critical for the Irish government because the preeminent planning authority, An Bord Pleanala, revoked partial planning permission for a $1.9 billion office, retail, and residential development in a pristine and exceptionally affluent inner suburb. The land for the development, which had as its centerpiece a 37-storey tower, was bought for $485 million in 2005. Dublin City Council had approved the bulk of the scheme but rejected the landmark building, much to the consternation of Sean Dunne, the flamboyant developer. In appealing the decision Dunne was banking on his capacity—and those of his backers—to bully the city into acquiescing in the destruction of the city's Georgian heritage. An Bord Pleanala disabused Dunne and his backers of their arrogance. The decision called into question the probity of the planning process in Dublin, the lack of due diligence within the banks in extending the loans to Dunne in the first place and the commitment of the government to ensuring transparency and accountability within the political and corporate sector.[47]

According to the planning authority, it was "not satisfied the proposed development would bring about a high-quality environment for

[45] Ibid, 24.
[46] Ibid, 32.
[47] See F. McDonald, "How An Board Pleanala Shot Down Dunne Plan and Buried Celtic Tiger," *Irish Times*, 31 January 2009, 8.

future occupants"; the density was criticized as "gross overdevelopment and over-intensification of the site," which is held was "highly obtrusive and [would] seriously injure the visual amenity of the area."[48] Crucially the authority found that the entire development conflicted with the City Council's own development plan. While it is not be expected that bankers should have a detailed knowledge of planning law, the grandiose ambitions of the project, its variance with the architecture of the affluent suburb that houses some of the most influential citizens in the state, made it far-fetched that approval would be given. It is perhaps not surprising that a subsidiary of Royal Bank of Scotland, Ulster Bank, is most exposed to the $312 million that Dunne sought and received for the site. The decision to comprehensively reject this kind of development is likely to have a sharp impact on commercial land values in the Irish capital, adding further to the liabilities faced by the banking sector.

The Irish government has attempted to quell investor concern about the viability of the major surviving Irish banks by authorizing a recapitalization valued at $8.98 billion, split between the Bank of Ireland and Allied Irish Bank. The move was immediately discounted by the credit rating agencies, which downgraded both banks. Moreover, the security of blanket guarantee seriously exposes the Irish exchequer. It is indicative that the cost of Irish debt is spiraling. The differential between ten-year Irish and German bonds now stands at 2.08%, six times that recorded in May.[49] Ireland has gone from poster child of globalization to the symbol of corporate, regulatory, and political failure.

The fate of Anglo Irish Bank and the "golden circle" of investors provide a fitting epitaph for the Celtic Tiger. A series of unanswered questions remain as to why the government made the decision to provide a blanket guarantee. In particular did it make the calculation solely on the basis of an evaluation of the Anglo accounts or were similar problems apparent in the other banks? To date the Irish government has not provided a convincing explanation as to why it will not disclose the names of the individuals provided with preferential borrowings from Anglo Irish to buy into the bank immediately prior to the blaknket

[48] O. Kelly, "Dunne Denied Permission For Ballsbridge Project," *Irish Times*, 31 January 2009, 8.
[49] D. Doyle, "Irish Outlook 'Appropriate' After Cuts Moody's Says," *Bloomberg*, 4 May 2009 (Online Edition) (reporting that Moody's Investment Services retained a "negative" watch rating on Irish debt, even after the announcement of $2.52 billion budget cuts from the public sector).

guarantee. The Supreme Court has already ruled that confidentiality cannot be assumed if there is a suggestion of wrongdoing and the public interest must be protected.[50] Until those questions are resolved it is unlikely that private capital will return to the Irish banking sector. This makes nationalization ever more likely at a time when the cost of servicing sovereign debt has escalated.

In short, the political and regulatory elite has lost all credibility in either identifying the problem associated with Contracts for Difference or fashioning a coherent response once the effects became clear. The extent to which Contract for Difference bets drove stock market activity in Ireland was reinforced by the decision in 2006 to amend the Finance Act to provide it with tax-free status. The amendment was put forward by the then Finance Minister, Brian Cowen, on what he termed official advice following representations from industry. Now Cowen clamors without irony for the Irish people not to "wallow in self-doubt" but reignite an "entrepreneurial can-do spirit that has brought us to where we are today."[51] Ireland's unemployment rate has mushroomed to 9.1%; according to the Taoiseach himself, living standards are expected to decline 10% and the country faces the real risk of bankruptcy. The Credit Default Swap market is now actively betting that Irish bonds will default. Significantly, the rating agencies have downgraded the state's own credit score, an indication that international markets are unconvinced that Ireland's political and regulatory elite have the capacity or willingness to affect meaningful change.

Moreover, blanket guarantees merely mask the problems associated with irresponsible lending. The drip feed of revelations and now the partial publication of the PriceWaterhouseCoopers report that the Minister did not even read demonstrate how problematic the initial decision to safeguard Anglo Irish was; not just for the country but also for the dynamics of European integration. Such mechanisms undermine European Union competition law. Following the Irish move, Greece, Denmark, Sweden, Austria, and Spain adopted similar strategies. Germany—which had been most vociferous in its initial objections—provided a political pledge to secure all banking deposits. The political decisions to place national banking security over European solidarity provided the most telling indications that contagion had become a

---

[50] *National Irish Bank v RTE* [1998] 2 ILRM 233 (allowing the national broadcaster to divulge information about a potentially illegal tax evasion scheme).
[51] Cowen, above n 35.

pandemic. Taken together, these initiatives also made a mockery of attempts in Paris to generate a coordinated response.

With the Irish government leading the unilateralist charge, the British government took the most comprehensive action. The indecision that had accompanied the policy response to Northern Rock the previous northern autumn was replaced by a steely determination to shore up the banking sector and the legitimacy of the overarching system of oversight that informed London's claim to challenge New York as the preeminent major global financial center. The British Chancellor of the Exchequer authorized the purchase of controlling interests in three of its major banks in a coordinated $600 billion rescue package that involved $64 billion in direct recapitalization, the provision of short-term loans and inter-bank lending guarantees.[52] The decision reflected a seismic change in governmental thinking about the efficacy of markets and undermined much of the theoretical cogency of the merits of associational democracy in the financial sector.

The calamitous events in Europe after the passage of emergency measures in Washington demonstrate the continued fragility of the banking sector. From Paris came the deeply embarrassing announcement that one of France's largest saving banks, Caisse d'Epargne, had lost $807 million in a trading strategy based on the erroneous belief that equity markets would stabilize. The loss was galling for the bank because it was in the process of closing down its proprietary trading unit.[53] It was, perhaps, more galling for the country because it followed a series of regulatory failures, most notably the exposure of an alleged rogue trading scandal at Societé Génèrale earlier in the year. Across the border in Germany the country's second largest bank, Commerzbank, received a $13.7 billion capital injection in return for a 25% government stake. If the banking sector was under siege within the European Union, outside it Iceland faced even more pressing problems.

The government, which nationalized the country's third largest bank, suspended all trading in major financial stock and proposed sweeping legislation because of an imminent threat of national bankruptcy. The crisis temporarily passed only when the International

---

[52] Government Statement on Financial Support, Department of Treasury (Press Release, London, 8 October 2008).
[53] S. Daneshkhu, "Latest Controversial Trading Bet Brings French Banks Into Question," *Financial Times*, 18 October 2008, 9.

Monetary Fund provided emergency financing.[54] Lack of controls was also apparent in Hong Kong. CITIC Pacific announced it had lost $1.89 billion on "unauthorized" trades on the direction of the Australian dollar to fund the expansion of the group's iron-ore business in Western Australia. This was not an example of a lack of oversight over a junior employee. The Group Finance Director authorized the trade. Both he and the Group Financial Controller were summarily dismissed and the Chinese state-controlled parent, CITIC, provided an immediate $1.5 billion loan to offset losses.[55]

Australia, which has been relatively well insulated from the impact of the credit crisis, in part because high interest rates dampened speculative activity and in part because of a well-regarded "twin-peak" system of oversight that splits regulatory authority between an aggressive securities regulator and a cautious prudential one, was not to prove immune. The niche financial engineers were decimated. Allco Finance, which led the private equity consortium to take control of Qantas, went into administration in November 2008 after posting a loss of AU$1.73 billion, one of the largest in Australian history. Macquarie Group, known colloquially as the "Millionaires Factory", flagged a profit downgrade as it sought to shore up its balance sheet by exiting the margin-lending sector. It announced that in the last quarter of 2008 "market conditions were exceptionally challenging for almost all of Macquarie's businesses, adversely impacting levels of business activity and profitability."[56] Its smaller rival Babcock & Brown faced imminent collapse because of conditions imposed by domestic and international banking syndicates.[57]

---

[54] The IMF approved a $2.1 billion emergency loan for Iceland on 24 October 2008, as well as $15.7 billion for Hungary (6 November) and $16.4 billion to Ukraine and has announced plans for a $2.4 billion rescue package for Latvia (19 December). The Icelandic government collapsed in January 2009.

[55] Y. Lee and L. Santini, "CITIC Pacific May Face Big Hit on Currency Wagers Gone Bad," *Wall Street Journal*, 21 October 2008, C2. At a closed meeting on 19 December 2008, shareholders approved CITIC's acquisition of HK $11.6 billion of convertible bonds and assumption of two thirds of the losses from the currency trade debacle. The bonds, if converted, would give CITIC a stake of 57.66%, double its initial position; see C. Chan, "Citic Pacific Bail-Out Is Best Option, Says Chairman," *South China Morning Post*, 20 December 2008, A2.

[56] S. Murdoch, "Macquarie's Woes Deepen," *The Australian*, 9 January 2009, 15.

[57] For background on the implosion of Babcock & Brown, see K. Maley, "Life on the Margin: How Green Blew Up Babcock," *Australian Financial Review*, 20 February 2009, 1.

In Australia the problems centered less on the commercial banks than on the implosion of critical residential and commercial property trusts. These promised excessive rates of return and engaged in excessive risk. In an effort to offset the potential risk associated with foreign banks scaling back their operations, the federal government announced the creation of an AU$4 billion package designed to shore up commercial real estate prices, despite concernss of the Reserve Bank of Australia. The package was justified on the grounds that it would protect construction jobs. The opposition leader, Malcolm Turnbull, himself a former Goldman Sachs executive, claimed, with reason, that the government was merely delaying a necessary and inevitable price correction.[58] A further problem is that the decision to intervene to allow the rolling over of commercial debt may make it easier for foreign banks to exit the market, secure in the knowledge that they would be made whole. The problems are magnified because a low deposit base requires the major domestic banks to enter into global commercial money markets. The freezing of this source of capital forced three major banks to tap the Future Fund for capital. The process, although defended as a commercial decision, remains clouded with secrecy. No information has been divulged about the size or terms of the loans; this cuts against international attempts to ensure that state-owned asset pools make decisions solely on commercial grounds.[59]

It is the United States and Europe, particularly Ireland and the United Kingdom, however, which continue to face the most severe practical and normative problems of banking oversight. The IMF released a devastating outlook report noting the need for "extraordinary public intervention to prevent a meltdown of the U.S. financial system....The disruptions in the U.S. financial system in September have heightened the risk of a systemic financial crisis in Europe further, though a full-blown crisis remains improbable and recent actions by the authorities should help in this respect. Nonetheless, additional banks may fail, as implied by their very high risk spreads and market doubts about

---

[58] P. Coorey and P. Hartchner, "Rudd Snubs Reserve Bank," *Sydney Morning Herald*, 28 January 2009, 1.
[59] D. Uren and S. Parnell, "Banks Turn to Future Fund," *The Australian*, 7 October 2008, 1. The Future Fund subsequently provided emergency financing following the sudden withdrawal of GMAC and GE from the domestic auto-market; see P. Maley, "Car Dealers Saved by $2 Billion Financing Package," *The Australian*, 5 December 2008, 1.

the viability of their business models."[60] Although the report suggested that the scale of intervention required to deal with the solvency issues are not as pronounced in Europe, it warned of "the serious risk of backtracking on European financial integration. Addressing the concerns raised by cross-border spillovers of actions taken by national authorities will require movement towards more joint responsibility and accountability for financial stability in Europe."[61] By December the IMF noted that the lack of consistency meant there was a profound need for coordinated financial market, fiscal and liquidity measures.[62] In the United Kingdom, the government sought to place the continuing dislocation in a global context. Gordon Brown warned of the profound risk of de-globalization and concomitant threats to global order unless action was taken to ensure that financial stability was restored.[63] It was, many in the markets feared, too little too late. A leading hedge fund manager warned that "the City of London is finished, the financial centre of the world is moving east. All the money is in Asia. Why would it go back to the West?"[64] The same applies to the retail sector. Many of the leading shopping chains on the British High Street are likely to be put on the market following the collapse of Bauger, an Icelandic retail chain. Bauger had expanded into Britain at the height of the boom to such an extent that it controls 10% of the high street. Bauger filed for credit protection after its leading lender, itself now nationalized by Reykjavik, withdrew funding. On the streets of the United Kingdom and other

---

[60] *Europe: Dealing with Shocks* (International Monetary Fund, Washington DC, October 2008) 8-9.

[61] Ibid, at 10.

[62] D. Strauss-Kahn, "The IMF and its Future" (Speech delivered at Banco e Espana, Madrid, 15 December 2008).

[63] On 19 January 2009 the government announced the establishment of a state-owned insurance scheme to enable banks to dispose of impaired assets. In a pre-announcement interview, Brown argued that "one of the necessary elements for the next stage is for people to have a clear understanding that bad assets have been written off.' See G. Parker, L. Barber, and J. Eaglesham, "Brown Orders British Banks to Come Clean," *Financial Times*, 17 January 2009, 1. The chair of the influential Treasury Select Committee, John McFall, was less diplomatic. "We have got to go back again with a bigger sum because, quite frankly, the banks in my opinion haven't been honest enough about the toxic assets on their books." See "Brown To Announce Bank Bailout Plan," *BBC News*, 18 January 2009; for domestic criticism of the plan, see "UK Banking Plan Faces Criticism," *BBC News*, 19 January 2009.

[64] J. Rogers, "View of the Day," *Financial Times*, 22 January 2009, 25.

countries across Europe, resentment is rising, with large-scale protests taking place from Moscow through Riga to Athens and on to Paris.

While disputation continues about what should be done, there has long been fundamental agreement on the severity of the crisis and its implications for regulatory design.[65] Ultimately, the seizing of the global securitization and wider credit markets stem from the combination of an emaciated conception of what constitutes effective corporate governance, skewed incentives that privilege chrematistic transactional-based banking and the flimsiness of a wider regulatory structure predicated on risk reduction rather than maintenance or strengthening of longer-term societal needs. Accountability proved elusive because of essentially ideographic and therefore incommensurable representations of what fealty to the concept entail. The problem intensifies as one cascades through the mechanisms used to measure performance.[66] The restraining power associated with enhanced transparency and disclosure within and among accountability dimensions has also been eroded.[67] The securitization of risk was, after all, perfectly legal. The risks were disclosed but discounted by allegedly sophisticated investors, who, in the main, jettisoned reason in the search for yield. The progressive revelation of such willful ignorance on the part of those entrusted to manage retirement savings is exceptionally disturbing. It is rendered even more so when assessed against a background in which these same institutional investors advocated raising the proportion of funds that could be invested in alternative asset classes.

Resolution of these issues requires close examination of the reasons behind failures within individual institutions. Limiting intervention to the micro-level of an individual bank or financial services firm without securing stewardship rights through guaranteed common

---

[65] For United States, see T. Geithner, "The Current Financial Challenges: Policy and Regulatory Implications" (Speech delivered at Council on Foreign Relations, New York, 6 March 2008); B. Bernanke, "Risk Management in Financial Institutions" (Speech delivered at Federal Reserve Bank of Chicago, Chicago, 15 May 2008); for Europe, see C. McCreevy, "International Financial Crisis: Its Causes and What to Do About It" (Speech delivered at Alliance of Liberals and Democrats for Europe, Brussels, 27 February 2008); for United Kingdom, see R. Lomax, "The State of the Economy" (Speech delivered at the Institute of Economic Affairs, London, 26 February 2008).

[66] M. Bovens, "Two Concepts of Accountability" (Paper presented at the Kettering Foundation, Dayton, Ohio, 23 May 2008).

[67] For critique suggesting that transparency does not necessarily improve oversight but rather can cloud it, see H. Tsoukas, "The Tyranny of Light: The Temptations and Paradoxes of the Information Society" (1997) 29 *Futures* 827.

equity stakes pre-ordains future failure. The accountability deficit transcends individual corporate stewardship, however. More fundamentally, it reveals a crisis in confidence in the rationale and structure of financial regulation itself. As such, the design of effective and flexible regulatory and corporate governance rules, principles and norms to address the interlinked and intractable problems in both the financial and real economies has become a global policy imperative. The extent of government intervention required to stabilize financial markets has fundamentally transformed the conceptual and practical dynamics. The power and influence of the state within the regulatory matrix has been augmented considerably. The unresolved question is what the state will do with this power. In the United States, the process will define the Obama presidency.

As the Bush administration entered into its final weeks, the chairman of the Securities and Exchange Commission, Christopher Cox, penned an extraordinary opinion piece that captured the enormity of the changes in the American corporate and political landscape.[68] Castigated throughout the crisis as ineffectual—the Republican presidential nominee had publicly called for his sacking in September—Cox appealed for the retention of the free market economy principles on which America was founded. Those principles underpin "our emphasis on private ownership [that] is directly tied to America's dedication to individual freedom. It is in our DNA….Our constitution is a brilliantly crafted system of checks and balances to prevent that abuse by limiting government's authority over individuals—including in the economic realm, where we're guaranteed our constitutional rights to liberty and property, to freedom from expropriation, and to freedom of contract."

Acknowledging the profound failures associated with the model, he posited the need to "take exceptional care to preserve the premise of well-ordered markets that underlies our enforcement and regulatory regime. Maintaining the arm's length relationship between government, as the regulator, and business, as the regulated, is essential. Otherwise, when the government becomes both referee and payer, the game changes dramatically for every other participant." For Cox, "it is incumbent upon federal policy makers to ensure that the extraordinary actions of the past months are understood to be temporary, and constructed so that they are self-liquidating. Since government programs do not on their own go

---

[68] C. Cox, "We Need a Bailout Strategy," *Wall Street Journal*, 11 December 2008, A16.

away, there has to be a deliberate design to eliminate them, and a relentless adherence to execution of that plan. Anything short of this will almost certainly guarantee eternal life for these vast new federal roles."

The extent to which large sections of the financial sector are now fully nationalized or are surviving because of public largesse raises profoundly difficult questions, particularly for those wedded to the narrow conceptions of corporate accountability found in the law and economics tradition. They tend to challenge the right of the state to intervene in the governance of a private entity. The democratic accountability deficit is displaced by the emphasis on the "sovereign" right of the shareholder to enter into a free association.[69] These private ownership rights are transferred to the collective, which is invested with a distinct, if artificial, legal personality. The normative emphasis remains on the "personality" component rather than its "artificiality." This emaciated conception of individual rights is given a democratic gloss through the corporate constitution.[70] Depending on political persuasion, autocracy or democratic centralism are perhaps better facsimiles for the reality of organizational control, albeit one that has limited recourse to the courts. Judicial intervention tends to focus on procedural rather than substantive matters. Adjudication of the consequences of organizational culture and the impact this has on (un) ethical decision-making is left to the corporation itself to decide because of the reluctance of the courts to second-guess business decisions taken within legal parameters (e.g. in good faith, with adequate cognizance of the long term interests of the corporation and without a material interest in the transaction).

The duties and responsibilities owed by the owners of the corporation to wider society are bypassed by characterizing the corporation as nothing more than a "nexus-of-contracts."[71] This

---

[69] R. Hessen, *In Defense of the Corporation* (1979) 115.

[70] For an approach suggesting the need to take the corporate constitution seriously, see S. Bottomley, "From Contractualism to Constitutionalism: A Framework for Corporate Governance" (1997) 19 *Sydney Law Review* 277; S. Bottomley, *The Constitutional Corporation, Rethinking Corporate Governance* (2007).

[71] See F. Easterbrook and D. Fischel, *The Economic Structure of Corporate Law* (1991). For an updated approach, see R. Kraakman, P. Davies, H. Hansmann, and G. Hertig, *The Anatomy of Corporate Law: A Comparative and Functional Approach* (2004). Although Kraakman and his co-authors view the corporation as encompassing more than a nexus of contracts, as the subtitle of the book suggests, they still couch company law in instrumental terms. Outside the narrow realm of corporate law, organizational theorists now conceive the corporation in much more complex terms; see, for example, R. Scott, *Organizations, Rational, Natural and Open Systems* (2003).

facilitates suspension of critical thinking about the social construction of the corporation. It also limits the grounds for intervention to whether an alleged breach is enforceable in the company law courts (which, in large measure, it is not unless explicitly forbidden under either standard or tailor-made articles of association). This conceptualization places arbitrary and artificial boundaries on the form and function of corporate law and capital market regulation. The emphasis on procedure over substance transacts around rather than resolves what should be the public policy response to the question of what constitutes the appropriate obligations for corporate ownership.[72] More perniciously, it limits the legitimacy of state intervention by suggesting a dichotomous relationship between the beneficence of economic freedom to contract and the deleterious consequences of regulatory intervention.[73] Indeed, it spawned an entire sub-disciplinary legal field, most notably through the work of Frank Easterbrook and Daniel Fischel. Their most celebrated essay postulates that the "corporation is a complex set of explicit and implicit contracts, and corporate law enables the participants to set the optimal arrangement for the many different sets of risks and opportunities that are available in a large economy."[74]

Easterbrook and Fischel maintain that wider social issues are and should remain outside the purview of the market, citing approvingly Adam Smith in defense of the proposition that "the extended conflict among selfish people produces prices that allocate resources to their most valuable uses."[75] In this context, the role of corporate law is solely "to establish rights among participants in the venture."[76] For Easterbrook and Fischel, the key normative advantage of such an approach is that it "removes from the field of interesting questions one that has plagued

---

[72] P. Ireland, "The Myth of Shareholder Ownership" (1999) 62 *Modern Law Review* 32 at 33.

[73] See JK Galbraith, *The Affluent Society* (1959); see also S. Marglin, *The Dismal Science* (2008).

[74] F. Easterbrook and D. Fischel, "The Corporate Contract" (1989) 89 *Columbia Law Review* 1416 at 1418.

[75] Ibid, 1422.

[76] Ibid, 1428 (Easterbrook and Fischel do note, however, circumstances where the corporate contract can be trumped. As the state, "the argument that contracts are optimal applies only if the contracting parties bear the full costs of their decisions and reap all of the gains. It applies only if contracts are enforced after they have been reached. The argument also depends on the availability of the full set of possible contracts. If some types of agreements are foreclosed, the ones actually reached may not be optimal": at 1436).

many writers: what is the goal of the corporation. Is it profit (and for whom). Social welfare more broadly defined. Is there anything wrong with corporate charity? Should corporations try to maximize profit over the long run or the short-run? Our response to such questions is: 'Who Cares?'"[77] This conceptual framework was always empirically questionable. The scale of intervention now required to stabilize global banking turns it into farce. The multifaceted nature of the contemporary crisis provides an opportunity to "rethink" the nature and function of the corporation and the capital markets in which it is nested. In particular, it focuses attention on the externality costs imposed by characterizing the corporation as an essentially private actor.

Notwithstanding the rhetorical power of the "invisible hand" metaphor, the laissez-faire contractual account of governance it ordains is, at base, a political construct. What constitutes the optimal level of intervention is contingent on the variable interaction of material and ideational factors. These include the depth, liquidity and importance of capital markets, interest group organizational power and international regulatory trends. The extent and direction of change are further determined by the environmental impact of professional norms and behavioral mores on the formal and informal nodes supporting the structural architecture. The complex interaction of these vectors determines who is given voice, authority and legitimacy within the overarching regulatory matrix. A critical mediating factor is the ideational terms of reference set by the wider political firmament. As Christopher Stone makes clear, legal frameworks operate within two distinct languages of control. One the one hand, there is "law's routine operating level: the language of rules and regulations, statutes and opinions. Transcending that is the legal meta-language of policy statements and principles, the chat of academicians, many of whose terms never descend into the operating language but which serve to assess, direct and nurture it."[78] Corporate responsibilities are framed by the capacity of institutional actors to influence what constitutes the limits of outside interference on capacities to contract within both domains. In this context, the falsification of the normative benefits of laissez faire economics extends far beyond what Hugh Collins terms "the productive

---

[77] Ibid, 1446.
[78] C. Stone, "Corporate Vices and Corporate Virtues: Do Public/Private Distinctions Matter" (1981) 130 *University of Pennsylvania Law Review* 1441 at 1442.

disintegration of private law."[79] To be truly effective, a regulatory system must operate with integrity (i.e. irrespective of whether the regime is rules-based or relies on an enabling system of oversight, it must be informed by a single, coherent set of overarching principles that delineate the rights and duties of all institutional actors).

The problems associated with a lack of integrity in capital markets are not new but the global financial crisis has made satisfactory resolution of them critical. As Edward Mason noted in 1958, the rise of the corporation had a profound impact on the "carefully reasoned" laissez-faire defense offered by classical economics, which held that "the economic behavior promoted and constrained by the institutions of a free market system is, in the main, in the public interest."[80] For Mason, the defense rested on foundations that "depended largely on the general acceptance of a reasoned justification of the system on moral as well as on political and economic grounds." The emergence of major corporations, immune from meaningful controls, along with its "apologetics" within the management literature "appears devastatingly to undermine the intellectual presuppositions of this system" without offering "an equally satisfying ideology for twentieth century consumption."[81] As such, "the entrepreneur of classical economics has given way to something quite different, and along with him disappears a substantial element in the traditional capitalist apologetic."[82] Despite Mason's misgivings, the economic conception of the corporation as a "nexus of contracts" extended well beyond the boundaries of the economics tradition. Alan Greenspan's admission that he was "partially" wrong in his deference to the capacity of the market to exercise necessary restraint marks a step forward. Greenspan, however, cautioned lawmakers not to rely on a command and control approach. "Whatever regulatory changes are made, they will pale in comparison to the change already evident in today's markets. Those markets for an indefinite future will be far more restrained than would any currently contemplated new regulatory regime."[83] Major job losses across the sector will

---

[79] H. Collins, *Regulating Contracts* (1999) 59.
[80] E. Mason, "The Apologetics of Managerialism" (1958) 31 *Journal of Business* 1 at 5. See also Galbraith, above n 63, 6–17.
[81] Ibid, 6. 9.
[82] Ibid, 10.
[83] Evidence to House Committee on Oversight and Government Reform, Washington DC, 23 October 2008 (A. Greenspan). For discussion of blame, see J. Reed, "Crisis Has Resulted From Honest Misjudgments By Finance Sector" (Letter to Editor), *Financial*

lengthen the restraining order. This is particularly important in New York. It is reported as many as 78,000 jobs could be lost.[84] While the securities industry (5% of total employment and 25% of earnings) has borne the public brunt of announced and planned job losses, the collapse of confidence has a wider spillover effect on professional and business services, including legal and accounting corporate advisory, as well as advertising.[85] A similar reality is dawning in London.[86] The challenge for a now weakened financial sector and for society is to build corporate governance and capital market regulation in ways that emphasize duties and responsibilities as well as corporate rights. Here progressive corporate law scholarship provides a useful starting point.[87]

Orts, for example, argues that it is impossible to "corporate law involves the simultaneous pursuit and coexistence of a number of ends or purposes, with the mix a predominance of different values depending on particular legal contexts."[88] For Orts then, "the technical rules of corporate law are primarily about structuring economic organizational power."[89] This, in turn, draws one's attention to the essential political nature of corporate governance design. It also suggests the need to take into account "a complex array of normative values, not only economic values which themselves are often divided and difficult to fathom but also values of abiding by the law and other principles of ethical business behavior."[90]

Untangling and ordering the precise public duties and responsibilities of an entity endowed with distinct contractual rights is inordinately complex. The policy problem is how to order those principles in a coherent and acceptable manner so as to strengthen political legitimacy. Legitimacy requires commitment at three interlinked

Times, 21 October 2008, 14; D. McDonald, "Crisis Caused By Negligence and Incredible Stupidity" (Letter to Editor), *Financial Times*, 24 October 2008, 10.

[84] J. Bram, J. Orr, and R. Rosen, *Employment in the New York-New Jersey Region: 2008 Review and Outlook* (Federal Reserve Bank of New York, 22 October 2008) 5.

[85] Ibid, 4 (The report further notes "each securities job is estimated to generate 2.3 other jobs by spurring demand for business and professional services...and real estate as well as other services such as hotels and restaurants": 5).

[86] A. McDonald and C. Bryan-Low, "Turmoil Batter's London's Status as Financial Center," *Wall Street Journal*, 22 October 2008, A1.

[87] E. Orts, "The Complexity and Legitimacy of Corporate Law" (1993) 50 *Washington and Lee Law Review 1565*.

[88] Ibid, 1566.

[89] Ibid, 1582.

[90] Ibid, 1612.

levels. At its most basic level, legal validity is necessary (based on the need for wide compliance to legal rules). At the middle level, there is a need to test for empirical legitimacy (i.e. the degree of warranted or unwarranted public confidence in the structure of economic relations). Overarching this is the need to assess systemic legitimacy (i.e. the extent to which the processes of corporate governance reform are tied to rational or ideational terms of reference').[91] This is, by necessity, an ongoing process. At any given moment, contingent resolution depends on the capacity of ideational forces to create, maintain, or undermine two critical and interlinked components: problem identification and problem parameters. The crisis has now produced a paradigmatic tipping point. The unprecedented nature of central bank intervention mirrors the admission by the chair of the most influential lobby group in investment banking that he "no longer believe[s] in the market's self-healing power."[92]

While it may be inopportune to engage in structural reform in the midst of a crisis, it is clear that the normative advantages of embedding a corporate form of associational democracy without reference or subservience to wider societal goals have been falsified. The critical policy challenge is to fashion an alternative framework that safeguards security without compromising innovation. Given the reality of globalization, it is not plausible to retreat to national-based uncoordinated approaches to financial regulation. Sustainable reform necessitates fundamental changes to both the structure and purpose of the global financial architecture. The necessary first step is to ascertain how the underlying problem is defined, to account for and order competing interpretations, and to evaluate the impact of proposed solutions. This requires, in turn, an investigation of how ideational terms of reference set the parameters of what constitutes rational policy responses. Methodologically, this requires a thorough anatomical investigation of the form, purpose, and substance of the complex legal reality that underpins corporate and regulatory decision-making.[93]

---

[91] Ibid, 1617; see more generally, J. Parkinson, "Legitimacy Problems in Deliberative Democracy" (2003) 51 *Political Studies* 180.

[92] Josef Ackerman, chairman of Deutsche Bank, quoted in J Randall, "When the Going Gets Tough, Banks Yell for Nanny," *Daily Telegraph* (London), 26 March 2008 (Online edition). See also L. Blankfein, "Do Not Destroy the Essential Catalyst of Risk," *Financial Times*, 9 February 2009, 13.

[93] The "institutional autopsy" heuristic is used to great effect in C. Milhaupt and K. Pistor, *Law and Capitalism* (2008) 45-46.

Chapter 2

The Price of Failure

The appropriate pricing of risk by private actors is arguably a commercial calculation. It is necessary, however, for the managers, board directors and owners of the providers of structured finance products to recognize responsibility for a systemic crisis of confidence. As the new US Treasury Secretary has pointed out, the "conventional risk-management framework today focuses too much on the threat to a firm from its own mistakes and too little on the potential for mistakes to be correlated across firms."[1] In somewhat plainer language, the European Commissioner for Internal Markets and Services refers to the consequences of imbibing with abandon a toxic cocktail of "stupidity, ignorance [and] misplaced optimism."[2] Commissioner McCreevy suggests the failure of internal risk management systems derives from the fact that senior corporate executives "of large financial institutions have admitted in their more candid moments that they did not understand many of the new products that their firms were designing, underwriting and trading."[3] The underlying risk associated with an expansion in securitization was not adequately considered. As a result, some of the most influential bankers on Wall Street have made inglorious exits, a process that culminated with the departure of John Thain from Bank of

---

[1] T. Geithner, "Reducing Systemic Risk in a Dynamic Financial System" (Speech at Economic Club of New York, 9 June 2008). Geithner further claimed that "innovation got ahead of risk management and restraint and prudence." See Confirmation Hearing, Senate Finance Committee, Washington DC, 21 January 2009.
[2] C. McCreevy, "International Financial Crisis: Its Causes and What to Do About It" (Speech delivered at Alliance of Liberals and Democrats for Europe, Brussels, 27 February 2008).
[3] Interview, Brussels, 15 May 2008; see more generally N. Taleb, *The Black Swan: The Impact of the Highly Improbable* (2007) 4 (in which the former options-trader argues that a "triplet of opacity" clouds understanding: "the illusion of understanding; the retrospective distortion; and an overvaluation of factual information").

America, just weeks after he effected an increasingly controversial merger with Merrill Lynch.[4] Thain has long had a reputation for repositioning financial institutions. He was recruited to lead the New York Stock Exchange following a scandal involving excessive executive compensation and poor governance. After Stan O'Neal's forced resignation from Merrill Lynch in the wake of multi-billion dollar losses associated with bad bets on the securitization markets, Thain was tasked with turning around the "thundering herd."[5] Realizing the enormity of the task, he instead negotiated an emergency sale. He has come in for ferocious criticism for paying executive bonuses in the final weeks of Merrill Lynch's existence as an independent entity and has been subpoenaed to give evidence in an investigation by the New York State Attorney General. The payments coincided with the disclosure that the investment house made a further $15.3 billion loss in the final quarter of 2008. His reputation for probity was further eroded by the revelation that he had lavishly refurbished his executive offices. In a memo, Thain defended his actions:

> I want to address several topics that have been inaccurately reported in the press. The first issue is our year-end bonus payments. Our 2008 discretionary bonus pool was 41% lower than 2007. The size of the pool, its composition (cash and stock mix), and the timing of the payments for both the cash and stock were all determined together with Bank of America and approved by our Management Development and Compensation Committee and our Board. The total bonus pool was also substantially less than the amount allowed under our merger agreement. The second topic is the losses in the fourth quarter, which were very large and unfortunate. However, they were incurred almost entirely on legacy positions and were due to market movements. We were completely transparent with Bank of America. They learned about

---

[4] Other high profile departures include those of Charles Prince at Citigroup (4 November 2007); Zoe Cruz, a co-president at Morgan Stanley (30 November 2007); and James Cayne, chief executive at Bear Stearns (9 January, 2008).

[5] See G. Morgenson, "How the Thundering Herd Faltered and Fell," *New York Times,* 9 November 2008, A1 (reporting that Merrill Lynch had entered the securitization business very late in the process and engaged in aggressive acquisition strategies combined with excessive risk taking in order to emulate the success of Lehman Brothers. According to John Kansas, the chief executive of Northfork Bancorp, which Merrill attempted to buy in 2005, the deal fell through because "unfortunately in the end, we were put off by the fact that we couldn't get comfortable with their risk profile and we could not get past the fact that we thought there was a distinct possibility that they didn't fully understand their own risk profile").

these losses when we did. The acting CFO of my businesses was Bank of America's former Chief Accounting Officer. They had daily access to our p&l [profit and loss]. Our year-end balance sheet target (which we more than met) was given to us by Bank of America's CFO. The final topic is the expenses related to my office. The $1.2 million reported in the press was for the renovation of my office, two conference rooms and a reception area. The expenses were incurred over a year ago in a very different environment. Nonetheless, they were a mistake in the light of the world we live in today. I will therefore reimburse the company for all of the costs incurred.[6]

While Thain can be accused of impaired judgment, responsibility for the financial crisis cannot be placed at the hands of individual myopic bankers alone. Rather, it reflects multiple accountability disorders across managerial, legal and political dimensions.[7] In the United Kingdom, the influential Treasury Select Committee held hearings at which leading former bankers at Royal Bank of Scotland and Halifax Bank of Scotland (HBOS) testified that they were sorry for the mistakes that led to the effective nationalization of the former and the government taking a major shareholding in a combined entity that subsumes the latter within the Lloyds TSB Group. The apologies did little to curb public anger. At no stage did the executives provide any convincing narrative as to the over-reliance on the wholesale money markets on the part of HBOS or an ill-timed takeover of ABN-Amro in the case of RBS, an acquisition that was rendered even more questionable because it was consummated after the credit crisis began to bite.[8] Tom McKillop, the former RBS chairman,

---

[6] John Thain "Memo to Merrill Lynch Staff," 26 January 2009 (Full text available online at: http://blogs.wsj.com/deals/2009/01/26/john-thain-memo-bank-of-america-knew-everything/); D. Fitzpatrick, S. Craig, and C. Mollenkamp, "Thain Ousted in Clash at Bank of America," *Wall Street Journal*, 26 January 2009. A1 (reporting that Thain lobbied behind the scenes for a multi-billion dollar bonus, which was not paid in part because of the disclosure of the negotiations); see also L. Story and J. Creswell, "For Bank of America and Merrill, Love Was Blind," *New York Times*, 8 February 2009, B1 (reporting internal divisions within Merrill Lynch about Thain's tenure that helped "splinter the carefully tended image of Merrill's chief executive, a man perceived during most of his career to be a robotic and circumspect number cruncher").
[7] B. Romsek and M. Dubnick, "Accountability in the Public Sector: Lessons from the Challenger Tragedy" (1987) 47 *Public Administration Review* 227. For application of accountability model to corporate sector, see M. Dubnick, "Sarbanes-Oxley and the Search for Accountable Corporate Governance" in J. O'Brien (ed), *Private Equity, Corporate Governance and the Dynamics of Capital Market Governance* (2007) 284–88.
[8] "Hearing on Banking Crisis," Treasury Select Committee, Houses of Parliament, Westminster, 10 February 2009.

accepted that in hindsight, the takeover of ABN was "a bad mistake," while the former chief executive, Fred Goodwin, bristled that it "is too simplistic to blame it all on me." At HBOS, both the former chairman and the chief executive had little banking experience. They determined that was unnecessary as they were surrounded with people of broad experience. The situation reached a critical point with the publication of a memo from the former head of Group Regulatory Risk, Paul Moore. Moore claimed that he had warned the then chief executive, Sir James Crosby, of excessive risk taking at HBOS. He claimed that his warnings were ignored.[9] His memo to the Committee is explosive.

> When I was Head of Group Regulatory Risk at HBOS, I certainly knew that the bank was going too fast (and told them), had a cultural indisposition to challenge (and told them) and was a serious risk to financial stability (what the FSA call "Maintaining Market Confidence") and consumer protection (and told them). I told the Board they ought to slow down but was prevented from having this properly minuted by the CFO. I told them that their sales culture was significantly out of balance with their systems and controls. I was told by the FSA, the Chairman of the Audit Committee and others that I was doing a good job. Notwithstanding this, I was dismissed by the CEO (he wrote that it was "...his decision and his alone"). I sued HBOS for unfair dismissal under the whistle blowing legislation. Ironically, I was also the "Good Practice Manager" for whistle blowing purposes at HBOS but could hardly report my case to myself! HBOS finally settled my claim against them for substantial damages in mid 2005. I was subjected to a gagging order but have decided so speak out now because I believe the public interest demands it.[10]

In his memo to the Committee, Moore claims that his replacement had no experience in risk management, in contravention of FSA guidelines. Furthermore, Moore claimed this was reported to the regulatory authorities and ignored.

---

[9] P. Moore, Memo to Treasury Select Committee, Westminster, 10 February 2009 ("My personal experience of being on the inside as a risk and compliance manager has shown me is that, whatever the very specific, final and direct causes of the financial crisis, I strongly believe that the real underlying cause of all the problems was simply this—a total failure of all key aspects of governance. In my view and from my personal experience at HBOS, all the other specific failures stem from this one primary cause.") The following day Crosby resigned as Deputy Chairman of the FSA. He denied that he had behaved inappropriately in relation to the termination of Moore.
[10] Ibid, 47.

My concerns on this appointment were reported to the FSA but
despite the clarity of their guidance on assessing fit and properness
they permitted the individual concerned to become an Approved
Person. It is extraordinary in my view that the FSA permitted this,
when this role is so important to the fulfillment of their statutory
objectives. Maybe they felt constrained, as James Crosby was a
non-executive director of the FSA at the time?[11]

The problems for the British government and its once admired and now
partially discredited flagship Financial Services Authority are intensified
because after his own departure from HBOS, James Crosby was knighted
and then appointed Deputy Chairman of the FSA and a senior advisor to
the Treasury on how to reform the regulation of the banking sector. The
Treasury Select Committee has resolved to further investigate Moore's
claims. At the very least, it raises profound questions about the close
relationship between the City and its regulator, a situation that is
replicated in a range of jurisdictions, including Ireland and the United
States. In the case of Ireland, the former chief executive of the Irish
Financial Regulatory Authority, Liam O'Reilly, became a board member
of Irish Life & Permanent, which is at the center of a major scandal
involving Anglo Irish Bank. O'Reilly, who also serves as chairman of
the Chartered Accountants Regulatory Board, was reportedly unaware of
a failure to monitor the $8.98 million in transfers between IL&P and
Anglo Irish Bank discussed in the previous chapter. The transactions,
which are now subject to regulatory investigation, have done much to
undermine the legitimacy of Irish banking and destroyed an already
tarnished international reputation. In the United States, the revolving
door between regulatory bodies and Wall Street is, if anything, even
more pronounced. The result is the dangerous inculcation of a common
set of beliefs in what constitutes the problem and how it should be
resolved.

I   MISMANAGING MANAGERIAL RISK

Financial crises happen with regularity. The current global financial
crisis is merely the latest if most catastrophic. The recurring problem is
that during a boom, it is not in the interests of any institutional actor to
seriously question whether the trading strategies being undertaken were

[11] Ibid.

either reasonable or sustainable. Indeed, given the profits that were occurring prior to the vaporization of credit markets in August 2007, any attempt by a publicly listed financial services firm to resist market practice would likely to have prompted negative comment from market analysts and from shareholders. Moreover, within the firm, hierarchical reporting structures coupled with unwillingness to challenge because of fear of retaliation have long been recognized in case study analysis of actual board performance.[12] At no stage in the Treasury Select Committee hearings into the causes of the credit crisis did any of the banking executives admit responsibility for the decisions that they personally took. No sins of omission or commission were admitted.

The industry-wide belief that risk could be tabulated through the use of quantitative measures was a chimera. Value at Risk (VaR) models calculated overall and subset portfolio exposure on a daily basis. The formulae, which were endorsed by the Securities and Exchange Commission and the Basel Committee on Banking Supervision, lacked historical depth. As a consequence of a reliance on short-term data, the models did not compute for systemic shocks or improbable events.[13] Furthermore, the assumptions underlying how individual firms measured particular risk salience lacked sufficient definition. Just as significantly, there was a failure to provide guidance as to whether the VaR models in fact worked. The partial nature of the disclosure was a major contributing factor to the severity of the financial crisis. It remains the source of continuing fear of counterparty risk. This is a global problem. Such is the continuing level of distrust about actual VaR performance that one major hedge fund manager, Jim Rogers, does not "think there is a sound UK

---

[12] For the impaired role of the board, see J. Pound, "The Promise of the Governed Corporation" in *Harvard Business Review on Corporate Governance* (2000) 89 at 95; see also M. Mace *Directors: Myth and Reality* (1971) 205–6 (outlining CEO dominance and limited value of board to act as corporate conscience), cited in O. Williamson, "Corporate Boards of Directors: In Principle and In Practice" (2007) 24 *Journal of Law, Economics & Organization* 247 (noting that "the board in practice is at a huge disadvantage to the top management of the corporation in information and expertise respects" and "the disparity between boards of directors in principle and corporate boards in practice is widely interpreted as a serious, perhaps the defining, illustration of the failures of capitalism": at 254, 267).

[13] A Federal Reserve study noted as early as 2000 that there was enormous variation in VaR models and furthermore "unclear connection with actual trading performance," cited in J. Lopez, "Disclosure as a Supervisory Tool" (2003) 22 *Federal Reserve Bank of San Francisco Economic Letter* 1 at 2.

bank now. At least, if there is one I don't know about it."[14] The precipitous decline in market capitalization across the global banking sector would appear to corroborate cynicism about bank values, material and moral. In the United States, the epicenter of the crisis, formal legal changes to corporate governance practices in the *Sarbanes-Oxley Act* (2002) offered little more than symbolic reassurance.[15] Passed in the immediate aftermath of the Enron and related financial reporting scandals, the legislation appeared to address the problems of deficient oversight in the corporate boardroom and ostensibly strengthened the fiduciary responsibility of external gatekeepers, particularly the audit profession but also, to a more limited extent, the legal community. Homogenous application of risk management procedures to attest internal controls—mandated under section 404 of the Act—discounted application of critical thinking within both the corporation and the provider of external audit services. The reforms offered a patina of legitimacy to a system of oversight that policymakers recognized was fundamentally flawed. The unresolved policy question is why, despite the recognition, attempts to exercise restraint failed?

Even before the implosion of the securitization market, there was mounting evidence of how defective our conceptions of corporate governance had become. Bankruptcies, excessive leverage, suspect trading with related parties, abusive use of tax shelters, failure of due diligence were not merely the prosecutorial outplaying of an unethical past. Rather they represented an unethical present. Take, for example, the battle for control of Hollinger International following (proven) allegations that its chief executive, (Lord) Conrad Black, had been provided with inappropriate payments. When sacked by his formerly supine board, Black lodged a defamation suit. Furthermore, he tried to convince the Delaware Court of Chancery that he had an untrammeled right to dispose of the company he had founded without reference to any underpinning fiduciary or stewardship obligations. The Delaware Court dismissed the application in a ruling that was unprecedented in its ferocity. Black was accused of being evasive and unreliable.[16] A report

---

[14] J. Rogers, "View of the Day," *Financial Times*, 22 January 2009, 25.

[15] M. Edelman, *The Symbolic Uses of Politics* (1964). For application of "symbolic lens" to Sarbanes-Oxley, see J. O'Brien, *Redesigning Financial Regulation* (2007).

[16] *Hollinger International Inc vs. Conrad Black, Hollinger Inc*, Case No 183-N, Court of Chancery of State of Delaware (24 February 2004). In a later ruling, Strine held that Hollinger was obligated to continue paying legal defense fees despite the conviction of Black in a criminal trial in 2007 over the improper spurious non-compete clauses; see

for the board by the former chairman of the Securities and Exchange Commission, Richard Breeden, went even further.

> To fully gauge the level of disregard for shareholders' interests, one must step back from individual transactions and note the myriad of schemes, fiduciary abuses and fraudulent acts that were used to transfer essentially the entire earnings outputs of Hollinger over a seven year period to the controlling shareholders [namely Black and his former chief operating officer]. In this case, more than most, one must not overlook the forest for the trees.[17]

The report tabulated that 95.2% of profits were improperly siphoned off. The company was "systematically manipulated and used by its controlling shareholders for their sole benefit and in a manner that violated every concept of fiduciary duty."[18] It was, Breeden concluded, nothing short of a corporate kleptocracy."[19] Black and his co-conspirator —who turned state witness against him—did not act alone. They required technical, legal and accounting expertise to facilitate deception on this scale. At no stage did any of the financial intermediaries alert regulatory authority. Moreover, their crimes continued even after the passage of Sarbanes-Oxley. In part, this could be traced to legislative timidity. As the judge who provided the negative ruling in the Delaware case noted, many reforms initiated in Sarbanes-Oxley "appear to have been taken off the shelf and put into the mix, not so much because they would have helped to prevent the scandals, but because they filled the perceived need for far-reaching reform and were less controversial than

---

Sun-Times Media Group f/k/a Hollinger International Inc v Conrad Black, John Boultbee, Peter Atkinson and Michael Kipnis, CA No 3518-VCS (Curtailing payment of legal fees in advance of final non-appealable conclusion of a proceeding would be "odd complex, inefficient and capricious": at 31). Black is currently serving a 78-month sentence in a federal prison in Florida. The demand for the non-advancement of legal fees to executives facing criminal charges was a critical factor in undermining the authority of the deferred prosecution mechanism adopted by the United States Department of Justice in the aftermath of the Enron scandal; see below n 37–60 and accompanying text.

[17] R. Breeden, "Report of Special Investigation by the Special Committee of the Board of Directors of Hollinger International" (Washington DC, 30 August 2004) 4–5.

[18] Ibid, 1.

[19] Ibid, 4. Breeden came to a similar view in an earlier investigation into WorldCom, where he found the board acquiesced in providing the CEO, Bernie Ebbers "imperial reign"; see R. Breeden, "Restoring Trust" (2003) 1.

other measures more clearly aimed at preventing similar scandals."[20] Most notably the reliance on independent directors, enshrined in US conceptions of corporate governance best practice, proved to be grossly deficient bulwark against malfeasance and misfeasance.

The Hollinger Board included a range of former statesmen from both sides of the Atlantic as well as prominent businessmen. The chairman of the audit committee was a former ranking official at the Department of Defense, Richard Perle. Perle received improper payments totaling $5.4 million from Black. According to the Breeden report, the former politician repeatedly breached his fiduciary duties.

> It is, of course, possible for a conflicted board member to act at least somewhat responsibly. As a conflicted Executive Committee member, however, Perle did not. Rather, his Executive Committee performance falls squarely into the "head-in-the-sand" behavior that breaches a director's duty of good faith and renders him liable for damages under Delaware law. Perle's own description of his performance on the Executive Committee was stunning. He informed the Special Committee that he considered the Executive Committee to be only a means of facilitating paperwork that would eventually be presented to the full Board. He could not recall the Executive Committee ever meeting in person. Rather, from time-to-time, Perle would simply receive a package of Executive Committee consents or resolutions to sign. Perle regarded these documents as mere formalities and signed them all since they appeared to be routine business of the Company. He said that he never discussed any of the consents with Black or [CFO] Radler before signing them. In fact, he admitted that he generally did not even read them or understand the transactions to which they applied. It is difficult to imagine a more flagrant abdication of duty than a director rubber-stamping transactions that directly benefit a controlling shareholder without any thought, comprehension or analysis.[21]

---

[20] L. Strine and W. Chandler, "The New Federalism of the American Corporate Governance System: Preliminary Reflections of Two Residents of One Small State" (2003) 152 *University of Pennsylvania Law Review* 953; see also R. Romano "The Sarbanes-Oxley Act and the Making of Quack Corporate Governance" (2005) 114 *Yale Law Journal* 1521 (criticizing the passage of "emergency legislation without deference to exiting empirical research": at 1528); for contours of the debate see D. Langevoort, "The Social Construction of Sarbanes Oxley" (2007) 107 *Michigan Law Review* 1817; see also J. Hill, "Evolving Rules of the Game" in J. O'Brien (ed), *Private Equity, Corporate Governance and the Dynamics of Capital Market Governance* (2007) 29.

[21] Breeden, above n 17, at 483–84. Furthermore, the report found that "the Special Committee believes that Perle's repeated failure to read, evaluate, discuss or attempt to understand the Executive Committee Consents before signing them evidences a complete

Black was well able to cow his so-called directors and entertained nothing but disdain for institutional investors, referring to critics as "corporate governance fascists."[22] Independence, therefore, is an exceptionally weak defense. As the late John Kenneth Galbraith put it, "the relationship [between independent directors and management] somewhat resembles that of an honorary degree participant to a member of a university faculty."[23] Fiduciary obligation is itself an insufficient buttress for probity and integrity; the latter requires board directors to take cognizance of empirical evidence and not rely on the fact that the corporation has designed a governance regime that conforms to self-designed principles of best practice. Take for example the case of Robert Rubin, who announced his resignation from Citigroup in January just before the announcement that the conglomerate was to split itself up. Rubin has been a pivotal figure at the intersection of Wall Street and Washington for decades. He steered through the *Financial Modernization Act* (1999), legislation that broke down the separation of investment and commercial banking, and retrospectively legalized the creation of Citigroup, whose failures have been talismanic of unethical practice. To the end Rubin denied any responsibility for either the failings within the conglomerate or with the integrated banking model he helped create and sustain.[24] Unless those failures are acknowledged, however, the search for a solution will be hopelessly compromised.

The implosion of Citigroup raises a further series of questions about deficient management of ethical issues.[25] The corporation has been

---

absence of good faith, a breach of loyalty and an abject failure to fulfill his fiduciary duties as an Executive Committee member. Such conduct subjects him to personal liability for breaching his duty of good faith": at 488).

[22] A. Neil, "Why It's Looking Black for Conrad," *The Scotsman*, 25 November 2006 (Online Edition).

[23] J.K. Galbraith, *The Economics of Innocent Fraud* (2004) 74–5.

[24] See E. Dash and J. Creswell, "Citigroup Saw No Red Flags Even As It Made Bolder Bets," *New York Times*, 23 November 2008, A1 (quoting an April 2008 interview in which Rubin argued "In hindsight, there are a lot of things we'd do differently. But in the context of the facts as I knew them and my role, I'm inclined to think probably not.") This reprised an argument made in his autobiography on the financial reporting scandals at the turn of the millennium; see R. Rubin, *In An Uncertain World* (2003) 337 ("The great bull market masked many sins, or created powerful incentives not to dwell on problems when all seemed to be going well—a natural human inclination"); for internal conflicts within the Clinton administration over the regulation of financial markets, see J. Stiglitz, *The Roaring Nineties* (2003) 159–62.

[25] See O'Brien, above n 15, 111–19.

at the center of a series of acrimonious disputes over deficiencies in its ethical culture. What makes the problems at Citigroup more difficult to comprehend is that the conglomerate introduced a totally revised code of conduct in 2005, three years after the passage of Sarbanes-Oxley. The then Chief Executive admitted that revision was necessary because "we emphasized the short-term side of the equation exclusively. We didn't think we had to say: "And by the way, don't violate the law." They were unspoken assumptions that need to be spoken."[26] The redesign was introduced, in part to stave off growing concern that the conglomerate was incapable of exercising restraint. The head of Citigroup in Tokyo, for example, was forced to issue a humiliating apology for an "aggressive sales culture whereby attention was not paid to the rules, even if those involved knew what the rules were. We acknowledge there was a fundamental flaw in our organization involving a weak culture of compliance and internal controls."[27] The executive accepted that there was no excuse for the transgressions.

In the United Kingdom, traders for the bank destroyed the MTS trading system on sovereign debt in an audacious trading bet that involved 100 different bonds in 13 different markets using 13 platforms, the majority of which were controlled by a consortium of banks, including Citigroup itself. Corporate headquarters consistently stated that the trade "did not violate any applicable rules or regulation." Nevertheless, following publication of an internal memo that outlined how the strategy could "kill off smaller rivals the bank accepted the language and the trade itself was 'inappropriate, unrealistic and juvenile...We failed to consider its potential impact on our clients and other stakeholders, including European regulators and treasuries, and because it did not meet our standards."[28] In each case, Citigroup acquiesced because there was no requirement to admit wrongdoing. When the Australian Securities and Investments Commission launched legal action against Citigroup over an alleged breach of fiduciary duties,

---

[26] R. Smith, "Citigroup CEO Pursues Culture of Ethics," *Wall Street Journal*, 2 March 2005 (Online Edition).

[27] D. Ibison, "Citigroup Promises to Compensate Japanese Clients," *Financial Times*, 30 November 2004 (Online Edition).

[28] P. Munter, "Citigroup Says Bond Traders Miscalculated," *Financial Times*, 2 February 2005 (Online Edition). Citigroup was eventually fined 4 million sterling and forced to disgorge a further 10 million to settle a (rare) regulatory action taken by the Financial Services Authority; see D. Reilly. "Citigroup to Take $25 Million Hit in Dr Evil Case," *Wall Street Journal*, 29 June 2005, C3.

it successfully defended the action. Its determination to contest the action was linked to both its protestation that the bank did not in fact owe fiduciary obligation in the case in question and an explicit rejection of the insider trading allegations but also because any settlement would have involved an admission of criminal guilt. The key issue for Citigroup is that it produced evidence in court of a mandate letter that explicitly revoked a fiduciary obligation. ASIC unsuccessfully argued that a reliance on this contractual clause could only be justified in the event that the investment bank had secured the informed consent of its client.[29] Success in the Australian federal court, however, does little to deal with the wider question of how better to manage potential conflicts.

The oversight issues at Citigroup demonstrate just how problematic it is to rely on monetary penalties alone. Civil sanctions through cease and desist orders are written off as the cost of doing business. Profit disgorgement represents an ineffective restraint, particularly for financial services firms. The potential for compliance programs to inculcate values has been undermined by the emphasis on maximizing share value, which tends to privilege an instrumentalist view of ethics.[30] Furthermore, the failure to align financial incentives with stated corporate priorities can create a reflexive environment that encourages derogation from publicly stated codes of ethics and other restraining forces provided by the articles of association. Adversarial systems, in turn, privilege a rules-based approach to compliance that is all too easily circumvented. The inflation of the securitization bubble required only collective amnesia in what was to become an age of credulity.

Politicians, including the Treasury Secretary, Henry Paulson, expressed alarm at the rapid growth of London and the emergence of regional financial markets in Dubai, Sao Paulo, and Shanghai.[31] The need

---

[29] See P. Hanrahan, "ASIC v Citigroup: Investment Banks, Conflicts of Interest and Chinese Walls" in O'Brien, above n 7, 117, 124-29.

[30] D. Quinn and T. Jones, "An Agent Morality View of Business Policy" (1995) 20 *Academy of Management Review* 22 at 25.

[31] See McKinsey Report, *Sustaining New York's and the US' Global Financial Services Leadership* (2007) (criticizing "the multi-tiered and highly complex nature of the US legal system...[and] the lack of coordination and clarity on the ways and means of enforcement...[can lead to a perception that it is] neither fair nor predictable": at 17). The McKinsey report endorses the findings of a separate investigation endorsed by the US Treasury; see Committee on Capital Markets Regulation, *Interim Report* (2006) (suggesting the "criminal enforcement system needs better balance": at xii). Both fed into

to safeguard innovation rather than security became the key indicator by which regulatory performance was measured. In many ways the emasculation of regulatory authority followed a well-worn pattern. Irrespective of ideological persuasion, incumbent governments rarely respond well to accusations of panic-derived policy design. In practice, this necessitates a preservation order mandating the maintenance of the external architecture.[32] While external sight lines remain unchanged, incremental change can hollow out the regulatory construct, fundamentally altering its purpose.[33] This is precisely what has happened to the Securities and Exchange Commission throughout the era of financial capitalism and to the Department of Justice in the aftermath of the passage of Sarbanes-Oxley.

II   WEAKENING PROSECUTORIAL AUTHORITY

Despite undoubted success in bringing abuse to light, regulatory, and prosecutorial agencies were unable to engineer lasting cultural change. Attempts to use creative enforcement strategies, such as negotiated prosecutions, to counteract creative compliance lacked coherent and consistent ordering. Populist discourse often bifurcated (without necessarily having a solid empirical grounding) between the accountable and responsive political party structure seeking to reduce regulatory burden and a didactic unaccountable bureaucracy which was

---

and amplified warnings by the then US Treasury Secretary to policymakers not to create or maintain "a thicket of regulation." See H. Paulson, "Remarks on the Competitiveness of US Capital Markets" (Speech delivered at National Economic Club of New York, 20 November 2006).

[32] For accounts that highlight the importance of politics, see J. Cioffi, "Revenge of the Law: Securities Litigation Reform and Sarbanes-Oxley's Structural Regulation of Corporate Governance" in M. Landy, M. Levin, and M. Shapiro (eds), *Creating Competitive Markets* (2007) 60 (emphasizing the contingent nature of interest group power). For how preferences are translated in policy outcomes more generally, see P. Gourevitch and J. Shinn, *Political Power and Corporate Control: The New Global Politics of Corporate Governance* (2005).

[33] Of equal importance was the passage of the *Private Securities Litigation Reform Act* of 1995 (Public Law 104–67), which made it more difficult to take securities litigation and the *Securities Litigation Uniform Standards Act* of 1998 (Public Law 105–33), which removed court adjudication of securities cases from state level. These developments reduced civil litigation at precisely the same time as public enforcement waned, managerial incentives to game the system increased, thus minimizing the efficiency of deterrence at precisely the same time as exuberance clouded investor judgment, see J. Coffee, *Gatekeepers, The Professions and Corporate Governance* (2006) 60–69.

undermining legislative intent by setting ill-considered strategic priorities. Critically, regulatory authority seeped away as business complained that excessive regulation was reducing the global competitiveness of New York as the epicenter of global finance. It repeated a dynamic seen in the dot.com boom. Throughout the 1990s, critical components of the regulatory architecture were weakened. In a much-cited 1998 speech, the then chairman of the SEC, Arthur Levitt, warned "the motivation to meet Wall Street earnings expectations may be overriding common sense business practices. Too many corporate managers, auditors, and analysts are participants in a game of nods and winks....Today American markets enjoy the confidence of the world. How many half-truths, and how much accounting sleight of hand, will it take to tarnish that truth?"[34] Levitt was ignored. Following the election of George Bush, leadership of the agency passed to Harvey Pitt, the avuncular former SEC operative who, in private practice, led the challenge from the accounting profession against attempts to strengthen the integrity of the audit. Enrollment rather than confrontation became the guiding leitmotif of the agency's interaction with industry. It is indicative that in 2002, the Division of Corporate Finance failed to fully review the annual reports of just under 50% of all firms in the past three years and, more seriously, did not bring under scrutiny the mandatory disclosure filings of firms that trumpeted new paradigms, such as Enron's notoriously complex and now discredited "asset-lite" trading strategy.[35]

---

[34] A. Levitt, "The Numbers Game" (Speech delivered at Center for Law and Business, New York University, 28 September 1998). For background on the development of meretricious accounting, see A. Berenson, *The Number: How the Drive for Quarterly Earnings Corrupted Wall Street and Corporate America* (2003) 129–49; A. Levitt, *Take on the Street* (2003) 128 (detailing how the chief executive of Arthur Andersen told the head of the SEC that any attempt to bar consulting for companies it audited would be seen as a declaration of "war").

[35] See Staff Report to Senate Committee on Government Affairs, "Financial Oversight of Enron: The SEC and Private Sector Watchdogs" (Washington DC, 8 October 2002), 13. The $50 billion trading scandal involving the former chairman of Nasdaq, Bernard Madoff, is just the latest example of this failure of oversight. According to court documents, Madoff admitted to senior employees (his sons) that the firm had been "all just a big lie, basically a giant Ponzi scheme." For overviews of the case and its implications for the SEC, see J. Chung, "Systemic Failure Turns More Ire on SEC," *Financial Times*, 15 December 2008, 18 (quoting John Coffee of Columbia Law School that "if the SEC cannot catch something like that, it is unclear what they can catch"); see also S. Labaton, "Yet Another Blow to SEC's Reputation," *International Herald Tribune*, 17 December 2008, 11; J. Gapper, "Wall Street Insiders and Fools Gold," *Financial*

The accounting scandal at Enron at the turn of the millennium centered on the trading of complex structured finance products and the dubious use of off-balance-sheet Special Purpose Entities. An investigation commissioned by the Enron Board found the entire arrangement by which the chief executive officer, Andrew Fastow, was given permission to self-deal and, as such, given explicit authority to derogate from the company's code of ethics "fundamentally flawed…and should not have been undertaken in the first place."[36] Enron's tactics were, however, far from unique. Congressional investigation demonstrated that the lack of credible enforcement meant that it was cost-effective for entities such as Enron to facilitate tax evasion and financial manipulation with the implicit and at time explicit approval of intermediaries subject to fiduciary obligation.[37]

A series of official reports explored the risks associated with off balance sheet reporting. Each highlighted the danger that the leading providers of corporate advisory services were hopelessly compromised because of inherent conflicts of interest. The Government Accountability Office, for example, noted that "since investment banks might be tempted to participate in profitable but questionable transactions when successful SEC prosecution is in doubt, it is especially important that regulators be alert to this possibility and be ready to use the rest of enforcement tools to deter such actions."[38]

Extraordinary civil litigation led by the Regents of the University of California against the major investment banks highlighted the dangers of the structural arrangement. The complaint bears revisiting in the wake of the global financial crisis. "This fraudulent scheme could not have been and was not perpetrated only by Enron and its insiders. It was

---

Times, 18 December 2008, 9 (noting that Madoff benefited from his status and, more significantly from the mores of "an age of credulity").

[36] W. Powers, "Report of Investigation by the Special Investigative Committee of the Board of Directors of Enron Corporation" (Houston, 1 December 2002) 9.

[37] Joint Committee on Taxation, "Report of Investigation of Enron Corporation and Related Entities Regarding Federal Tax and Compensation Issues and Policy Recommendations" (JCS-3-03, Washington DC, February 2003) 23.

[38] Government Accountability Office, "Investment Banks, The Role of Firms and Their Analysts with Enron and Global Crossing" (GAO-03-511, Washington DC, March 2003), 39; see also Powers, above n 16 ("Many of the most significant transactions were designed to accomplish favorable financial statement results, not to achieve bona fide economic objectives or transfer risk…They allowed Enron to conceal from the market very large losses resulting from Enron's merchant investments by creating an appearance that those investments were hedged": at 4).

designed and/or perpetrated only via the active and knowing involvement of Enron's banks, including JP Morgan, Citigroup, Credit Suisse First Boston, Merrill Lynch, Deutsche Bank, Barclays, Lehman Brothers and Bank of America."[39] The complaint argued that these firms significantly enriched themselves by, for example, advancing funds "that enabled Enron to preserve its liquidity and continue to operate while helping Enron sell billions of dollars of securities to public investors to utilize to pay down Enron's short-term commercial paper and bank debt, again to keep the Enron Ponzi scheme in operation and the banks also played an indispensable role in helping to inflate and support Enron's stock price by issuing research reports that contained false and misleading information about Enron's business, finances and future prospects."[40]

The most credible attempt to change this reality involved exporting deterrence models from the criminal justice system, including deferred and non-prosecution deals.[41] The reconfigured and contested enforcement battleground can be traced, in part, to the significant increase in financial penalties and custodial sentences provided by Sarbanes-Oxley. It rekindled the interest of the Department of Justice in the prosecution of corporate offenders. The key structural change centered on the establishment of a Corporate Crime Task Force, which

---

[39] *Mark Selby et al v Enron Corporation*, "Consolidated Claim Against Violations of Securities Law, " cited in J. O'Brien, *Wall Street on Trial* (2003) 77.

[40] Ibid, 77. The complaint was settled in May 2006 for $6.7 billion as the jury in the criminal trial, held in an adjacent court, deliberated on the personal guilt of Ken Lay, the charismatic chairman of Enron, and his former chief executive, Jeffrey Skilling. Andrew Fastow, the former chief financial officer, who organized the trading strategies and interacted more closely with the investment banks, pleaded guilty in return for a reduced sentence.

[41] This has spawned a voluminous literature; for useful surveys see *Corporate Crime Reporter*; see also "Crime Without Conviction: The Rise of Deferred and Non-Prosecution Agreements" *Corporate Crime Reporter*, 28 December 2005 (noting that deferrals "undermine the general deterrent and adverse publicity impact that results from corporate crime prosecutions and convictions": at 3); B. Greenblum, "What Happens to a Prosecution Deferred? Judicial Oversight of Corporate Deferred Prosecution Agreements" (2005) 105 *Columbia Law Review* 1863 (criticizing discretion and lack of accountability); C. Christie and R. Hanna, "A Push Down the Road of Good Corporate Citizenship: The Deferred Prosecution Agreement Between the US Attorney for the District of New Jersey and Bristol-Meyers Squibb Co" (2006) 43 *American Criminal Law Review* 1043 (articulating goal of wider demonstration effect by reforming industry practice); F. Warin and A. Boutros, "Deferred Prosecution Agreements: A View From the Trenches and a Proposal for Reform" (2007) 93 *Virginia Law Review* 107 (noting the lack of transparency in ascertaining the number as well as content of the agreements).

reinforced the primacy of the Justice Department.[42] Its goals went far beyond bringing individual malefactors to the courts. Instead, the Deputy Attorney General, Larry Thompson, suggested it had become a federal policy imperative to charge the corporation itself for demonstration effect. The effectiveness of the mechanism is predicated on the threat of criminal sanction to institutionalize the wider inculcation of operating and ethical norms.[43] In exchange for a decision to defer criminal or civil prosecution or sentencing, the corporation agrees to a narrative provided by prosecutors, provides evidence to secure convictions against identified executives, makes traditional financial restitution and, crucially, in most cases agrees to significant governance reforms.

According to Thompson, "the substantial risk of great public harm" caused by financial fraud could necessitate "a substantial federal interest in charging the corporation."[44] In a memo circulated to all Attorneys' Offices across the United States, Thompson provided the impetus and broad authorization to consider charging, deferring or offering a non-prosecution deal with conditions to corporations under investigation depending on the calculation of nine non-weighted factors. These were "the nature and seriousness of the offence; the pervasiveness of wrongdoing including the complicity of corporate management; the corporation's history of similar conduct; its disclosure of wrongdoing and its willingness to cooperate in the investigation of its agents, including, if necessary, the waiver of corporate attorney-client and work product protection; the existence and adequacy of the corporation's compliance program; the corporation's remedial actions (which includes the implementation of an effective corporate compliance program or attempts to improve an existing one, the replacement of management, the extent to which those involved were either disciplined and fired, willingness to pay restitution and to cooperate with the relevant government agencies); an evaluation of the collateral consequences; the adequacy of the prosecution of individuals responsible for the

---

[42] C. Wray and R. Hur, "Corporate Criminal Prosecution in a Post-Enron World" (2006).
43 *American Criminal Law Review* 1095 at 1133 (highlighting cooperation between the Department and civil regulatory agencies).
[43] It also meshes with earlier calls for law to formally alter lines of authority within private firms and ensure the continual disclosure of how decisions are made; see C. Stone, *Where The Law Ends: The Social Control of Business* (1975) 217–27.
[44] L. Thompson, "Principles for Prosecution of Business Organizations" (Department of Justice, Washington DC, 20 January 2003).

corporation's malfeasance; and the adequacy of remedies such as civil or regulatory enforcement actions."[45]

From a regulatory perspective, the negotiated prosecution offers a range of advantages. First, individual executives are made amenable to the courts, thereby serving the public policy imperative of individual legal accountability. Second, the corporation is forced to ensure that control deficiencies highlighted by the investigation are adequately addressed. Third, the regulatory authority is given explicit operational veto over implementation by the requirement that the corporation accept ongoing (but time-limited) external monitoring and adjudication of effectiveness.[46] Fourth, by committing to the process, the corporation is shielded from uncertainty and ongoing negative publicity. Fifth, through demonstration effect, the pre-trial diversion triggers a dynamic non-prescriptive process that has the potential to inculcate cultural change across particular sectors. Of critical significance was the manner in which the memorandum provided a mechanism to reinvigorate the form and function of compliance. Each agreement to end (threatened or real) prosecutorial action contained specific provisions designed to enhance the quality of ethical decision-making and transcend a technical approach to compliance. As such, the mechanism and its application were consistent with guidance offered in speeches from Securities and Exchange Commissioners' in the aftermath of the passage of Sarbanes-Oxley.

Cynthia Glassman, for example, termed corporate governance the manifestation of "corporate conscience."[47] Harvey Goldschmid declared that "the modern corporation—if it is to be effective in the long run—should be operating with an ethical culture" and this required corporate counsel to report any potential infringement of securities law and resile from, if necessary, a fiduciary duty to uphold strict confidentiality. For Goldschmid, "an absolute emphasis on confidentiality is incomprehensibly out of balance. Think of the

---

[45] Ibid.

[46] See Stone, above, n 43 ("To the executive and his business community peer group, losing a law suit does not involve the same loss of face as does a new model that does not sell": at 73). He suggests instead a process of "selective intrusion": at 75. This has been achieved primarily through the appointment of external corporate monitors. Contestation continues over the process of how these monitors are selected and the degree to which there is consistency in the way in which they interpret their brief.

[47] C. Glassman, "Sarbanes-Oxley and the Idea of Good Governance" (Speech delivered at American Society of Corporate Secretaries, Washington DC, 27 September 2002).

enormous human cost of Enron, WorldCom, and other corporate scandals on employment, college plans, retirement plans, etc. Are the economic and psychological harms of those scandals—to thousands upon thousands of individuals and families—really less deserving of protection than threats to the life or physical health of one individual? An absolute emphasis on confidentiality for lawyers in financial fraud situations is contrary to the duties that the securities and corporate laws now place on accountants and corporate directors."[48]

How, therefore, did a mechanism designed with such promise lose its legitimacy? In part, this can be traced to overuse and inexperience, in part to discretion it provided, discretion that was in no way mitigated by formal accountability structures. The expansive nature of the memo, coupled with a skeptical approach to business assertions of the efficacy of existing programs, emboldened prosecutors across the United States. The deployment raises a series of inter-connected questions over the limits of regulatory authority.[49] Does the mechanism enhance or subvert democratic accountability? How can the rights of the corporation be protected from the twin threats of executive malfeasance and prosecutorial ambition?[50] The emphasis on cooperation masks disproportionate prosecutorial leverage. This advantage extends throughout the process. Prosecutors not only investigate potential crime (with the complicity of the corporation) but also adjudicate on guilt and determine the degree of penalty. The agency determines whether to offer deferral and scopes the extent of internal change required and the degree of subsequent external oversight. Furthermore, the prosecuting authority alone determines whether a breach has taken place.[51] Crucially, the entire negotiation takes place outside the formal juridical arena with a waiver of client-attorney privilege and work product not explicitly required but

---

[48] H. Goldschmid, "A Lawyers Role in Corporate Governance: The Myth of Absolute Confidentiality and the Complexity of the Counselling Task" (Speech delivered at the Association of the Bar of the City of New York, New York City, 17 November 2003).

[49] For a trenchant critique by the US Attorney credited with its first application, see "Interview with Mary Jo White" 19 *Corporate Crime Reporter* 48 (11) 12 December 2005.

[50] J. Baker, "Reforming Corporations Through Threats of Federal Prosecution" (2004) 89 *Cornell Law Review* 310.

[51] C. Wray, "Remarks to the ABA White Collar Crime Luncheon Club" (Speech delivered at American Bar Association, Washington DC, 25 February 2005); see, more generally, C. Wray & R. Hur, above n 43 (suggesting the memo was both justified and effective: at 1135).

implicitly expected.[52] The US Sentencing Commission went further by inserting into the commentary accompanying guidelines the following suggestion.

> Cooperation must be timely and thorough. To be timely, the cooperation must begin essentially at the same time as the organization is officially notified of a criminal investigation. To be thorough, the cooperation should include the disclosure of all pertinent information known by the organization. A prime test of whether the organization has disclosed all pertinent information is whether the information is sufficient for law enforcement personnel to identify the nature and extent of the offense and the individual(s) responsible for the criminal conduct....Waiver of attorney client privilege and of work product protections is not a prerequisite to a reduction in culpability score...unless such waiver is necessary in order to provide timely and thorough disclosure of all pertinent information known to the organization.[53]

Critics argued that this amounted to an extrajudicial contract that serves to foster "a climate of suspicion" within the organization and between it and its counsel.[54] Others suggest it legitimates the emergence of an inquisitorial prosecutorial system without countervailing and necessary checks and balances.[55] In addition, there are concerns about the corrosive impact of "reverse whistle-blowing" on requisite levels of trust required for organizational development.[56] While the negotiated prosecution enhances capacity, therefore, it also makes threats (if misapplied) to institutionalize a discriminatory mechanism that undermines due process. As with any conflict, the legitimacy of the policy response to business malfeasance is predicated on its proportionality, appropriateness and the clarity of the rules of

---

[52] Wray, "ABA Speech above n 51 (Waiving the privilege is *not* a requirement or a litmus test for cooperation. But it *is* a very valuable and helpful action that goes a long way toward persuading us that a company's cooperation is authentic" (emphasis in original).

[53] United States Sentencing Commission, *Guidelines Manual* Section 8C2.5, commentary Note 12 (November 2004). The language was deleted from the 2006 edition of the guidelines.

[54] Greenblum, above n 41 at 1865, 1881.

[55] G. Szott Moohr, "Prosecutorial Power in an Adversarial System: Lessons from Current White Collar Cases" (2004) 8 *Buffalo Criminal Law Review* 165 at 167.

[56] See W. Laufer, "Corporate Prosecution, Cooperation and the Trading of Favors" (2002) 87 *Iowa Law Review* 643.

engagement. Not only should the outcome be governed by the principle of fairness, so too should the procedures.

It is appropriate to require accountability from regulators, the eroding of regulatory authority has significantly weakened our capacity to re-engineer corporate behavior. Arguably, regulatory and prosecutorial authorities have only themselves to blame. The failure to define precisely the determinants of acceptable conduct undermined both authority and credibility. In the process, a unique opportunity to renegotiate the parameters of corporate accountability was lost. The critical turning point was a devastating rebuke to the Southern District of New York over its handling of a deferred prosecution negotiated with KPMG.[57] Justice Kaplan admonished the government for allowing its "zeal to get in the way of its judgment. It has violated the constitution it has sworn to defend."[58] The case centered on KPMG's provision of abusive tax shelters, which the partnership settled through a deferred prosecution. Individual partners implicated in the scandal countersued on constitutional grounds: the right to a fair trial and adequate representation. KPMG was accused of violating its "implied contract" with the partners, which was consistent with Delaware law (the partnership's domicile) and wider public policy objectives as necessary to obtain and retain executive talent. More damaging were their claims this could be traced directly to imperatives emanating directly from the Thompson Memo.

Justice Kaplan found three significant failings. First, calculating cooperation on (non) payment of legal fees did not facilitate "just charging decisions." Rather, it disregarded corporate practice, public policy goals and legally endorsed precedent. As such, it amounted to a form of pre-trial "economic punishment...[which] is not a legitimate

---

[57] For details of the underlying case, see O'Brien, above n 15, 141–57. Charges against thirteen defendants were dismissed, as was the underlying conspiracy case; see Editorial, "A Conspiracy Theory Debunked," *Wall Street Journal*, 20 December 2008, A14 (describing the prosecution of KPMG over a tax shelter case as a "regrettable, and abusive episode" deriving from an "Alice-in-Wonderland logic").
[58] *United States of America* vs. *Jeffrey Stein et al*, S1 05 Crim.0888 (LAK), 27 June 2006 at 8. While careful to place the blame on Washington for formulating a policy lacking in propriety, Kaplan argued that the USAO for the Southern District was at best economical with the truth in its submissions to the court. Its claim that the legal fee decision was made without "'coercion' or 'bullying'...can be justified only by tortured definitions of those terms": at 81).

governmental interest. It is an abuse of power."[59] Second the open-ended
language of the memorandum compounded the difficulties. The judge
rejected arguments from the Department of Justice that the provision was
only meant to apply if the payment of legal fees was explicitly designed
to impede an investigation.[60] According to Kaplan, the difficulties lay
with the excessive discretion provided to prosecutors. He conceded that
the prosecutors were following established policy. He held, however, that
this was insufficient. Thirdly, the overarching policy on which
prosecutorial actions were based could not in itself be justified because it
amounted to a violation of due process. The "reckless disregard" of the
government that this was a profound possibility meant that "it is not
unfair to hold it accountable."[61] Justice Kaplan ruled that it was
premature to dismiss the indictment on grounds of prosecutorial
misconduct, but reserved the right to do so if the questions of fees could
not be resolved. The doctrine of sovereign immunity, however, meant
that only KPMG could pay the costs, with or without governmental
prodding, which the judge suggested was desirable.[62]

Although the ruling was limited to the payment of fees, the
rebuke provided increasing traction for those calling for a radical
overhaul of both the Memo and the assumptions on which it is based.
Influential interest groups including the American Chamber of
Commerce, the Association of Corporate Counsel, and the National
Association of Criminal Defense Lawyers formed a coalition to lobby for
far reaching change. The ruling gave judicial weight to attempts to
influence the Senate to rethink the practical basis and theoretical
implications of the Thompson Memo, including criticism provided by a

---

[59] Ibid, 49–50.
[60] Ibid, 52 (Justice Kaplan further suggested that this was in any event immaterial. "The
Court holds that the fact that advancement of legal fees occasionally might be part of an
obstruction scheme or indicate a lack of full cooperation by a prospective defendant is
insufficient to justify the government's interference with the right of individual criminal
defendants to obtain resources lawfully available to them in order to defend themselves,
regardless of the legal standard of scrutiny applied": at 60). A similar logic informed the
ruling by the Delaware Court of Chancery in its determination that Hollinger
International was under an obligation to continue advancing legal fees to its now
imprisoned former CEO; see above n 13 and accompanying text.
[61] Ibid, 56.
[62] Ibid, 79.

former head of the Enron Task Force, who on returning to private practice rethought the benefits accruing from application.[63]

The Kaplan ruling provided cover for policymakers to revisit both the underlying law and its interpretation by executive agencies. Opponents of the expansion of deferred prosecutions gained the support of the Treasury Secretary, Hank Paulson. The shift was comprehensively signaled in a pivotal speech delivered to the Economic Club of New York. Paulson warned that three critical dysfunctions threatened the competitiveness of US capital markets: "a complex and confusing regulatory structure and enforcement environment"; the costs associated with the implementation of governance reform, particularly internal controls mandated by Sarbanes-Oxley; and continued litigation risk. Paulson was careful to endorse the need for criminal and civil law enforcement. He raised, however, serious concerns that competition between state and federal agencies to demonstrate muscularity in enforcement against corporate entities had become counter-productive. The pursuit of wrongdoing was deemed "worthy, necessary and acceptable." A vital caveat was introduced, however. "When multiple jurisdictions and entities are involved, each with their own objectives and approaches, the enforcement environment can become inefficient, and, to the regulated, can appear threatening and confusing." The Treasury Secretary criticized the tendency for US policymakers to respond to scandal by adding layers of legal and institutional complexity. By not "focusing on the broader objective of regulatory efficiency," policymakers had created a "thicket of regulation that impedes competitiveness."[64]

Throughout the speech, he damned the regulators with faint praise. A particular target was the Department of Justice, which has gone further than the Securities and Exchange Commission in using innovative enforcement techniques to force behavioral change. For Paulson, "if it appears that changes are warranted, in the public interest and consistent with the need to safeguard the integrity of our economic system, I am confident that the Justice Department will revise its policy." Decoded, this suggested that the Justice Department's intrusions into individual corporate governance regimes through enforced compliance are neither warranted nor in the public interest. The Justice Department

---

[63] See A. Efrati, "Former Enron Prosecutor Speaks Out: Criminal Charges Shouldn't Be So Easy," *Wall Street Journal*, 21 November 2008 (Online Edition).
[64] Paulson, above n 31.

acquiesced and a made clear in a major policy revision that privileged information should only be requested in extreme circumstances and even then only if the decision was referred upwards and signed off by the most senior legal officer in the District Attorney Office and the Assistant Attorney General of the Criminal Division of the Department of Justice.[65] No guidance was provided on what those circumstances should be, and the lack of accountability meant that legitimacy was undermined.

This rejection of discretion was further underscored by the findings of the Committee on Capital Markets. Funding for the study came, in part, from the Starr Foundation, a charitable institution controlled by Maurice Greenberg, the disgraced former chairman of American International Group. Greenberg was ousted from control of the global insurer because of a scandal involving accounting manipulation. This blunted, but only partially, the power of the central message: the regulatory pendulum had unleashed its own Perfect Storm, an analogue to the greed and ethical failure that coalesced at the turn of the millennium. In this context, therefore, with regulatory authority diminishing, it is hardly surprising that the financial sector sought and largely succeeded in its aim to bypass the formal regulatory apparatus. Attempts to regulate private equity, hedge funds or complex derivate instruments sold only to sophisticated investors were routinely dismissed as evidence of over-zealous bureaucrats who misunderstood and undervalued innovation.

III   WILLING DEFENESTRATION

By 2004, it was clear that the business quiescence in regulatory innovation had come to an end. The then chairman of the Securities and Exchange Commission, William Donaldson, was warning of the propensity of managers "to pursue questionable activity right up to technical conformity with the letter of the law, and some will step over the red line, either directly or with crafty schemes and modern financial technology that facilitates deception."[66] As with Levitt before him, Donaldson was overruled and replaced by the much more emollient Christopher Cox, whose deleterious stewardship prompted the republican

---

[65] P. McNulty, "Memorandum on Principles of Business Organizations to the Heads of Department Components" (Department of Justice, Washington DC, 12 December 2006).
[66] W. Donaldson (Speech delivered at Business Roundtable, Washington DC, 14 October 2004).

challenger for the White House to call for his immediate sacking. The Ponzi trading scheme involving Bernie Madoff, the former chairman of Nasdaq, further tarnished the reputation of the agency and indeed the quality of due diligence procedures within instutions that invested in or provided finance for a trading operation that has seen multi-billion dollar losses and the forced closure of charitable foundations from Palm Beach to Tel Aviv.

The extent of the failure was underscored in remarkable testimony to the House Financial Services Committee by Harry Markopolos, a portfolio manager who assembled a team of private investigators to probe the Madoff scheme and who had alerted the SEC as early as 2000 that the investment strategies used by the former chairman of NASDAQ were quite possibly fraudulent. Markopolos argued that SEC securities" lawyers [in Boston and the regional office in New York] colluded to mantain large frauds such as the one to which Madoff later confessed, if only through their investigative ineptitude and financial illiteracy."[67] In prepared remarks to the Committee, senior SEC officials retreated to an account that highlighted the changing structure of the organization. They maintained that they were "not authorized to provide specific information about matters under active investigation or past regulatory activities in this matter. We cannot jeopardize the process of holding the perpetrators accountable."[68] While the protocols governing the SEC's diclosure prevented commenting on the specifics, the hearing degenerated with the chairman accusing the agency personnel of obstruction.[69]

The SEC has belatedly (and only partially) recognized its own failings. Negative reviews by the agency's Inspector General have punctured the myth of a robust regulator. One recent report, for example, focused on an investigation into how Bear Stearns valued and marketed securities. It found that the agency failed to "vigorously" enforce its

---

[67] Evidence to US House of Representatives Committee on Financial Services, "Hearing on Assessing the Madoff Ponzi Scheme and Regulatory Failures," Washington DC, 11 February 2009 (H. Markopolos) 4–5.

[68] Evidence to US House of Representatives Committee on Financial Services, "Hearing on Assessing the Madoff Ponzi Scheme and Regulatory Failures," Washington DC, 11 February 2009 (A. Donohue, L. Richards, E. Sirri, L. Chatman Thomsen, A. Vollmer) 2.

[69] D. Henriques, "Anger and Drama at a House Hearing on Madoff," *New York Times*, 5 February 2009, B1 (reporting that the new head of the SEC later wrote to the Committee conceding that the protocols could lead to understandable frustration and offering private meeting).

remit. The Office of the Inspector General's report, although concentrating primarily on the Bear Stearns collapse, was a damning indictment of a failed regulatory system. In evidence to a Senate committee, Christopher Cox, noted that the Bear Stearns failure was "unprecedented. For the first time, a major investment bank that was well-capitalized and apparently fully liquid experienced a crisis of confidence that denied it not only unsecured financing, but short-term secured financing, even when the collateral consisted of agency securities with a market value in excess of the funds to be borrowed."[70] This is, however, a self-serving and contestable reading of events.

Throughout the boom, the SEC appeared not just powerless but complicit in its own loss of authority. The agency had emerged as the key regulator of US investment banks in 2004 through the Consolidated Supervised Entity (CSE) program.[71] By entering a voluntary program of oversight with the SEC, US institutions avoided more invasive regulation from the European Union, which had produced a directive that financial conglomerates required single regulatory supervision, with compliance on internal controls, capital adequacy, intra-group transactions and risk concentration assessed through a combination of quantitative and qualitative measures.[72] The CPE was presented as an opportunity to provide US banks with a competitive advantage. In allowing mark to market pricing for on-balance sheet reporting, leverage restrictions were loosened and the capital required for compliance with minimum requirements set out by Basel Committee on Banking Supervision finessed. The SEC press release announcing the changes is exceptionally revealing of the reality governing capital market regulation in the United States. It gives the illusion of a robust oversight regime and reinforces the supremacy of market-based control mechanisms.

> Under the alternative capital computation method, the broker-dealer
> will be allowed to compute certain market and credit risk capital
> charges using internal mathematical models. The CSE will be

---

[70] Evidence to US Senate Committee on Banking, Housing, and Urban Affairs, Washington DC, 3 April 2008 (C. Cox).

[71] The CSE program covered seven entities: Bear Stearns, Citigroup, Goldman Sachs, JP Morgan, Lehman Brothers, Merrill Lynch, and Morgan Stanley. The SEC did not, however, have direct oversight over Citigroup or JP Morgan, who were under the supervision of the Federal Reserve.

[72] Office of Inspector General, *SEC's Oversight of Bear Stearns and Related Entities: The CSE Program* (Report No 446-A, Washington DC, 25 September 2008) 4.

required to comply with rules regarding its group-wide internal risk management control system and will be required periodically to provide the Commission with consolidated computations of allowable capital and risk allowances (or other capital assessment) prepared in a form that is consistent with the Basel Standards. Commission supervision of the CSE will include recordkeeping, reporting, and examination requirements.[73]

Compliance with Basel Committee on Banking Supervision requires the integration of three restraining pillars: minimum capital requirements; effective supervision and market discipline. Each mechanism failed. First, the capital requirements require that banks have a 10% equity cushion. The capital must be appropriately stress tested against the entire set of liabilities accrued by the banks in the event of an unlikely but conceivable deleterious market event. As Wall Street clamored to buy sub-prime debt, financial engineering ensured that much of the liability was siphoned to off-balance sheet entities. That the growth of securitization was predicated on a concomitant expansion of the shadow banking system meant that functional regulation proved worse that sub-optimal. It undermined the credibility of supervisory review, the critical second pillar in the Basel framework.

The banking sector lobbied that mark to market accounting provided a critical risk and governance control mechanism. The SEC transferred responsibility for deciding appropriate capital charge levels to the investment banks themselves. This had the effect of transacting around prescriptive leverage limits. Although the rule change was unanimous, two commissioners—from very different ideological perspectives—did voice concern. According to Harvey Goldschmid, who has since returned to teach at Columbia Law School, "if anything goes wrong, it's going to be an awfully big mess."[74] A second commissioner, Roel Campos, said he was "very happy to support it and I keep my fingers crossed for the future."[75] The SEC was at best naïve in relying on the internal mathematical modeling provided by the investment banks. Moreover, an investigation by the inspector general for the agency revealed that responsibility for managing a combined $5 trillion asset

---

[73] "Broker-Dealer and Affiliate Supervision on Consolidated Basis" (Press Release, Securities and Exchange Commission, Washington DC, 28 April 2004).
[74] Cited in S. Labaton, "Agency's '04 Rule Let Banks Pile Up New Debt," *New York Times*, 3 October 2008, A1.
[75] Ibid.

portfolio was delegated to a team comprising just seven staff, which had functioned without a director since March 2007.[76] The SEC instead relied on the market to provide an early warning system. Market discipline, however, was designed to complement, not replace, effective supervision.

The third pillar leverages market discipline through enhanced public disclosure by individual banks about how their operations and conditions impact on capital adequacy. Given the complexity of modern banking, and the limits of regulatory capacity, complementary reliance on professional investors and financial analysts can have practical value.[77] The problem is that both the market and the SEC itself ignored detailed information about obvious weaknesses in bank balance sheets and earnings. This was particularly evident in the oversight of Bear Stearns. According to the Inspector General, the Trading and Markets Division of the SEC "became aware of numerous potential red flags prior to Bear Stearns' collapse, regarding its concentration of mortgage securities, high leverage, shortcomings of risk management in mortgage backed securities and lack of compliance with the spirit of certain Basel II standards and did not take action to limit these risk factors."[78]

Among the findings were "a lack of expertise by risk managers in mortgage-backed securities at various times, lack of timely formal review of mortgage models; persistent understaffing, a proximity of risk managers to traders suggesting a lack of independence; turnover of key personnel during times of crisis; and the inability or unwillingness to update models to reflect changing circumstances."[79] In addition, the Division of Trading and Markets allowed critical audit work on risk management to be carried out by internal rather than external auditors, in

---

[76] Ibid.

[77] See, however, Lopez, above n 9 (noting under the Basel framework, "disclosures need not be audited by an external auditor, unless otherwise required by accounting standard setters, securities regulators, or other authorities, but management should ensure that the information is appropriately verified": at 3).

[78] Office of Inspector General, *SEC's Oversight of Bear Stearns and Related Entities: The CSE Program* (Report No 446-A, Washington DC 25 September 2008) ix (The Inspector General quotes internal memoranda from the Trading and Markets Division that Bear Stearns consistently asked for authority to enhance "balance sheet and risk taking authority despite six limit increases since 2001." Furthermore, SEC staff recognized that the Adjustable Rate Mortgage business within Bear Stearns "continues to operate in excess of allocated limits, reaching new highs with respect to the net market value of its positions": at 18).

[79] Ibid, x.

contravention of the rules governing the CSE program. Furthermore, it failed to assess risk tolerance at board level.[80] Bear Stearns, for example reduced its capital ratio from 21.4 per cent to 11.5 per cent in the period April 2006 to March 2008. While it was still compliant with the terms of the program, the Inspector General held that the Trading and Markets Division failed to exert influence over Bear Stearns because of a technical reading of the rules.[81] As a consequence, it failed to institute an adequate supervisory regime under pillar two of the Basel Standards.

> In particular, the SEC failed to address credit risk concentrations, how they are managed and the extent to which the bank considers them in its internal assessment of capital adequacy under Pillar 2. Such assessments should include reviews of the results of a bank's stress tests. Supervisors should take appropriate actions where the risks arising from a bank's credit risk concentrations are not adequately addressed by the bank.[82]

The SEC responded that the report was "misleading, and all too often relies on speculation and innuendo to support its harsh conclusions."[83] The SEC has now abolished the CPE initiative. In a statement Cox admitted that "the past six months [April 2008— September 2008] have demonstrated that voluntary regulation does not work."[84] The problems caused by a technical reading of legislation and

---

[80] Ibid.

[81] Ibid ("In this sense, TM [Trading and Markets Division] acted as though it did not believe it had a mandate to compel Bear Stearns to raise additional capital as long as its capital ratio was greater that 10%...[A]lthough the Commission has maintained that liquidity (not capital) problems caused Bear Stearns' collapse, this audit found that it is entirely possible that Bear Stearns' capital levels could have contributed to its collapse by making lenders unwilling to provide Bear Stearns the funding it needed": at 12).

[82] Ibid, see also Basel Committee on Banking Supervision, *International Convergence on Capital Measurement and Capital Standards* (June 2006), para. 777. According to the Inspector General, "notwithstanding these 'red flags' that TM knew about, and warnings in the Basel standards, TM did not make any efforts to limit Bear Stearns' mortgage securities concentration": at 18).

[83] K. Scannell, "SEC Watchdog Faults Agency in a Bear Case," *Wall Street Journal*, 11 October 2008, B6. The SEC is now under investigation for allegedly revealing material information to the chief legal counsel of JP Morgan on the status of a second investigation into misleading practices at Bear Stearns immediately prior to the bank's decision to buy the battered franchise, see J. Chung, "Senator Probes SEC Role in Bear Rescue," *Financial Times*, 23 October 2008, 2.

[84] Securities and Exchange Commission, "Chairman Cox Announces End of Consolidated Entity Program" (Press Release, Washington DC, 28 September 2008).

policy documents were reinforced by pro-cyclical and ultimately sub-optimal enforcement strategies.[85] The hubris of its corporate actors was matched only by the arrogance of the custodians of economic policy. As this chapter has demonstrated, a range of factors can influence the use or neglect of discretionary power. Within a regulatory agency, these can include differential political support, internal strategic imperatives and staff enthusiasm or longer-term career ambition.[86] In the absence of decisive leadership, resolve can weaken at each organizational level and at each stage of engagement with regulated entities. What matters is less the formal architecture but rather how the regulator (or its delegated authority), corporate executives and financial intermediaries conceive and apply specific control mechanisms.[87] This is essentially a political rather than an economic efficiency argument. The problem was that the process was reversed as the mores and logic of financial capitalism was inculcated and disseminated by the custodians of economic policy.

---

[85] See A. Aviram, "Counter-Cyclical Enforcement of Corporate Law" (2008) 25 *Yale Journal on Regulation* 1, 7-11 (suggesting that "cognitive biases may play a role in exacerbating the perception of fraud during downward trends and under-estimating the risk during upward trends": at 7).

[86] See M. Lewis and D. Einhorn, "The End of the Financial World as We Know It," *New York Times*, 4 January 2009, B1 (noting caustically that "a casual observer could be forgiven for thinking that the whole point of landing the job as the SEC's director of enforcement is to position oneself for the better paying one on Wall Street").

[87] See J. Lerner and A. Schoar, "Does Legal Enforcement Affect Financial Transactions? The Contractual Channel in Private Equity" (2005) 120 *Quarterly Journal of Economics* 223.

Chapter 3

Apportioning Blame

As equity markets continued to fall throughout October, the House of Representatives began ascertaining the causes. From the start, it was apparent that a narrative based on greed would play a central role. Much was made, for example, of a $440,000 bill accrued by a subsidiary of American International Group at the luxurious St Regis Hotel in Monarch Beach, southern California. According to its website, the hotel is "a landmark resort of legendary proportions."[1] It features a private beach where guests can avail themselves of personalized surf butlers, and bespoke spa and poolside rental cabanas for an additional $300 per day. The portfolio, released by the House Committee on Oversight and Government Reform, included $7,000 in golf outings and $23,000 on spa treatments during a seven-day retreat for high-performing sales staff. While executive pampering is commonplace, the expenditure came immediately after the federal government advanced $85 billion to prevent the collapse of the parent firm, one of the most interconnected in global finance. The committee chairman, Representative Henry Waxman of Los Angeles, was incredulous: "Average Americans are suffering economically yet less than one week after the taxpayer rescued AIG, company executives could be found wining and dining at one of the most exclusive resorts in the nation."[2] By displaying photographs of the ornate St Regis lobby, Representative Waxman conjured up images of continued profligacy, which inevitably dominated subsequent media coverage.[3]

---

[1] http:///www.stregismonarchbeach.com

[2] Opening Statement, "Hearing on the Causes and Effects of the AIG Bailout," House Committee on Oversight and Government Reform, Washington DC, 7 October 2008 (H. Waxman).

[3] See, for example, S. Kirchgaessner, "Profligacy of AIG's Executives Draws Fire," *Financial Times*, 8 October 2008, 3. AIG subsequently said it would cancel most

As with hearings the previous day into the bankruptcy of Lehman Brothers, the AIG investigation focused on three lines of enquiry: first, whether the internal compensation model was fair and reasonable; second, whether the company—and wider system—was brought down by ineptitude or the confluence of external factors beyond the corporation's control; and third, whether the same executives had failed to disclose material financial information to the firm's auditors or the market, thus breaching the legislative requirements of the *Public Company Accounting Reform and Investor Protection Act* (2002), the previous attempt by Congress to instill restraint in corporate America. The overarching purpose, however, was to hold individuals to account. This was to be achieved by reprising a time-honored exercise in ritualized humiliation.[4] The committee chairman, for example, decried Lehman Brothers' decision to "squander millions of dollars in executive compensation" even as the company hurtled towards bankruptcy.[5] Lehman, it was revealed somewhat breathlessly, paid out over $16 billion in performance bonuses, with the chief executive alone taking total compensation of $260 million. Performance-related payments, primarily in the form of deferred stock options, comprised $40 million. According to Waxman, the strategy ensured that as "executives were

---

functions; see E. Holm and H. Son, "AIG Host With Most to Explain," *Sydney Morning Herald*, 11 October 2008, 42.

[4] The most famous example of this integrated approach was the Pecora Hearings into investment bank complicity in the 1929 stock market crash; see C. Geisst, *Wall Street* (1999) 196–244. There have been many calls for a similar set of hearings; see, for example, Evidence to House Committee on Financial Services, "Systemic Risk: Examining Regulators Ability to React to Threats in the Financial System," House of Representatives, Washington DC, 2 October, 2007 (R. Kuttner). In a subsequent book, Kuttner, the editor of *American Prospect*, doubted Democrats' resolve to order such a sweeping approach; see R. Kuttner, *The Squandering of America: How the Failure of Our Politics is Squandering Our Prosperity* (2008), 160. The banking literature has adopted a much more skeptical approach to the value of the Pecora Hearings and the "efficiency" of regulation more generally; see C. Calomiris, *US Bank Deregulation in Historical Perspective* (2006) xii (noting that "limits—especially restrictions placed on bank consolidation from the mid-nineteenth century through the early 1990s, and the separation of commercial and investment banking beginning in 1933—are artifacts of specific historical events and associated political battles in which facts and economic logic often took a bad seat to special interest politics and occasionally to populist passions": at xii and associated references).

[5] Waxman, above n 2.

getting rich, they were steering Lehman Brothers and our economy towards a precipice."[6]

Greed and incompetence narratives may play well to a confused and wary electorate. They downplay, however, the extent to which the crisis derives from the elevation of short-term value over long-term values across a range of personal, commercial, and political settings in the United States.[7] The journey to the edge was one that everyone involved in the process undertook willingly. There was a perverse rationality to the systematic inflation of the bubble. Integrity was compromised, willingly, at each stage. Take, for example, the emergence of "liar loans," known by the acronym NINJA—No Income, No Jobs or Assets. These reflected a decline in effective risk management. The risk was exacerbated by the reliance on mathematical models that relied on historical data. This approach failed to take into consideration the statistical likelihood of default rising in direct correlation with a slackening of lending standards. They also demonstrated a decline in trust, the key foundational principle for an effective banking and wider financial services system. Blame can be apportioned to those who designed and used the products, to those who added the accelerant by providing unreasonable or unsustainable ratings or insurance, to ineffective shareholders and regulators unwilling or unable to understand the systemic risks being undertaken, and to those who derived financial support for political campaigns and failed to rein in excess because of a blind and ultimately erroneous faith in the power of markets to deliver social good. Throughout, regulators and policymakers retained myopic faith in an increasingly questionable conception of regulatory form and purpose, thus exacerbating an overarching systemic failure that derives from an abdication of personal, corporate, executive and political

---

[6] Ibid. The numbers are, to be sure, significant. It is also important to note, however, that the payments were designed to align the interests of management with the corporation. Furthermore, when Lehman collapsed, employees not only lost their jobs, but also a large proportion of their savings. Such factual niceties were not a concern of a committee looking for villains.

[7] A similar populist dynamic was apparent in Britain, where Gordon Brown castigated poor governance practices and "irresponsible behavior" in the City; see G. Parker and J. Pickard, "Brown Goes on the Road to Sell Rescue Plan to Skeptical Voters," *Financial Times*, 10 October, 2008, 3. Many of the British bankers involved in the crisis, past and present, appeared before the Treasury Select Committee. The former CEO of HBOS, Andy Hornby, accepted that the bonus culture played a part in exacerbating systemic risk; see Evidence to "Hearing on Banking Crisis", Treasury Select Committee, Westminster, 10 February 2009 (A. Hornby).

responsibility. In this regard, responsibility for the inflation of the housing bubble mania in the United States and beyond lies with us all. This is not to suggest that as a consequence, culpability can be minimized. Rather, it is to underline the fact that the blame game on both Capitol Hill and in Westminster has too narrow a focus.

The producers, financiers, and consumers of a highly leveraged variant of the American dream failed to appreciate the dynamics of integrating desire, delusion, and greed with lower opportunity costs. Excess liquidity generated huge risk distortions. Arbitraging the differential between the cost of debt and rising house prices was enhanced by the power of leverage. The process and its rationale percolated throughout society. From the boardrooms of Manhattan to the inner cities of the United States, no barrier to lending was imposed. Just as low-documentation loans became pervasive in the sub-prime housing market, multi-billion dollar lines of credit were extended to corporate entities with little or no covenants. As Wall Street moved decisively into the securitization of mortgage debt, leverage ratios spiraled out of control.[8] This is a responsibility to be shouldered primarily by those with direct exposure to corporate risk, namely the shareholders. While its board was particularly weak, the strategy adopted by Lehman Brothers in riding the expansion of the mortgage bubble was far from unique. Focusing on the scale of executive compensation alone as the driving force for irresponsibility risks missing the point.

Although the crisis initially centered on the sub-prime sector of the United States residential market, it is important to emphasize that this was a symptom rather than the cause of the maelstrom. The search for sustainable reform risks failure unless the investigation tackles the underlying causes. This requires, in turn, an analysis of the form, substance, and rationale of corporate governance within specific institutions. In particular it requires cognizance of how board decisions are informed (and constrained) by weakened conceptions of what effective performance entails. Poor governance aside, attention must also focus on how the structure of the financial architecture influences and is, in turn, influenced by wider corporate behavior. These conceptions were, in turn, actively encouraged by a political culture that now seeks to minimize its own complicity by engaging in a contemporary version of the Salem witch-hunts.

---

[8] See M. Lewis, "The End of Wall Street's Boom," *Portfolio*, November 2008 (Online Edition).

I   PRIDE AND PREJUDICE: THE FALL OF LEHMAN

The price of failure has been further inflated by what now appears to be a major policy mistake: the decision by the Treasury and the Federal Reserve to send a message to the markets by allowing Lehman Brothers to fail. It is a market cliché that investors are unwise to catch a falling knife. The attempts by Lehman Brothers to minimize its liabilities throughout the second and third quarter of 2008, taken in consultation with the Federal Reserve and the Securities and Exchange Commission, were insufficient to persuade investors to reach out. On 15 September, after being told that no government or market participant help would be forthcoming, Lehman accepted the inevitable and filed the largest corporate bankruptcy in history. This marked an inglorious end to a firm that only two years previously garnered the highest corporate performance in an annual survey conducted by the influential finance magazine *Barron's*. In 2007 Lehman Brothers collected the Fortune award for "Most Admired Securities Firm." However, the bank, which had thrived on its maverick reputation, was the architect of its own downfall.

The House Oversight Committee Chairman, Henry Waxman, noted, "if Wall Street had been less reckless, or thorough regulators had been more tentative, the [initial] financial crisis could have been prevented."[9] While concentrating his attack on Lehman's own mismanagement, he castigated the misjudgments of the Treasury Secretary and the Chairman of the Federal Reserve. They had testified that "our financial system could handle the collapse of Lehman. It now appears they were wrong." The critical lesson from the fall of Lehman Brothers is not whether policymakers could have avoided systemic failure by adopting more imaginative solutions. Even if successful, such an approach would have only slowed the onset of a progressively debilitating but ultimately terminal condition. Rather, the Lehman collapse marked the moment that the credibility and legitimacy of an entire model of capitalism could no longer be sustained.

Even as its competitors were announcing multi-billion dollar falls in the values of asset-backed portfolios, Lehman Brothers stalled. It

---

[9] Opening Statement, "Hearing on the Causes and Effects of the Lehman Brothers Bankruptcy," House Committee on Oversight and Government Reform, Washington DC, 6 October 2008 (H. Waxman).

relied on spin and sassy presentation to deflect growing criticism from institutional investors, if not initially the media. In the spring of 2008, Lehman Brothers' newly appointed chief financial officer, Erin Callan, was feted for her communication skills and for the possibility that the glass ceiling preventing the elevation of a female to lead a New York investment house might shatter. The business media paid much less attention to her lack of an accounting background.[10] The black arts of media manipulation are, however, a poor substitute for technical knowledge and expertise. The increasingly widespread view that Lehman was less than forthcoming about the value of its mortgage-backed securities portfolio made it inevitable that attempts to woo institutional investors, including the Korea Development Bank, would fail. The campaign was further undermined by hedge funds, which consistently shorted the stock in the wake of the Bear Stearns collapse and, as the year progressed, publicly called into question the chief financial officer's commitment to transparency and accountability.[11] A belated credit rating downgrade by Moody's Investor Services sealed Lehman's fate.

The falling knife severed an artery of global finance. The subsequent hemorrhaging was an inevitable consequence of the calculated but erroneous risk by regulators and self-serving market participants that Lehman lacked the strength to inflict serious damage. The fateful decision was taken over the course of weekend negotiations overseen by the Federal Reserve Bank of New York at its offices in Lower Manhattan and attended by representatives of the major banks as well as the Department of Treasury. The regulators adopted an uncompromising approach to their private sector charges. In so doing, they reprised the strategy used in emergency talks a decade earlier over the future of Long Term Capital Management. The crisis derived from a

---

[10] For flattering profiles, see S. Kolhatkar, "Wall Street's Most Powerful Woman," *Portfolio*, April 2008 (Online Edition); S. Craig, "Lehman's Straight Shooter," *Wall Street Journal*, 17 May 2008 (Online Edition). The CFO was forced to resign on 12 June 2008, along with the president, Joe Gregory. Both were blamed for failing to assure investors that sufficient action had been taken to recapitalize the bank. Callan, who was a frequent guest on business television, is, at time of writing, head of global hedge fund business at Credit Suisse.

[11] The most prominent critic was David Einhorn, who regularly flailed Lehman for failing to account for its potential losses; see M. Barnett, "An Einhorn in Her Side," *Portfolio*, 23 May 2008 (Online Edition); M. Barnett, "I Am Short-Seller, Hear Me Roar," *Portfolio*, 12 June 2008 (Online Edition); J. Eisinger, "Diary of a Short Seller," *Portfolio*, 12 May 2008 (Online Edition).

market failure; it was up to the market to sort it out.[12] The scale of the contemporary crisis was much more serious, however, than the fate of an individual, if substantial, hedge fund. At stake was the stability of the entire US investment banking system. The banks, although fearful and distrustful, reluctantly agreed to create a $10 billion insulation fund. They refused, however, to risk the capital on their most vulnerable member unless the government provided a backstop against further undisclosed losses. The government's refusal to repeat the offer made to JP Morgan when it bought the ravaged Bear Stearns earlier in the year with a $21 billon guarantee changed the dynamics over any planned purchase of Lehman.

The two suitors in most advanced discussions, Bank of America and Barclays, recognized their own short-term self-interest dictated caution. By not proceeding, Bank of America positioned itself to take advantage of the trepidation felt by Merrill Lynch, the investment bank next most exposed to negative sentiment. Recognition that public defenestration awaited once the markets digested the fact that no investment bank was deemed to big too fail, Merrill Lynch negotiated a frantic merger. The decision to buy Merrill Lynch, coming after the acquisition of Countrywide, a leading mortgage provider, gave the Charlotte-based Bank of America a retail broking presence and lending franchise it had coveted for a decade.[13] The risk was further minimized because Merrill had earlier offloaded $31 billion of impaired securities at a fire sale price of 22 cents in the dollar. Lehman, by contrast, retained enormous exposure to future losses because of unsustainable valuations of its mortgage-backed securities. For Barclays, the Lehman collapse allowed it to pick up the investment banking franchise for pennies in the dollar.

Neither market nor regulatory participants addressed the externality costs that non-intervention would have on wider market confidence. The government appeared to take comfort from the fact that

---

[12] For the most complete account of the LTCM failure, see R. Lowenstein, *When Genius Failed* (2000); see also M. Lewis, "How the Eggheads Cracked," *New York Times Magazine,* 24 January 1999, reprinted in M. Lewis (ed), *Panic* (2008) 124–144.

[13] For background on Bank of America's rationale, see P. Muolo and M. Padilla, *Chain of Blame* (2008) 251, 269–70. The acquisitions, however, raise enormous governance questions. Bank of America has received an emergency injection of funds from the TARP program to cover worsening earnings figures from Merrill Lynch in the final quarter of 2008. Furthermore, the chief executive, Ken Lewis, publicly talked up Bank of America's prospects while secretly negotiating with the government over the terms of the bailout.

the surviving banks had created the insulation buffer. In an interview, the Treasury Secretary, Hank Paulson, said he had pleaded with the Lehman CEO to sell his company. He also maintained that neither the Treasury nor the Federal Reserve had the power to intervene because loans could only be advanced against performing assets.[14] This implied that Lehman had misrepresented its trading position to the market in advance of the weekend talks at the Federal Reserve. According to Paulson "there was no buyer for the bank" and "we did not have the wind-down authorities that we needed for...non-banking financial institutions."[15] The remaining investment banks, Morgan Stanley and Goldman Sachs, were not going to make the same mistake. They reached a separate sidebar agreement with the Federal Reserve to transform themselves into bank holding companies, thus marking the demise of the independent Wall Street merchant house. It was, however, too little to late. Maladroit hedge funds suddenly found that they could not redeem billions of dollars "parked" in Lehman Brothers' accounts, particularly in London. Fearful that they themselves would be unable to meet redemption from nervous institutional clients, leading hedge funds started withdrawing funds from the remaining investment banks. In essence, the Lehman collapse sparked not just a run on one bank or even the investment banking sector but the entire multi-trillion dollar credit market. The crisis metastasized further when the Reserve Primary Fund, which had $64 billion under management, confirmed its inability to repay its investors in full because of an un-hedged $785 million exposure with Lehman Brothers. By "breaking the buck," the commercial paper industry instantaneously disintegrated. Huge stock losses were merely the public face of a flight to safety. A staggering $290 billion was withdrawn from the money markets in just two days. The global head of prime services at Swiss Bank UBS captured the mood in an interview with the *New York Times*: "it felt there was no ground beneath your feet. I didn't know where it was going to end."[16]

---

[14] J. Nocera and E. Andrews, "Struggling to Keep Up as the Crisis Raced On," *New York Times*, 23 October 2008, A1. The incoming Treasury Secretary, Timothy Geithner, has corroborated this version by describing at his confirmation hearing the rationale for the implosion of Lehman as tragic.
[15] A. Bull, "Lehman Failure Seen as Straw Which Broke Credit Market," *The Guardian*, 9 October 2008 (Online Edition).
[16] J. Nocera, "As Credit Crisis Spiraled, Alarm Led to Action," *New York Times*, 2 October 2008, A1.

The decision to allow Lehman Brothers to fail turned the sub-prime housing scandal into a major global catastrophe. Belated recognition of market panic forced the US federal authorities into a series of immediate policy reversals. As the chief economist of the International Monetary Fund, Olivier Blanchard, explained, the decision to allow Lehman to go to the wall "was a bet. It was lost."[17] In such circumstances, it was not surprising that the Lehman CEO, Richard Fuld, would be unapologetic. In written testimony to the House Oversight and Government Reform Committee he maintained that Lehman Brothers, as the smallest investment bank, could not withstand a "financial tsunami" that had generated "a storm of fear."[18] No one institution could be held responsible for the unintended consequences of belatedly recognized deleterious market and policy choices. Rather, Lehman was "overwhelmed, others were overwhelmed and still other institutions would have been overwhelmed had the government not stepped in to save them."[19] Accordingly, Lehman was an innocent victim of a collective failure to foresee a once in the lifetime crisis.

The evidence failed to impress the Oversight Committee. Representative Waxman castigated Lehman Brothers as "a company in which there was no accountability for failure."[20] This is true. It is also true, however, that there was very little accountability within any major institutional actor on Wall Street and the City of London. The collapse of Lehman Brothers, the forced sale of Bear Stearns and Merrill Lynch and the calamitous failure of Royal Bank of Scotland and HBOS reflect grossly deficient internal risk management systems, cosmetic compliance, poor ethical training and exceptionally weak external oversight at both individual firm and wider systemic level.[21] This failure

---

[17] See Bull, above n 15.

[18] Evidence to House Committee on Oversight and Government Reform, "Hearing on the Causes and Effects of the Lehman Brothers Bankruptcy," Washington DC, 6 October 2008 (R. Fuld). This choice of metaphor was also deployed by Alan Greenspan to deflect responsibility; see Evidence to House Committee on Oversight and Government Reform, "Hearing on the Role of Federal Regulators in the Financial Crisis," Washington DC 23 October 2008 (A. Greenspan).

[19] Fuld, above n 19.

[20] Opening Statement, "Hearing on the Causes and Effects of the Lehman Brothers Bankruptcy," House Committee on Oversight and Government Reform, Washington DC, 6 October (H. Waxman).

[21] For wider problems and lack of oversight on Wall Street, see C. Morris, *The Trillion Dollar Meltdown* (2007); G. Soros, *The New Paradigm of Financial Regulation* (2008); for lack of political oversight in the United States, more generally, see J. K. Galbraith,

destroyed not only the corporate reputation of many storied firms and individual financiers but also the trust on which a credible banking system is founded.

II   RATING FAILURE

At a political level, securitization could and was presented as an example of how innovation allowed an even greater proportion of the population to attain the benefits of home ownership. Within the academy, early articles referred approvingly to its alchemistic properties.[22] The mechanism proved exceptionally alluring for providers of housing capital through Residential Mortgage Backed Securities (RMBS) and Commercial Mortgage Backed Securities (CMBS). The originators benefited in three ways. First, out-sourcing the debt from underlying balance sheets reduced the reserves required to remain in compliance with capital adequacy requirements. Second, the capital released generated funding for further loans, which could, in turn, be securitized. Third, the risk of default was passed on to third parties with little no knowledge of the specific circumstances of individual mortgagees. If the risk was outsourced, so too was any degree of responsibility.

The critical design flaw was that the outsourcing was less than complete. As a consequence the system could not withstand a calamitous decline in confidence. Rather than providing a social good, the alchemy corroded the authority of financial capitalism. Nowhere was this more apparent than in the mismanagement of the conflicts of interest facing

---

The Predator State (2008); C. Milhaupt and K. Pistor, *Law and Capitalism* (2008) 47–66. For problems in the British banking sector, see P. Moore, "Memo to the Treasury Select Committee," Westminster, 10 February 2009 (the author, former head of regulatory risk at HBOS, argued that there was a need for more detailed policy guidance from the FSA on the form and content of ethics training within banking corporations. He says it is essential to introduce "a more detailed policy and rules which allows the FSA to test the cultural environment of organizations they are supervising e.g. tri-annual staff and customer survey. There is no doubt that you can have the best governance processes in the world but if they are carried out in a culture of greed, unethical behavior and indisposition to challenge, they will fail. I would now propose ***mandatory*** (emphasis in original) ethics training for all senior managers and a system of monitoring the ethical considerations of key policy and strategy decisions within the supervised firms": at 53).

[22] See, for example, S. Schwartz, "The Alchemy of Securitization" (1994) 1 *Stanford Journal of Law, Business and Finance* 133; L. Kendall and M. Freeman, *A Primer on Securitization* (1996).

the credit rating agencies.[23] It was these same entities that transformed inherently risky products into ostensibly secure products in the first place, thus legitimating the entire pyramid scheme. The implosion of the securitization market calls into question the normative value of transferring oversight to public corporations with no accountability for the social risks of systemic failure. Economic and political orthodoxy, after all, had maintained that the social responsibility of the corporation was to maximize profits for shareholders. The housing collapse exposed the corrupting influence of this compact on the mortgage industry. As public and private legal actions multiply, the search for institutional scapegoats has focused primarily on the US-based firms that dominate the industry, Moody's Investment Services and Standard & Poors. According to the House Oversight and Government Reform Committee chairman, these firms had violated a "bond of trust" while "federal regulators ignored the warning signs and did nothing to protect the public."[24] Understanding how this occurred requires a detour into the mechanics of the mortgage business.[25]

There are four main mortgage categories in the United States. "Prime" loans are offered to applicants with high credit rating scores who place a significant equity stake in the property. "Jumbo" loans form the second most secure form. These conform to agency requirements in every respect but size. "Alt-A" loan are provided to those with lower credit ratings. While the applicants may not have any prior credit problems, the loans fail to conform to generic prudential lending standards. The borrower may, for example, have substantially less equity, or none at all. The fourth form was "Sub-Prime" generally

---

[23] See T. Sinclair, *The New Masters of Capital* (2005) 61–69 (noting that "rating is not the technical activity it is thought popularly to be. Instead it is highly indeterminate, qualitative and judgment laden....The bond rating agencies tend to promote specific frameworks of investment practices, knowledge forms, and governance systems. In any other context, these views would be readily recognizable as instances of political ideology": 61–62).

[24] Opening Statement, "Hearing on the Credit Rating Agencies and the Financial Crisis," House Committee on Oversight and Government Reform, Washington DC, 22 October 2008 (H. Waxman).

[25] See G. Dell'Ariccia, D. Igan, and, L. Laeven, "Credit Booms and Lending Standards: Evidence from the Sub-Prime Mortgage Market" (International Monetary Fund, Washington, DC, WP/08/06, April 2008); For general overviews of corrupt practices at mortgage broker level, see R. Bitner, *Confessions of a Sub-Prime Lender* (2008); for the collapse of Countrywide, one of the largest sub-prime specialists and its relationship with Wall Street, see Muolo and Padilla, above n 13.

offered to those with the poorest credit record. Yet from 2000 to 2007, it grew by 800%. As it mushroomed, so too did the Alt-A market. By 2006 the combination accounted for 30% of the entire US housing market.[26]

The Adjustable Rate Mortgage, first authorized in the 1980s, proved to be a critical accelerant.[27] It allowed originators to offer low introductory repayment levels, thus expanding the range of retail customers. The design remained effective as long as the mortgage was refinanced no less than one year after the introductory period expired.[28] The structure was explicitly designed to ensure constant rolling over of debt but on terms set by the lender. Despite high pre-repayment penalties, both borrower and lender stood to gain as long as house prices continued to rise. In the process, addictive tendencies began to take root. Misrepresentation, falsification and fraud became rampant across large swathes of the industry. From the borrower through to the broker, the original lender and the manufacturer of the residential mortgage backed securities, credibility and probity became compromised because of a naïve faith that housing growth was sustainable.[29] If the initial loans were not necessarily predatory, the refinancing dimension certainly was.[30]

Mortgage brokers, largely unregulated, had a vested interest in pushing the lines of credit that attracted most personal gain. A sizeable proportion of their income was based on commission. Riskier classes attracted higher inducements from the investment banks.[31] The absence of fiduciary duty—or meaningful liability—meant the broker had no incentive to worry about default risk.[32] Paradoxically, as competition for the riskier components increased, lending standards on "Prime" applications simultaneously tightened. This forced, in turn, a herding

---

[26] G. Gorton, "The Sub-Prime Panic" (2008) *European Financial Management* (forthcoming) 4.
[27] This was first legislated for in 1982 through the *Alternative Mortgage Transaction Parity Act* (1982). The legislation allowed differential mortgage rates, including the use of balloon payments.
[28] Bitner, above n 25, 31.
[29] Figures released by the Mortgage Industry Data Exchange showed that fraud incident submissions increased by 30% between 2005 and 2006; one industry insider notes that 70% of loan applications made to his wholesale lending firm were fraudulent; see Bitner, above n 25, 45.
[30] For a devastating account, see P. Boyer, "Eviction," *The New Yorker*, 24 November 2008, 48.
[31] The same commission logic applied to the bond salesmen in the investment banks creating the CDO; see Muolo and Padilla, above n 13, 9.
[32] See Bitner, above n 25, 4, 32.

dynamic towards what an IMF sponsored report termed systemic "gambling on speculative borrowers."[33] Moral compunction did not feature, either in the back streets of Ohio or the canyons of midtown Manhattan. As Christopher Dodd, the chair of the Senate Committee on Banking Housing and Urban Affairs, noted following the collapse of New Century, one of the leading purveyors of sub-prime markets, "frankly, the fact that any reputable lender could make these kinds of loan so widely available to wage earners, to elderly families on fixed incomes, and to lower-income and unsophisticated borrowers, strikes me as unconscionable and deceptive. And the fact that the country's financial regulators could allow these loans to be made for years after warning flags appeared is equally unconscionable."[34]

When sub-prime mortgages reset, the cost is based on the London Inter-Bank Offered Rate (LIBOR)—the rate at which banks lend to each other—plus a variable supplement. With the LIBOR trading at exceptionally high rates, a vicious circle begins to spin. Higher repayment costs compromise the capacity of borrowers; forced sales lower prices and depress remaining equity and thus capability to refinance. Accounting rules force the banks to recognize rising default. As a consequence, already precarious solvency levels are further threatened.[35] As the cycle spins, the share price of the bank most exposed faces concerted deliberate short-selling assault in those countries that allow the practice. A credit rating downgrade in such circumstances serves to further depress prices and threatens viability.[36] It is this baleful reality that ultimately led to the meltdown in mortgage providers such as Countrywide, the forced fire-sale of Bear Stearns and ultimately, following the collapse of Lehman Brothers, the destruction of the investment banking model. The critical question is why the rating agencies, which were given delegated authority to monitor the quality of

---

[33] Dell'Ariccia et al, above n 25, 11–12.

[34] Opening Statement, "Hearing on Mortgage Market Turmoil: Causes and Consequences," Senate Committee on Banking, Housing and Urban Affairs, Washington DC, 22 March 2007 (C. Dodd).

[35] The rise in losses is linked to legal rulings that the lenders held a prudential obligation to vet the representations; see *National City Bank v. Hill*, United States Bankruptcy Court, Northern District of California, A.P. 07-4106 (May 28, 2008), cited in A Efrati, "Are Borrowers Free to Lie?" *Wall Street Journal*, 31 May 2008, B2.

[36] This was precisely the defense offered by the Lehman chief executive in testimony to Congress.

corporate bonds, failed to stop the cycle from starting in the first place. The warning signs were there from the start.

Risk was magnified because many banks established Special Investment Vehicles (SIV) that were designed by one London-based boutique firm named, perhaps appropriately, Gordian Knot.[37] The SIV issued securities on the undiluted value of a pool that typically contained between 1,000 and 25,000 individual but related mortgages in a mechanism termed a Collateralized Debt Obligation (CDO). Despite the inherently unstable nature of the core ingredients, the parcels were provided with implausible and unsustainable credit rankings because of the epistemic authority of agencies.[38] This enabled the SIV to market the CDO to institutional investors, who like everyone else in the system, remained convinced of a low risk of default. After all, they were provided with three further layers of comfort.

First, the bonds were designed to appeal to differential risk appetites across the market. As noted above, each CDO was made up of broadly similar mortgage types. Furthermore, the CDO itself was sliced, with each component carrying a differential rating. The safest component—Senior Debt—received a rating that suggested that the default risk was minimal. With yield spreads ranging between 5 and 800 basis points, it was rational for institutional investors to include CDO exposure within a diversified asset management strategy. Institutional actors, precluded by governance mandates from holding products with a less than investment-grade valuation, followed hedge funds into products in which the ownership of economic risk was, at best, unclear. The faith placed in these products and in the ratings system now appears grossly unwarranted.

As with those involved in providing mortgages or brokering finance, the rating agencies were themselves inherently conflicted. For example, as early as 1996, Standard & Poors had made its proprietary risk default model available to clients. According to the former head of the Residential Mortgage Backed Securities Ratings Department, the decision gave issuers greater certainty about how an individual CDO

---

[37] C. Mollenkamp, D. Solomon, R. Sidel, and V. Bauerlein, "How London Created a Snarl in Global Markets," *Wall Street Journal*, 18 October 2007, A1.

[38] Sinclair, above n 23 (noting that while the epistemic authority of the agencies is embedded and failures routinely written off, it is also "bivariate" and could be lost in the event of "a persistent record of perceived failure or by a change in the relationship between raters and those who use ratings—a change in the structure of capitalism": at 65).

would be rated. For the executive in question, "it was critical [however] to maintain the best models as they were the lynchpin of the rating process."[39] In evidence to the House Oversight and Government Reform Committee, he maintained that "things began to change in 2001 as the housing market took off—a new version of the model was developed using approximately 2.5 million loans with significant performance information. This model was by far the best developed but it was not implemented due to budgetary constraints."

Although the company questioned the computer program's effectiveness, insider testimony that "improving the model would not add to S&P's revenues" struck a cord with legislators. So too did the publication of a series of memos over how to value an early CDO called "Pinstripe." When the executive asked for detailed information about the performance of the underlying mortgages, he was rebuffed:

> Any request for loan level tapes is TOTALLY UNREASONABLE!!! Most investors don't have it and can't provide it. Nevertheless we MUST produce a credit estimate. It is your responsibility to provide those credit estimates and your responsibility to devise some method for doing so [emphasis in original].[40]

As the value and amount of individual transactions increased, the mechanisms for evaluating risk became even more problematic. The rating agencies calculated default through proprietary models provided by the financial engineers. Integrity was further compromised precisely because risk was calculated on the credit rating of the individual bank rather than the underlying asset. The public illusion could only be sustained as long as real estate markets defied gravity. Privately, however, unease was becoming apparent. In a reprise of the conflicts of interest investigations on Wall Street research at the turn of the

---

[39] Evidence to House Committee on Oversight and Government Reform, "Hearing on the Credit Rating Agencies and the Financial Crisis," Washington DC 22 October 2008 (F. Raiter) 4.

[40] The executive's written response was to protest that "this is the most amazing memo I have ever received in my business career." In a response to subsequent media queries, S&P offered the following explanation. "It has long been the practice of S&P to review loan level data for new RMBS securities. The e-mail in question reflects a discussion regarding the appropriate analytic treatment for a CDO rating of an underlying asset that has been rated by another credit rating agency." See G. Morgenson, "House Panel Scrutinizes Rating Firms," *New York Times,* 23 October 2008, B1.

millennium,[41] the House Oversight Committee released a series of damning electronic exchanges. These helped build a case that centered on a "colossal failure" to manage the competing imperatives of maintaining the integrity of the rating and the demand to secure business.[42]

Considerations of the impact on probity were ignored. At Standard & Poors, for example, one of those involved in the actual analysis reasoned, "let's hope we are all wealthy and retired by the time this house of cards falters." Just how degraded the process had become was captured in this instant message exchange between two members of its structured finance department.

> Rahul Dilip Shah: BTW [By the Way]—that deal is ridiculous.
> Shannon Mooney: I know right…model def[initely] does not capture half the risk
> Rahul Dilp Shah: We should not be rating it.
> Shannon Mooney: We rate every deal. It could be structured by cows and we would rate it.
> Shah: But there's a lot of risk associated with it—I personally do not feel comfy signing off as a committee member.[43]

Standard & Poor's president, Deven Shama, conceded to Congress that the language was inappropriate. He denied, however, that it reflected core corporate culture, a view echoed by his counterpart at Moody's Investment Services. Documentary and oral evidence contradict the veracity of this account. Jerome Fons, the former director of Credit Policy at Moody's, testified that "the business model prevented analysts from putting investors' interests first." Frank Raiter of S&P put it even more bluntly: "Profits were running the show."[44] So too, however, was politics. The growth of the mortgage-backed securities business in the United States stemmed from reasonable attempts to hedge against government demands that the privilege of home ownership be expanded to communities that could not afford them. Executive agencies failed, however, to adopt a holistic approach to the risks involved in this process.

---

[41] See generally, J. O'Brien, *Wall Street on Trial* (2003), 141–73.
[42] Waxman, above n 24.
[43] Ibid.
[44] Ibid.

As Robert Shiller has pointed out, "the very people responsible for oversight were caught up in the same high expectations for future house-price increases that the general public had."[45] Shiller, one of the most respected housing specialists in the country, put the calculations down to exuberance rather than connivance. Congress itself, however, may not deserve such a charitable judgment. The most senior Republican on the committee noted in a rare moment of congressional forthrightness, "members from both parties and both chambers not only tolerated, but encouraged the steady erosion of mortgage-lending standards."[46] This was most apparent in the oversight of Freddie Mac and Fannie Mae. These ostensibly public corporations proved impervious to market or executive branch political discipline.[47] Buoyed by unsustainable bond ratings, they rapidly became the main secondary providers of housing credit. Their success derived from an implicit government guarantee. Congress reinforced this by accepting annual reports from the Office of Federal Housing Enterprise Oversight (OFHEO). The OFHEO was established with a specific mandate to ensure the insulation of Freddie and Fannie from any systemic impact associated with irresponsible lending in the commercial sector. The agency ensured that its charges only bought and securitized conforming loans and had developed stress-testing models. The problem was that these capped national price declines at a maximum of 13.4%. As with the rating agencies, the efficacy of the model was used to tabulate risk was compromised by reliance on short-term historical data. It was delusional.

Throughout the lending boom attempts to enhance the accountability of Freddie Mac and Fannie Mae failed to gain sufficient traction.[48] The power of their lobbyists to frame discourse appears undiminished. When the financial crisis hearings were first proposed, the Oversight Committee omitted the Government-Sponsored Enterprises

[45] R. Shiller, *The Sub-Prime Solution* (2008) 53.
[46] Opening Statement, 'Hearing on the Causes and Effects of the Lehman Brothers Bankruptcy," House Committee on Oversight and Government Reform, Washington DC, 6 October (T. Davis).
[47] Evidence to House Oversight and Government Reform Committee, "Hearing on Collapse of Fannie Mae and Freddie Mac," Washington DC, 9 December 2008 (T Stanton) noting "their market power gave them political power...that political power, in turn entrenched their market power": at 4.
[48] Evidence to House Committee on Oversight and Government Reform, "Hearing on the Role of Federal Regulators in the Financial Crisis," Washington DC, 23 October 2008 (J. Snow).

from those who would be held to public account. This was, however, unsustainable. Failing to call the senior executives of major government sponsored enterprises to give evidence about a scandal that has cost the US taxpayer $750 billion risked undermining the credibility of the entire process. The calculated political decision was then made to delay hearing evidence about the governance of the Government Sponsored Enterprises until after the presidential election. The decision ensured the temporary evasion of difficult questions about whether payments to Democrats, in particular, but also to Republicans impacted the capacity or willingness of Congress to exercise effective oversight. As a Republican representative put it during a particularly tense exchange, the hearings had been hijacked. It was, he said, akin to tiptoeing around the tulips while someone had driven a bulldozer through the garden. When the hearings were eventually held, Representative Waxman argued that documentary evidence showed that "the CEOs of Fannie and Freddie made reckless bets that led to the downfall of their companies. Their actions cost taxpayers hundreds of billions of dollars. But it is a myth to say they were the originators of the sub-prime crisis. Fundamentally, they were following the market, not leading it."[49] As with other executives paraded before the committee room, the chief executive of Fannie Mae, Daniel Mudd, used the "perfect storm" defense. In an interview with the *New York Times,* Mudd argued that "it is not fair to

---

[49] Opening Statement, House Committee on Oversight and Government Reform, "Hearing on Collapse of Fannie Mae and Freddie Mac," Washington DC, 9 December 2008 (H. Waxman), citing a presentation from the CEO of Fannie Mae, Daniel Mudd, in which the strategy is set out: "We face two stark choices: (1) Stay the course; or (2) Meet the market where the market is." Similarly, Freddie Mac's CEO, Richard Syron, ignored a warning from his chief risk officer that "the potential for the perception and reality of predatory lending with this product is great," ibid. Expert testimony provided to the committee noted the "clear and unambiguous support for the proposition that Freddie Mac consciously undertook the acquisition of loans with poor underwriting processes in spite of factual evidence, both from the past and the current market experience, that led its own risk managers to recommend raising auditing standards and scaling back their involvement in these loans." See Evidence to House Committee on Oversight and Government Reform, "Hearing on the Collapse of Fannie Mae and Freddie Mac," Washington DC, 9 December 2008 (C. Calomiris) 3. Professor Calomiris went further, however, by stating that "accounting transparency has never been a strength at the GSEs": at 8. This occluded the scale of the risk that was taking place. The GSEs became market makers as "originators of subprime and Alt-A mortgages knew that the GSEs stood ready to buy their poorly underwritten instruments, and this GSE legitimization of unsound underwriting practices gave assurance to all market participants that there was a ready source of demand for the new product" at 8.

blame us for not predicting the unthinkable. Almost no-one expected what was coming."[50] Furthermore, he argued that blame, if apportioned at all, should focus on the demands of Congress to ensure that the agencies were meeting ambitious goals of homeownership, and on Wall Street, where its main level of interaction occurred, meaning that the organization was not aware of significant problems in the housing industry. This is an implausible defense. As the *New York Times* reported in the same article, a former loans director at Fannie Mae, conceded, "we didn't really know what we were buying. This system was designed for plain vanilla loans [the acquisition of individual mortgages] and we were trying to push chocolate sundaes through the gears."[51]

The forced nationalization of Fannie Mae and Freddie Mac has ensured that the United States government is now underwriting a majority of housing mortgages. Unlike a corporate provider, the federal government's capacity to foreclose is a political impossibility. This makes it essential that a broader solution is put in place. This, in turn, cannot be done without first insuring that the integrity of bond rating is restored. The credit rating agencies and the Government Sponsored Enterprises connived in creating the circumstances for a rapid expansion of the residential mortgage boom. As noted above, however, the contemporary credit crisis reflects a much more systemic failure, one that was internally generated by the financial engineers in Wall Street. The critical ingredient was the development of the multi-trillion dollar Credit Default Swap market.

III   INADEQUATE INSURANCE: THE CASE OF AIG

The Credit Default Swap (CDS) completed the flight from reality in the oversight of the securitization market. The CDS provided a further apparent diversification of risk. Designed by the purveyors of the underlying Mortgage-Backed Securities (MBS) and Collateralized Debt Obligations (CDO), when applied to the housing market, it functioned as a pseudo-insurance contract. The distinction is essential. By definition the CDS was not insurance and therefore did not fall under the direct responsibility of state-based regulators. Furthermore, the global nature of the market meant that opacity increased at precisely the same time as

---

[50] C. Duhigg, "Pressured to Take More Risk, Fannie Reached Tipping Point," *New York Times*, 5 October 2008, A1.
[51] Ibid.

underlying risk was accelerating. Regulatory arbitrage created artificial circuit breakers that impeded information flows within individual entities and across jurisdictions. There was no requirement for the buyers of CDS protection to hold an ongoing stake in the entity insured. As a result, it legitimated the most egregious form of "naked" short selling. Investment banks and institutional investors now had the opportunity and incentive to deliberately cause corporate default.[52] Operating without supervision, the market expanded rapidly in size to $58 trillion.

The now failed AIG is exceptionally problematic in this regard. AIG, one of the largest insurance and general global financial services firms has offices in more than 130 countries, employs more than 116,000 employees and until its collapse had assets in excess of $1 trillion. Its disastrous foray into the CDS market was managed out of London, rather than corporate headquarters in New York. The insurance colossus appeared oblivious to the potential risk if even a fraction of the hundred of billions of cover it was underwriting through London and Paris was called. During the boom, AIG benefited enormously from the rise in the securitization market. Institutional investors bought the CDO on the basis of a rating, which we have seen was hopelessly compromised. They sought (rationally enough) to minimize any residual risk through the purchase of a CDS contract.

By the end of 2006, the London office of AIG Financial Products had underwritten contracts valued at $500 billion. Unfortunately, the insurance cover was just as compromised as the underlying product. The profits booked appeared reasonable, on the face of it, because the underlying CDO was deemed to have a default risk as low as US Treasury bonds. Furthermore, AIG did not have to post collateral because of its own high rating. The entire arrangement was at best hopelessly naïve. At worst, it bordered on fraud. As the levels of default grew, AIG was forced to post collateral it did not have in order to cover actual losses. With the parent teetering on the edge of collapse in mid-September 2008, the decision by the credit rating agencies to downgrade the stock rather than await the result of a restructuring left AIG with a

---

[52] The Securities and Exchange Commission has now recognized that the failure to regulate the CDS market was a critical accelerator. It has repeatedly called on Congress to allow for expansion of oversight capabilities; see Evidence to Senate Committee on Banking, Housing and Urban Affairs, Washington DC, 23 September 2008 (C. Cox); Evidence to House Committee on Agriculture, Washington DC, 15 October 2008 (E. Sirri).

profound liquidity problem as Lehman Brothers faced imminent bankruptcy.

With the authorization of the New York State Governor, David Paterson, the State Insurance Superintendent, Eric Dinallo, spent the weekend of 12–14 September—the same weekend that investment banks were frantically trying to save themselves—working out an emergency salvage plan. The plan provided regulatory approval for an internal transfer of assets with the capacity to release $20 billion in order to meet collateral obligations due to the rating downgrade. According to Dinallo, "we were willing to consider allowing AIG to effectively sell some US AIG life insurance companies to some of AIG's property insurance companies. In exchange for the stock of the life insurance companies, the property insurance companies would have transferred a lesser value of certain liquid assets, specifically municipal bonds, to the parent. The municipal bonds would have been used by AIG to provide the collateral it needed."[53] Dinallo stressed to Congress that no state money was involved in the temporary transfer. The state insurance companies remained in compliance with statutory risk-based capital requirements. He further noted that the temporary transfer was one component of a three-pronged strategy, which also involved the sale of other AIG assets and a capital injection from either private equity firms or a bank syndicate. It became immediately apparent when the markets opened on the day of the Lehman bankruptcy that the $40 billion raised would not be sufficient. With AIG unable to obtain commercial funding, the federal government stepped in with an $85 billion bridge loan. For Dinallo, "the risks of allowing AIG to file for bankruptcy were in my opinion just too great."[54]

There is considerable merit in Dinallo's contention. It also raises difficult questions, however, about why the risks were not addressed by regulatory authorities. The Balkanization of regulatory oversight provides only a partial explanation. The fact that the CDS market was unregulated provides greater traction but here the unresolved question remains why such a broad systemic risk did not trigger regulatory questions. To date the bailout of AIG has cost the US taxpayer $150 billion. Attempts to reduce liabilities through the sale of flagship subsidiaries such as the Asian life assurance business are proving

---

[53] Evidence to House Committee on Oversight and Government Reform, "Hearing on the Causes and Effects of the AIG Bailout," Washington DC, 7 October 2008 (E. Dinallo) 4.
[54] Ibid, 6.

inordinately difficult because of complex valuations, a lack of potential buyers and a lack of credit. As a consequence, the government retained its overarching 79.99% control but loosened significantly the onerous terms imposed on the corporation. First the loan term was increased from a two to a five year term. Second, the interest premium over the London Interbank Overnight Rate (LIBOR) was reduced from 8.5% to 3.5%. Third, the government has invested $30 billion in two entities designed to buy the CDOs on which AIG had an exposure through its CDS operation. AIG is to invest $5 billion in the venture, which is attempting to buy the CDOS at a rate of 50 cents in the dollar. This is well in excess of the 22.5 cents in the dollar paid by Lone Star in its deal with Merrill Lynch. Even so, there is no guarantee that the banks will exit the market at this price. Even if they do, the government faces enormous exposure if the levels of default continue to rise.

The lack of credible oversight is even more worrisome because AIG was under intense regulatory scrutiny at precisely the time it ratcheted up its CDS exposure. Its use of reinsurance contracts to manipulate corporate earnings for others and for itself had prompted wide-ranging civil and criminal investigations. The then New York State Attorney General, Eliot Spitzer, and the federal Department of Justice were involved in multiple cross-cutting investigations that led to the forced ousting of the chief executive, Hank Greenberg.[55] The company paid a fine of $126 million to settle charges of misconduct. While not admitting liability, AIG entered into a deferred prosecution that was explicitly designed to improve its risk management processes. The promise proved worthless. Joseph Cassano,the head of the London-based subsidiary at the heart of the debacle, AIG Financial Products, told investors that the exercise had improved risk management with the company. Cassano claimed that quality control was assured through a committee that "I sit on along with many of the senior managers at AIG and we look at a whole variety of transactions that come in to make sure that they are maintaining the quality that we need to. And I think the things that have been put in at our level and the things that have been put in at the parent level will ensure that there won't be any of those kinds of mistakes again."[56] The collapse of AIG is therefore best conceptualized

---

[55] The State Insurance Superintendent, Eric Dinallo, was a senior investigator with the State Attorney General.
[56] See G. Morgenson, "Behind Insurer's Crisis, Blind Eye to a Web of Risk," *New York Times*, 28 September 2008, A1.

as the result of a grossly deficient corporate governance and financial regulation paradigm. It highlights the limitations of functional regulation. The omission from integrated oversight of critical components of the shadow banking system—such as the CDS market, as well as hedge funds and private equity firms—means that regulators are incapable of engaging in effective preemptive strategies. Behind a robust façade, the regulatory regime was hopelessly compromised, particularly in the United States.

IV   THE DEMISE OF AUTHORITY

Financial capitalism literally as well as practically inverts Joseph Schumpeter's famous model of "creative destruction."[57] For Schumpeter, the perennial gale of change "incessantly revolutionizes the economic structure from within, incessantly destroying the old one, incessantly creating a new one. This process of Creative Destruction is the essential fact about capitalism."[58] Change emanates from the impact on the existing order of "the competition from the new commodity, the new technology, the new source of supply, the new type of organization." The challenge "strikes not at the margins of the profits and the outputs of the existing firms but at their foundations and their very lives."[59] Change of this magnitude is far from unproblematic. Change can weaken loyalty, trust and institutional knowledge. Contemporary ethnographies of the corporation highlight the internal social dislocation and anxiety this process generates for employees (including middle management).[60] As Schumpeter warns, "no social system can work in which everyone is supposed to be guided by nothing except his short-term utilitarian ends....The stock market is a poor substitute for the Holy Grail."[61] This, however, was precisely the vision of society championed by the former chairman of the Federal Reserve, Alan Greenspan. His defenestration in Congress provides a telling example of how the inculcation of an ideological worldview created a self-deception of catastrophic proportions.

---

[57] J. Schumpeter, *Capitalism, Socialism and Democracy* (1943).
[58] Ibid, 84.
[59] Ibid.
[60] See R. Sennett, *The Culture of the New Capitalism* (2006) 57, 181.
[61] Schumpeter, above n 57, 137.

Throughout his career, Greenspan had been feted by the political
and market elite. He served as head of the Council of Economic Advisors
under President Ford and presided—to wide acclaim—over the Federal
Reserve under both Democratic and Republican administrations. On his
retirement, President Bush described Greenspan as a "legend" who "has
dominated his age like no central banker in history."[62] In November
2005, the central banker was awarded the Presidential Medal of
Freedom, the nation's highest civil award. The medal is awarded 'to any
person who has made an especially meritorious contribution to (1) the
security or national interests of the United States, or (2) world peace, or
(3) cultural or other significant public or private endeavors." In
announcing the award, the White House lauded Greenspan as "an
extraordinary leader."[63] The citation was, if anything, even more
gushing.

> Alan Greenspan has been a steadfast and effective manager of
> United States monetary policy. With prudence and wisdom, he
> has helped shepherd our economy through stock market crashes,
> global financial crises, recessions, and national disasters. During
> his nearly two decades of principled work at the Federal
> Reserve, he has become the standard by which central bankers
> are measured. The United States honors Alan Greenspan for his
> outstanding career of public service and for enhancing the
> character and prosperity of our Nation.[64]

Greenspan returned to Capitol Hill exactly three years later. The
sprightly eighty-two year old entered the committee room just before ten.
Ever the consummate professional, Greenspan immediately worked the
room. He bounded up the steps, shook hands with the most senior
politicians and nodded sagely to all present. Greenspan looked in
command of his brief; apparently secure in the esteem in which he had
previously been held. At first, he was listened to patiently. The five-
minute limit for opening statements was waived, as Greenspan sought to
explain the causes and consequences of "a financial tsunami" that, he
conceded, disturbed him greatly.

---

[62] "President Appoints Dr Ben Bernanke for Chairman of the Federal Reserve" (Press
Release, White House, Washington DC, 24 October 2005).
[63] "Presidential Medal of Freedom Recipients" (Press Release, White House, Washington
DC, 3 November 2005).
[64] "Citation for 2005 Presidential Medal of Freedom" (Press Release, White House,
Washington DC, 9 November 2005).

A Nobel Prize was awarded for the discovery of the pricing
model that underpins much of the advance in derivatives
markets. This modern risk management paradigm held sway for
decades. The whole intellectual edifice, however, collapsed in
the summer of last year because the data inputted into the risk
management models generally covered only the past two
decades, a period of euphoria. Had instead the models been
fitted more appropriately to historic periods of stress, capital
requirements would have been much higher and the financial
world would be in far better shape today, in my judgment.[65]

This account fails to take into consideration why the Federal Reserve
itself did not input more historical data. Over the course of four hours,
Greenspan's confidence waned. In the face of extremely hostile
questioning, his age began to show. He saw his record mocked, and his
prior contributions to public policy belittled. Legislators repeatedly
claimed that Greenspan was a slave to the market rather than its master,
so enthralled by an ideological worldview that he failed in this primary
duty: to protect the country.

What remains staggering is that economic policymakers were
aware from as early as 2004 that a speculative bubble was being inflated.
It could only be sustained by the expansion of low introductory rates, a
process actively encouraged by the then chairman of the Federal
Reserve. Alan Greenspan claimed that "American consumers might
benefit if lenders provided greater mortgage product alternatives to the
traditional fixed-rate mortgage. To the degree that households are driven
by fears of payment shocks but are willing to manage their own interest
rate risks, the traditional fixed-rate mortgage may be an expensive
method of financing a home."[66] By late October of the same year,
Greenspan was again trying to quell concern. In a speech to the
Community Bankers conference, he remarked that "debt leverage of all
types is often troublesome when one judges the stability of the economy.
Should home prices fall, we would have reason to be concerned about
mortgage debt; but measures of household financial stress do not, at least

---

[65] Evidence to House Committee on Oversight and Government Reform, "Hearing on the
Role of Federal Regulators in the Financial Crisis," Washington DC, 23 October 2008
(A. Greenspan).
[66] A. Greenspan, "Understanding Household Debt Obligations" (Speech delivered at
Credit Union National Association Annual Conference, Washington DC, 23 February
2004).

to date, appear overly worrisome....In addition, improvements in lending practices driven by information technology have enabled lenders to reach out to households with previously unrecognized borrowing capacities. This extension of lending has increased overall household debt but has probably not meaningfully increased the number of households with already overextended debt."[67] Notwithstanding his "shocked disbelief" at the willful destruction of shareholder value, the Greenspan doctrine weakened regulatory defenses across the world. Furthermore, Greenspan's after the fact assertion that it is impossible to have a perfect model of risk is, to put it mildly, self-serving.[68]

---

[67] A. Greenspan, "The Mortgage Market and Consumer Debt" (Speech delivered at America's Community Bankers Annual Convention, Washington DC, 19 October 2004).
[68] A. Greenspan, "We Will Never Have a Perfect Model of Risk," *Financial Times*, 17 March 2008, 13.

Chapter 4

The Moral Hazard of Intervention

There is now incredulity on Wall Street at the enormity of personal and professional costs imposed by acquiescing in the neglect of restraint. Dennis Berman has captured the sense of shellshock in a memorable dispatch. According to Berman, "inside what's left of Wall Street, investment bankers are doing all they can to cope with a business that is disappearing before their eyes. Yes, there are tens of thousands of people still with jobs. They just don't have much work. Debt and stock markets are virtually shut, merger volume is down by 28%, and whole lines of structured finance are closed for good. Investment banking has since become a phantom realm, where everyone is busy but no one is doing anything."[1] The declines in revenue and reported losses pose serious questions about the viability of business models, in particular the use of proprietary trading. The decision by the last surviving investment banks to seek security by submitting themselves to Federal Reserve regulation makes it even more difficult to engage in risky (if potentially rewarding) trading strategies. Moreover, it not only marks the demise of the independent New York merchant house. It also draws attention to the grossly inadequate oversight regime that legitimated regulatory arbitrage across and between deficient and antiquated structures.

If confidence is to be returned, it is essential that a new order is put in place. One key mechanism to ensure that risks are minimized is to

---

[1] D. Berman, "On the Street, Disbelief and Resignation," *Wall Street Journal*, 9 December 2008, C3. It is indicative of the scale of the crisis that Goldman Sachs posted its first quarterly loss since going public. Although the loss, at $2.12 billion, was much smaller than those reported by its rivals, revenues dropped by 52% and earning suffered an 80% decline; see G. Farrell, "Goldman Hit By Quarterly Loss," *Financial Times*, 17 December 2008, 13. The following day, Morgan Stanley reported losses of $2.2 billion; see F. Guerrera, "Morgan Stanley Hit by 'Savage' Downturn'", *Financial Times*, 18 December 2008, 16.

ensure that the board of directors within a specific financial services firm takes its fiduciary obligations seriously. This forms the cornerstone of state corporation law. The existence of a business judgment rule makes it exceptionally difficult to second-guess a board's exercise of what constitutes best practice. This suggests that ongoing supervision of risk management requires that the government exercise direct ownership rights, including, where appropriate board seats. While such a step cuts against established political realities in the United States, it is necessary to break the desultory cycle of regulatory reform that sees the promise of reform inevitably founder as immediate crisis recedes. The crisis is intensified precisely because despite enormous capital injections, credit conditions remain difficult. Banks are hoarding the cash rather than dispersing it. In this context, the initial policy preferences enshrined in the *Emergency Economic Stabilization Act* (2008) represented a missed opportunity. The decision to take preference share stakes is a step in the right direction; the decision not to take board seats, however, weakens oversight and directional capacity.

I   CONTROLLING THE CORPORATION

The financial crisis coincided with the most sensitive time in the electoral calendar. Along with the upcoming presidential contest, one third of the Senate as well as the entire House of Representatives faced the electorate. Castigating Wall Street, of course, has a long and storied, if episodic, history in the United States. The gap between the rhetoric and reality of the market is pronounced in the very architecture of the New York Stock Exchange. As the cultural commentator Simon Fraser has noted, above the inscription of "Business Integrity Protecting the Industries of Man," "integrity," personified as a woman, dominates the neo-Grecian façade, with "her outstretched arms hovered protectively over sculptured figures frozen in a choreography of productive labor; to her left, Agriculture and Mining; on her right, Science, Industry, and Invention. Beneath Integrity's solicitous gaze, a harmonious Commerce reigned."[2] This benign vision has long been questioned in popular culture, most recently

---

[2] S. Fraser, *Wall Street, A Cultural History* (2007) 221 (further noting that "Wall Street, once a scarlet woman, a disreputable habitueé of capitalism's badlands, was here miraculously beautified": at 221–22). The interpretation of Wall Street's "supreme accomplishment is as a harlot" underpins the classic account of the 1929 Crash; see J.K. Galbraith, *The Great Crash* (1954, 1975 edition) 48.

in the eponymous movie *Wall Street* (1987) and Tom Wolfe's biting satire *Bonfire of the Vanities* (1987). In sharp contrast, political support for market-based solutions to regulatory failure gained bipartisan support, a process reinforced by the centrist policies adopted by the Clinton administration throughout the 1990s. This substantially reduced capacity to engage in a sustained preemptive discussion with industry over what constitutes or should constitute integrity. A narrow conception of regulatory and prosecutorial purpose to deal with white-collar crime was reinforced.[3] This contrasted "deviants" with those engaged in the respectable pursuit of legally mandated (if integrity-challenged) business.[4] Such a myopic approach ignores how the deleterious inculcation of amoral values compromises the efficacy of compliance. Moreover, undue deference to legally permitted but ethically questionable market actions leads to an abdication of political responsibility.[5] The global financial crisis has, at last, punctured the power of that myth, exposing in the process the degree of political culpability.[6]

As with fall-out from the Enron-related financial reporting scandals, policymakers in Washington sought to benefit from (or insulate themselves against) an increasingly irate American public, scandalized at the excess of Wall Street and the desultory failure of executive agencies and political oversight. The provision of a lifeline to those responsible for generating the crisis at a time of record foreclosures and increased

---

[3] For a discussion of the moral ambiguity inherent in the definition and prosecution of white-collar crime more generally, see S. Green, *Lying, Cheating and Stealing* (2006) 24–9.

[4] See M. Levi, "Suite Revenge? The Shaping of Folk Devils and Moral Panics about White Collar Crimes" (2009) 49 *British Journal of Criminology* 48. Creating and sustaining an "us" and "them" dynamic carries substantial political risks; see C. Tilly, *Credit and Blame* (2008) 53–60 (noting further that the "use of public power to fix credit and blame writes us-them divisions into political life. It also reinforces the operation of the same divisions in private life....Be very careful when you call for the authorities to back up your assignments of credit and blame": at 151).

[5] See J. Braithwaite and V. Braithwaite, "Democratic Sentiment and Cyclical Markets in Vice" (2006) 46 *British Journal of Criminology* 1110 ("Demand is built through creating or appealing to an emotional need in individuals that can be satisfied intermittently through the supply the good or service in question....The important question is what is being demanded and supplied, with what consequences for the well-being of society": at 1117).

[6] For recent critiques of market mechanisms on practical and normative grounds, see L. Brown and L. Jacobs, *The Private Abuse of the Public Interest* (2008); S. Marglin, *The Dismal Science: How Thinking Like an Economist Undermines Community* (2008).

economic uncertainty was always going to be a difficult sell.[7] At a series
of hearings, the nation's financial custodians claimed that failure to
provide emergency funding through a Troubled Assets Relief Program
(TARP) would prompt catastrophe.[8] The decision to advocate a $700
billion solution was accompanied by belated and half-hearted recognition
that the policy choices heretofore adopted were, at best, based on an
optimistic, if not naïve, reading of what was fast becoming a global
financial crisis. At each stage they had maintained that the credit crunch
was contained and containable, that markets were stable, that institutions
were viable and that the existing regulatory structures were sufficiently
robust. With the credit markets paralyzed, systemically important
financial institutions falling, and contagion spreading, this was not, they
argued, a time for recrimination or reflecting on moral hazard of
providing bailouts to those guilty of reckless disintermediation; necessity
required providing Treasury with what amounted to a blank check.[9]

The Federal Reserve Chairman, Ben Bernanke, accepted the
need for a more far-reaching reorganization of regulatory structure and
purpose but argued that "at this juncture, in light of the fast-moving
developments in financial markets, it is essential to deal with the crisis at
hand." The Treasury Secretary, Henry Paulson, was even more direct: "I
am convinced that this bold approach will cost American families far less
than the alternative—a continuing series of financial institution failures

[7] It also prompted concern, particularly on the left, of a democratic deficit; see W.
Greider, "Economic Free Fall," *The Nation*, 18 August 2008, 18 (arguing that
Washington's selective generosity for influential financial losers is deforming democracy
and opening the path to an awesomely powerful corporate state: at 20).
[8] See J. Toobin, "Barney's Great Adventure," *The New Yorker*, 12 January 2009, 37
(reporting an emergency meeting called by the Treasury Secretary with senior
congressional Democrats to secure support for the bailout legislation. The House
Speaker, Nancy Pelosi, is quoted as saying that the meeting—held on Thursday 18
September just after the collapse of Lehman Brothers and the emergency rescue of AIG
—was necessary because Paulson claimed "if we don't act now we may not have an
economy on Monday night": at 44).
[9] For compelling overview of the decisions taken by the Federal Reserve, see J. Cassidy,
"Anatomy of a Meltdown," *New Yorker*, 1 December 2008, 49; for an examination of the
role played by the Treasury, see Government Accountability Office, "Troubled Asset
Relief Program" (GAO-09-61, Washington DC, December 2008); Congressional
Oversight Panel for Economic Stabilization, "Questions About the $700 Billion
Emergency Economic Stabilization Funds" (Washington DC, 10 December 2008).

and frozen credit markets unable to fund everyday needs and economic expansion."[10]

The initial plan contained a range of flaws, most notable of which was a total lack of accountability. The draft contained a provision that precluded judicial review. Not surprisingly, opposition encompassed the entire political spectrum. These opposing opinions were nicely put in the op-ed page of the *New York Times*. The influential Democrat-leaning economist Paul Krugman, recipient of the 2008 Nobel Prize for Economics, fretted that Treasury was provided with far too much discretion and that, in any event, the plan was unlikely to provide necessary solvency unless the taxpayer overpaid.[11] A leading conservative writer, William Kristol, condemned the proposal as "the panicked product of a discredited administration, an irresponsible Congress and a feckless financial establishment, all of which got us into this fine mess."[12] While there is truth in both assertions, there was enormous pressure for immediate action from the political establishment, the market and increasingly fearful governments across the world. The latter contrasted dramatically with domestic revulsion. Constituents bombarded talk radio as well as congressional switchboards with angry denunciations of what was seen as policy devoid of principle. Over the course of the deliberations on Capitol Hill, the mood alternated between hope and despair as the calculation of political risk constantly shifted. When the negotiations were completed, in time for the opening of Asian markets, the mood in Washington remained bleak. Democrats argued that greater accountability was secured. President Bush, cognizant of continued Republican antipathy, warned again that failure to ratify the legislation could spell disaster.

Once given authority, the Treasury Secretary embarked on a series of contradictory strategies which were never adequately explained. As a consequence, public confidence in the integrity of the TARP program and the accountability of the Treasury Department was compromised, a fact accepted by the incoming Treasury Secretary in his confirmation hearing, which was marred by revelations that he had failed

---

[10] Evidence to Senate Committee on Banking, Housing, and Urban Affairs, Washington DC, 23 September 2008 (B. Bernanke and H. Paulson).
[11] P. Krugman, "Cash for Trash," *New York Times*, 22 September 2008, A29.
[12] W. Kristol, "A Fine Mess," *New York Times*, 22 September 2008, A29.

to pay taxes.[13] Acknowledging past failure and designing credible programs that have the capacity to engineer meaningful change in corporate and regulatory governance are, however, very different things. The evidence to date is that confusion and incoherence still inform regulatory responses in the United States and elsewhere.

II   BRINGING THE STATE BACK IN

Examining the provisions of a bill that transmogrified from a three-and-a-half-page imperial command into a 451-page Act is exceptionally revealing of regulatory dynamics in the United States. First, earmarks, distinctly American legislative adornments that incorporate stunningly unrelated measures, were required to secure passage.[14] These included the

---

[13] Geithner was confirmed in post despite admitting an error in failing to pay $34,000 in taxes accrued while working at the IMF. Two of Obama's other senior nominees (Health Secretary, Tom Daschle, and Chief Performance Officer, Nancy Killefer) withdrew their nominations over failure to pay back taxes. As with Geithner, Daschle paid a benefit-in-kind debt of $142,000 after his nomination. Killefer's transgressions, although minor—$946 lien for underpaying household help tax, which was paid in 2005 (the year in which it accrued)—was deeply embarrassing to the administration. As an Assistant Secretary of Treasury in the Clinton administration, Killefer was involved in modernizing the Internal Revenue Service and was later appointed to the IRS Oversight Board. The withdrawals followed that of first pick for Commerce secretary, Bill Richardson. The former Arizona governor is under investigation for payments made by a contributor who subsequently received a major state contract. The lapses—along with the appointments of lobbyists which required waivers from newly announced guidelines—temper the euphoria associated with the rhetoric of a new culture of responsibility; see P. Baker, "Obama's Ethics Reform Pledge Faces an Early Test," *New York Times*, 3 February 2009, A1 (reporting "the Obama team finds itself being criticized by bloggers on the left and the right, mocked by television comics and questioned by reporters about whether Mr. Obama is really changing the way Washington works or just changing which political party works it.")

[14] If not corruption, earmarking is certainly corrupting of public life. Opposition to the practice has played a pivotal role in Senator John McCain's presidential campaign. Before the Senate vote, the Republican candidate stated categorically, that "it is completely unacceptable for any kind of earmarks to be included in this bill. It would be outrageous for legislators and lobbyists to pack this rescue plan with taxpayer money for favored companies. This simply cannot happen." In the event, Senator McCain and Senator Obama both voted in favor of the legislation; neither queried the earmarks involved. A spokesperson for the McCain campaign said a national emergency overcame principle; see M. Shear, "With Bailout Vote, McCain Voted For Earmarks," *Washington Post*, 3 October 2008 (Online Edition); P. Abrams, "Loopholes v Earmarks," *Huffington Post* (Washington), 6 October 2008 (Online Edition).

provision of $192 billion in rebates to rum producers in Puerto Rico[15] and the US Virgin Islands and tax incentives of $478 million to film and television producers to use domestic locations in upcoming productions.[16] Second, as with the first incarnation, the legislation's purpose is "to immediately provide authority and facilities that the Secretary of the Treasury can use to restore liquidity and stability to the financial system of the United States." This is to be achieved by a series of potentially conflicting imperatives. As the lead agency, Treasury is asked to ensure that such authority and such facilities are used in a manner that—(a) protects home values, college funds, retirement accounts, and life savings; (b) preserves homeownership and promotes jobs and economic growth; (c) maximizes overall returns to the taxpayers of the United States; and (d) provides public accountability for the exercise of such authority.[17]

The Treasury Secretary is mandated to provide guidelines outlining the criteria and mechanisms for purchasing and pricing assets and procedures for hiring asset managers within two days of the first purchase (or forty-five days after enactment).[18] In addition, a Financial Stability Oversight Board is to be established. The board is to meet monthly and report to Congress every six months. It is made up of the chairman of the Federal Reserve, the Director of the Federal Home Finance Agency, the Chair of the SEC and the Secretary of Housing along with the Secretary of the Treasury, who is precluded from serving as chair.[19] The reporting mechanism specifically calls for congressional notification within seven days of expenditure reaching $50 billion trigger intervals. This reporting requires "a description of all of the transactions made during the reporting period; (b) a description of the pricing mechanism for the transactions; (c) a justification of the price paid for and other financial terms associated with the transactions; (d) a description of the impact of the exercise of such authority on the financial system, supported, to the extent possible, by specific data; (e) a description of challenges that remain in the financial system, including any bench marks yet to be achieved; and (f) an estimate of additional actions under the

---

[15] *Emergency Economic Stabilization Act* (2008), Section 502.
[16] Section 308.
[17] Section 2.
[18] Section 101 (d).
[19] Section 104 (b-e).

authority provided under this Act that may be necessary to address such challenges."[20]

The plan bore an uncanny resemblance to proposals first mooted the previous northern autumn when major banks, including Citigroup, began posting colossal losses. Those plans, which were ultimately rejected by the market, involved establishing what was termed a Master Liquidity Enhancement Conduit. As with the current plan, its aim was to allow the banks most exposed to progressively unwind their positions. This strategy, designed by the contributing banks but endorsed by the Treasury, failed because market participants deemed it impossible to ascertain true value. This problem, it will be recalled, was central to the BNP Paribas calculation to suspend withdrawals from its hedge funds the previous August. Despite the passage of time, there is no indication that policymakers at the Treasury are going to be any more effective in divining actual prices. Moreover, a close reading of the legislation suggests that claims of fettered discretion are somewhat overblown.

The Secretary is mandated to make "such purchases at the lowest price that the Secretary determines to be consistent with the purposes of this Act through mechanisms such as reverse auctions."[21] When making direct purchases, the Secretary is given discretion subject only to undefined "additional measures to ensure that prices paid for assets are reasonable and reflect the underlying value of the asset."[22] This creates, in turn, two further inter-linked policy dilemmas. First, forcing the banks to sell the assets at market prices could have the effect of worsening the solvency problem. Second, it potentially legitimizes retrospectively the abdication of responsibility that saw investment bankers create conduits to introduce and disseminate toxicity with careless disdain for the consequences. Furthermore, the Treasury Secretary has the right to request non-voting or preferred stock warrants but not an obligation to demand them if the cumulative total of investment is less than $100 billion.[23] Indeed the evidence to date is that it has overpaid already.[24]

---

[20] Section 105 (b) (1).

[21] Section 113 (b).

[22] Section 113 (b).

[23] Section 113 (d).

[24] The chair of the Congressional Oversight Panel, Elizabeth Warren, told a Senate Banking Committee that the price differential was significant, see M. Crittenden and D. Solomon, "Watchdog Says US Overpaid For Troubled Assets", *Wall Street Journal*, 6 February 2009, C3 (reporting Warren's assertion that Treasury paid $254 billion for preference shares and warrants that had a market value of $176 million).

The criteria for corporate governance and executive compensation are equally nebulous. Corporations taking advantage of the scheme to offload toxic products are required to meet "appropriate standards".[25] These include:

> (A) limits on compensation that exclude incentives for executive officers of a financial institution to take unnecessary and excessive risks that threaten the value of the financial institution during the period that the Secretary holds an equity or debt position in the financial institution;
> (B) a provision for the recovery by the financial institution of any bonus or incentive compensation paid to a senior executive officer based on statements of earnings, gains, or other criteria that are later proven to be materially inaccurate; and
> (C) a prohibition on the financial institution making any golden parachute payment to its senior executive officer during the period that the Secretary holds an equity or debt position in the financial institution.[26]

It is far from clear that the Treasury has used its power to ensure that the banks will change practice. Indeed its lack of consistency has enhanced the power of the banks to thwart further intervention. On 13 October, the Treasury announced that $250 billion would be invested in preferred stock. On November 12, the Treasury Secretary noted that the $700 billion fund would not, in fact, be used to purchase asset-backed securities directly. Yet less than two weeks later the Treasury, along with the Federal Reserve, approved a rescue package for Citigroup, which had the effect of providing backing for $306 billion in loans and securities. Under the terms of the agreement, Citigroup is liable for only the first $29 billion in losses. After that, the government will assume 90% of future liabilities. No time-limitation has been imposed. The following day, the Treasury changed tack again. It offered financing to private investors willing to purchase (allegedly) highly rated asset-backed securities, while continuing to invest directly into the banks through the Capital Purchase Program. Those most exposed to asset-backed securities blamed the policy reversal on direct purchases of continued losses, most notably Morgan Stanley, which complained that "markets

---

[25] Section 111 (b) (1).
[26] Section 111 (b) (2). It is hard to see, in the absence of direct involvement in the development and execution of a risk management system, how the Treasury could second-guess management on what constitutes "unnecessary and excessive risk."

had a savage reaction the likes of which we have never seen before".[27] At time of writing, the Treasury Department is reconsidering its decision not to establish a "toxic bank," in part because of the decision by the United Kingdom to contemplate this approach in a desperate attempt to force lenders to reopen lines of credit.

The Capital Purchase Program has now invested $115 billion in senior preferred shares of eight of the largest financial institutions and a further $139 million in smaller banks. The Government Accountability Office noted, however, that the Treasury had not instituted robust oversight and monitoring functions. As a result, it argued, "Treasury's ability to help ensure an appropriate level of accountability and transparency will be limited."[28] A further damning report was released by the Congressional Oversight Panel, which was established to provide a further layer of accountability.[29] The Panel—chaired by Elizabeth Warren, a professor at Harvard Law School—demanded that the Treasury "articulate its vision of the problem, its overall strategy to address that problem, and how its strategic shifts since September 2008 fit into that strategy."[30] In other words, the Panel saw no vision, no strategy and no coherence.

According to the Panel, "Congress provided substantial flexibility in the use of funds so Treasury could react to the fluid and changing nature of the financial markets. With these powers goes a responsibility to explain the reason for the uses made of them. With these monies goes a responsibility to ensure that the support to the economy from each dollar spent is maximized consistent with the purposes of the Act."[31] The Panel found, however, that the Treasury has not conducted a detailed audit of the impact of the $254 billion already disbursed through the Capital Purchase Program nor had it been "seeking to monitor the use

---

[27] Guerrera, above n 1.

[28] GAO, above n 9, 7.

[29] Section 125.

[30] Congressional Oversight Panel, above n 9, 13. For insight into the views of the chairman, see E. Warren and A. Warren Tyagi, "Protect Financial Consumers," *Harpers*, November 2008, 39 (arguing for the need for a Consumer Product Safety Commission). After early success in setting the agenda, the work of the Panel has begun to come under intense scrutiny, particularly over the age and lack of experience of staffers and what was been termed Warren's reputation as "a sharp-elbowed ideological infighter," see S. Schmidt, "Policing TARP Proves Tricky," *Wall Street Journal*, 20 February 2009 (Online Edition).

[31] Congressional Oversight Panel, above n 9, 13.

of funds provided to specific financial institutions." As with the GAO, the Panel found the Treasury's reliance on general economic indicators unacceptable. For the Panel, "using general metrics could be a substitute for using no metrics at all, thus committing taxpayer resources with no meaningful oversight."[32]

A major part of the perceived legitimacy problem is that little action has been taken on the rise of foreclosures. The provisions on foreclosure reduction are, at best, optimistic. The Treasury is mandated "to implement a plan that *seeks to maximize* assistance for homeowners and use the authority of the Secretary *to encourage* the servicers of the underlying mortgages...to minimize foreclosures. In addition, the Secretary *may* use loan guarantees and credit enhancements to facilitate loan modifications to prevent avoidable foreclosures (*emphasis added*)."[33] Evidence to the Senate Banking Committee in the closing days of the Bush presidency opened fissures between Treasury and the Federal Deposit Insurance Corporation on how to proceed. The Treasury representative wanted to give the banks latitude. He maintained it was not in society's interest to micro-manage these institutions.[34]

The chair of the FDIC, Sheila Blair, was much more forthright. "We need to act quickly and we need to act dramatically."[35] This, she claimed, may involve economic incentives for the banks to modify loans to reduce foreclosure rates, which had risen by over 70 per cent since the crisis began. The Treasury representative would not commit itself to this course of action, although with unemployment levels forecast to rise to over 7%, it may have to revisit this reticence.[36] The Congressional Oversight Panel is exceptionally critical of Treasury's actions to date, most notably its failure to make funding conditional on foreclosure relief for existing borrowers and apparent opposition to proposals put forward

---

[32] Ibid, at 20; see also GAO, above n 9, 10, 25. For initial Treasury response, see GAO above n 9, 64–65.
[33] Section 109 (a).
[34] See J. Politi, "Senators Question Bank Oversight Plan", *Financial Times*, 24 October 2008, 6 (reporting derision with this caution from Senator Charles Schumer of New York, who charged that the Treasury was "leaning to far in giving them desert and not enough in making them eat their vegetables").
[35] Ibid.
[36] J. Politti, "US Grapples With Shift of Mood in Jobs Markets," *Financial Times*, 24 October 2008, 6.

by the FDIC. It asks "the Department to explain how its broad authority reflects the purposes of the Act."[37]

Similar problems have now become apparent in the ongoing regulatory arbitrage between the United States and other key jurisdictions. The legislation allows the Treasury to buy securities from foreign owned banks and explicitly calls for coordination to work toward the establishment of similar programs.[38] What is also clear, however, is that regulatory arbitrage remains a significant risk. Following the British decision to inject capital directly into its banks, the US Treasury Secretary partially followed suit. Hank Paulson summoned representatives of nine of the most important banks to a meeting in Washington and demanded that each accept government funding.[39] The funding, however, was offered at substantially less punitive rates than those imposed by the British government.

The Congressional Oversight Panel noted that while "the Act provides the Treasury with broad authority to set the conditions under which companies may receive aid...the public has a right to know to what extent conditions have been imposed on financial institutions receiving public funds, and if not, why not."[40] The Panel concluded by arguing that the policies lack strategic direction and impose nowhere near the normative changes demanded by the London government. "It is critical for Congress and the public, including participants in the banking industry, to understand exactly what the criteria are for receiving money under the TARP programs, what the strategic intentions of the criteria are, if any, what the strategic effects of the criteria are, and how the criteria advance the purposes of the Act."[41] The failure to engage in more invasive monitoring represented the continued power of the banking lobby in the United States. It also foregrounds the risk that international coordination will be much more difficult to achieve than previously understood.

The report, along with the publication of the GAO findings, prompted extremely hostile questioning to the Treasury Under Secretary,

---

[37] Congressional Oversight Panel, above n 9, 18, 19.

[38] Section 112.

[39] For detailed accounts, see D. Paletta, J. Hilsenrath, and D. Solomon, "At Moment of Truth, US Forced Big Bankers to Blink," *Wall Street Journal*, 15 October 2008 (Online Edition); M. Landler and E. Dash, "Drama Behind a $250 Billion Banking Deal," *New York Times*, 15 October 2008 (Online Edition).

[40] Congressional Oversight Panel, above n 9, 27, 28.

[41] Ibid, at 30.

Neel Kashkari, from members of the House Financial Services Committee, including its chairman, Barney Frank, who condemned the "blatant refusal [by the Treasury] to enforce any lending obligations on individual institutions, the continued policy of ignoring the clear intent of the EESA to aid in the reduction of foreclosures put the Treasury perilously close to a breach [of] faith with those who responded to the bush Administration's request to establish the program."[42] In a somewhat grudging profile, Barney Frank is quoted as saying that "we are at a moment now when liberalism is poised to have its biggest impact on America since Roosevelt....You know Hegel. Thesis: No regulation at all. Antithesis. Now the Government owns the banks. What I gotta do next year [2009] is the synthesis. Unfortunately, how to achieve this remains undetermined."[43]

The problems intensified with the publication of the Congressional Oversight Panel's second report in January 2009. The Panel found that a lack of consistency and coherence still animated Treasury decision-making process, a situation that was exacerbated because of the failure to provide a detailed analysis of the causes of the crisis. "For the Panel, it was important for the Treasury and our financial services regulators to have an analysis of the causes and nature of the financial crisis to be able to craft a strategy for addressing the sources, and not solely the symptoms, of the problem or problems."[44] Foremost among them is the issue of executive pay.

The new Obama administration has promised significant action to strengthen oversight and reduce contestation over the payment of bonuses to executives in banks that avail of the bailout. On 4 February 2009, President Obama announced that pay would be capped at $500,000 for the most senior executives in any corporation that received exceptional assistance in the future, with share incentives paid only after the government has been repaid in full. He described the payment of bonuses totaling $18.4 billion in 2007 (itself a reduction of 44% on the 2007 round) as a "shameful" practice. The changes were not, however, be retrospectively applied. Senior Democrats have called for and managed to legislate further action. The chairman of the Senate Banking

---

[42] B. Frank, "Statement on GAO TARP Report" (Press Release, Washington DC, 3 December 2008).

[43] Toobin, above n 8, 47.

[44] Congressional Oversight Panel, "Accountability for the Troubled Asset Relief Program" (Second Report, Washington DC, 9 January 2009) 9.

Committee, Christopher Dodd, tabled an amendment to the TARP program through the *American Recovery and Reinvestment Act* (2009) that mandates the Treasury Secretary "to review bonus awards paid to executives of TARP recipients to determine whether any payments were excessive, inconsistent with the purposes of the Act or the TARP, or otherwise contrary to public interest and, if so, to seek to negotiate with the recipient and the subject employee for appropriate reimbursement to the Government."[45] It underscores the extent of popular revulsion with bailing out Wall Street and demonstrates just why the planned redesign of the TARP program, announced by the Treasury Secretary the previous week proved so disappointing to markets and politicians on the left alike.

On 10 February Timothy Geithner, unveiled what he termed rather grandiosely, a new Financial Stability Plan. This was necessary, he argued, because of the failure of piecemeal attempts to reform the financial system.

> There were systematic failures in the checks and balances in the system, by Boards of Directors, by credit rating agencies, and by government regulators. Our financial system operated with large gaps in meaningful oversight, and without sufficient constraints to limit risk. Even institutions that were overseen by our complicated, overlapping system of multiple regulators put themselves in a position of extreme vulnerability. These failures helped lay the foundation for the worst economic crisis in generations. When the crisis began, governments around the world were too slow to act. When action came, it was late and inadequate. Policy was always behind the curve, always chasing the escalating crisis. As the crisis intensified and more dramatic government action was required, the emergency actions meant to provide confidence and reassurance too often added to public anxiety and to investor uncertainty.[46]

Geithner argued that it was necessary for comprehensive, forceful, and sustained intervention to prevent an intensification of the financial crisis. He made clear that "access to public support is a privilege not a right" and that "government support must come with strong conditions to protect the taxpayer and with transparency that allows the American people to see the impact of those investments." The Secretary further

---

[45] "Dodd Commends Administration's Announcement on Executive Pay" (Press Release, Senate Committee on Banking, Housing and Urban Affairs, Washington DC, 4 February 2009).
[46] T. Geithner, "Remarks Introducing the Financial Stability Plan" (Speech delivered at US Department of the Treasury, Washington DC, 10 February 2009).

argued that moving forward, "polices must be designed to mobilize and leverage private capital, not to supplant or discourage private capital." The plan has four major components. First, a comprehensive stress test is to be conducted to evaluate the health of specific banks and "initiate a more consistent, realistic, and forward looking assessment about the risk on balance sheets, and we're going to introduce new measures to improve disclosure." No further detail was provided as to how this intervention will ensure greater lending. Second, the Treasury is to set up a Public Private Investment Fund to target legacy loans and stalled securitization markets.

> By providing the financing the private markets cannot now provide, this will help start a market for the real estate related assets that are at the center of this crisis. Our objective is to use private capital and private asset managers to help provide a market mechanism for valuing the assets. We are exploring a range of different structures for this program, and will seek input from market participants and the public as we design it. We believe this program should ultimately provide up to one trillion in financing capacity, but we plan to start it on a scale of \$500 billion, and expand it based on what works.[47]

Here again, however, no detail was provided about how the mechanism would work, the proportion of public to private contribution or whether the investment would come from traditional investors or Sovereign Wealth Funds and, if the latter, whether this injection would require legislative change. Moreover, the policy framework suggests that the critical question is one of illiquidity borne of panic rather than a systemic solvency problem. As a consequence, the plan suggests that government intends prop up "zombie" banks and serves to undermine Obama administration's claim to inculcate change we can believe in.[48] Senior Senate Democrats, including Chris Dodd, influential chairman of the Senate Banking Committee, however, have indicated that nationalization may be necessary, suggesting fissures within the party. The third

---

[47] Ibid.

[48] See M. Wolf, "Why Obama's New Tarp Will Fail to Rescue the Banks," *Financial Times*, 11 February 2009, 13 (suggesting that by imposing "three arbitrary self-imposed constraints: no nationalization; no losses for bondholders; and no more money from Congress" the administration has acted with "timidity" and is taking a "huge gamble"). The editorial writers are even more forthright; see Editorial, "Son of Tarp Follows in Father's Footsteps," *Financial Times*, 11 February 2009, 12 ("Saving the financial system will take more money and a greater degree of public control than the government is yet willing to admit").

component of the plan was to commit up to $1 trillion to support what was termed a Consumer and Business Lending Initiative, designed to jumpstart the securitization markers for small business lending, consumer and auto finance, and commercial mortgages. Again no detail was provided nor was any provided on how the government plans to bring down mortgage payments and reduce mortgage interest rates. If nothing else, Secretary Geithner was frank:

> But I want to be candid: this strategy will cost money, involve risk, and take time. As costly as this effort may be, we know that the cost of a complete collapse of our financial system would be incalculable for families, for businesses and for our nation. We will have to adapt our program as conditions change. We will have to try things we've never tried before. We will make mistakes. We will go through periods in which things get worse and progress is uneven or interrupted.[49]

The market reaction was immediate. Stocks fell by 4% as the realization sank in that the Obama administration had failed to deliver on expectations. Moreover, the fourth component, the expansion of the TARP program to the automotive industry raises enormous exit problems for the government moving forward. Providing emergency funding helped stave off the risk of an unruly bankruptcy for Chrysler and General Motors. It also opened a range of questions about what should be the purpose and limits of government intervention. At the time of writing those problems have intensified, not just in the United States but also in Europe and Australia, where GM has embarked on a strategy of extensive retrenchments and 'corporate begging.'[50]

III   DRIVING A BARGAIN

Federal reach over industry expanded dramatically by the decision by President Bush to overrule Senate Republicans and disperse $13.4 billion in emergency funding to Detroit automakers. A further $4 billion was to be provided in February, subject to congressional approval. In return, the automakers were mandated to develop business plans, provide the

---

[49] Ibid.
[50] Editorial, "Beggars Make For Bad Policy," *Australian Financial Review*, 20 February 2009, 58. Despite cash injections by the Australian government into Holden, the GM subsidiary, its longer-term future is less than assured. In Europe, GM has already forced Saab to seek bankruptcy protection in Sweden following failure to persuade Stockholm to invest in the company.

government with warrants for non-voting stock and demonstrate to the incoming administration that they were viable institutions by the end of the first quarter of 2009. If these conditions were not complied with, the recipients would, in theory, be required to return the loans. The binding terms restrict executive compensation and eliminate the capability of the firms to provide dividends while in receipt of government loans. In addition, the carmakers are to dispose of corporate jets. The government is given the power to review books and records and, in addition, has the power to block any transaction over the value of $100 billion. Curiously, these far exceed the restrictions placed on the financial services firms that arguably caused the contraction of credit in the first place. The non-binding terms call on the manufacturers to reduce unsecured debt by two thirds (by transferring it into equity) and, more controversially, make wages and work rules competitive to foreign auto-manufacturers operating in the United States by the end of 2009. To a large extent the conditions are, as the *Wall Street Journal* reported, "much more porous" than those contained in legislation struck down by Senate Republicans earlier in December.[51] Most notably, that legislation contained a provision that, if enacted, would have banned any further provision of federal aid if Congress adjudicated that viability was not adequately demonstrated. The passage of time has intensified the crisis facing the new administration.

The then president George Bush justified the initial intervention on the grounds that these were extraordinary times and the rescue package was limited in scope. The sums made available were substantially less than the $34 billion initially requested by the Detroit chairmen when they ill-advisedly traveled to Washington on corporate jets to demand emergency funding. Furthermore he emphasized that the expenditure was approved only because of the failure of the legislative branch to act. It represented a rebuke to Senate Republicans and an attempt to ensure that his already tarnished presidency was not completely de-legitimized by comparisons to Herbert Hoover, a Republican predecessor who had famously decried all government intervention in the aftermath of the Great Crash. President Bush also

---

[51] J. McKinnon and J. Stoll, "US Throws Lifeline to Detroit," *Wall Street Journal*, 20 December 2008, A1. There have been persistent suggestions that Republican senators from the southern states where many of the foreign-owned car manufacturers are based struck down the measure on state rather than national interest; see A. Ward, "Republicans Face Battle for Party's Ideological Soul," *Financial Times*, 18 December 2008, 4.

emphasized the limited purpose of the rescue package. It was approved only because of the failure of the carmakers to make the legal and financial preparations necessary to carry out an orderly bankruptcy that could lead to a successful restructuring.

> This is a difficult situation that involves fundamental questions about the proper role of government....If we were to allow the free market to take its course now, it would almost certainly lead to disorderly bankruptcy and liquidation for the automakers. Under ordinary economic circumstances, I would say this is the price that failed companies must pay - and I would not favor intervening to prevent the automakers from going out of business. But these are not ordinary circumstances. In the midst of a financial crisis and a recession, allowing the U.S. auto industry to collapse is not a responsible course of action.[52]

The bumpy interaction between Wall Street and Main Street was evidenced in a sidebar arrangement between the US Treasury and GMAC, an auto-financing firm co-owned by General Motors and the private equity consortium headed by Cerberus Capital Management, which controls Chrysler. As with the investment banks, GMAC sought to stabilize by transforming itself into a bank holding company. This was to be achieved by raising $30 billion from bondholders. Despite missing two deadlines to raise the required capital, the Treasury provided emergency funding of $5 billion, a decision that allowed the Federal Reserve to claim that GMAC had sufficient capital to be transformed into a bank holding company. The decision, announced on Christmas Eve, was justified on what the Federal Reserve termed "the successful efforts of management of GMAC to raise capital; the experience of senior management of GMAC in other organizations that are regulated as bank holding companies; ...and the public benefits that would accrue from approval of this proposal."[53] Furthermore, the Federal Reserve waived public notice claiming that "in light of the unusual and exigent circumstances affecting the financial markets, and all other facts and

---

[52] "President Bush Discusses Administration's Plans to Assist Automakers" (Press Conference, Washington DC, 19 December 2008). No mention was made of the fact that Cerberus, which bought Chrysler from Daimler at the height of the boom, had failed to inject further capital. As such the intervention marked the first time that that the TARP had been used for this alternative asset class as well as non-financial purposes.

[53] "Order Approving Formation of Bank Holding Companies and Notice to Engage in Certain Non-Banking Activities" (Press Release, Federal Reserve, Washington DC, 24 December 2008) 5.

circumstances, the Board has determined that emergency conditions exist that justify expeditious action on this proposal."[54]

The only condition imposed on GM and Cerberus was to reduce their holdings. GM was to reduce its equity stake to less than 10% of the voting and total equity interest, which is to be transferred to a trust that has a trustee acceptable to the Board and the Department of the Treasury, who will be entirely independent of GM and have "sole discretion to vote and dispose of the GMAC equity interests."[55] In addition GM is to remove any restrictions on GMAC's ability to engage in transactions with unrelated third parties and to ensure that GMAC has complete discretion to set the terms of its financing arrangements. Cerberus is mandated to distribute its equity interests in the company to its respective investors, ensuring that "the aggregate direct and indirect investments controlled by Cerberus and its related parties would not exceed 14.9% of the voting shares or 33% of the total equity of GMAC LLC."[56] This distribution, that limits individual holding that are less than 5% of the voting rights or 7.5% of the total equity, was justified on the basis that "the investors that receive shares in the distribution from the Cerberus funds are each sophisticated investors and are independent of Cerberus and independent of each other."[57] The Federal Reserve argues "Cerberus has made a number of commitments previously found by the Board to be helpful in limiting the ability of an investor to exercise a controlling interest over a banking organization."[58] Unfortunately, the press release does not disclose what these are.

When the Detroit leaders returned to Congress, in late February, they demanded an extra $24 billion in emergency funding. The White House did not make any formal commitments but hinted that the companies would not be allowed to fail. As the press secretary, Robert Gibbs, put it, "it is clear going forward, more will be required from everyone involved-creditors, suppliers, dealers, labor and auto executives themselves-to ensure the viability of these companies going forward."[59] Republicans, however, noted that Cerberus as a private equity company with access to its own capital, should be forced to inject more first. The

---

[54] Ibid, 2–3.
[55] Ibid, 6.
[56] Ibid.
[57] Ibid.
[58] Ibid, 7.
[59] White House Press Release (Washington DC, 17 February 2009).

administration is currently reviewing the revised plans put forward by the auto manufacturers. In a statement, the US Department of Treasury outlined both the scale of the problem and the scale of ambition.

They argued that it was essential to "address financial and operational restructuring, improving competitiveness of wage and benefit structures and progress towards creating clean competitive car of the future."[60] The press release referred to the need for a fundamental restructuring of the car industry, a goal that appeared to be progressed by the historic decision to let Chrysler file for bankruptcy protection on 30 April. A deal brokered by the government envisages that Chrysler will enter a partnership with Fiat, the European auto-manufacturer known for its fuel-efficient small car range. Of equal significance is a consortium of banks receiving bailout funds from the federal government agreed to substantially reduced payments. Other financiers argued that the payments, of less that 30 cents in the dollar did not reflect fair value in a liquidation. Moreover, the argued that the deal, which envisages unions receiving more that 50% control of the company if it emerges from bankruptcy upending settled bankruptcy protection laws. These concerns were dismissed by the Administration as the baseless claims of speculators.

Despite the severity of the problems facing both the auto industry and the wider credit markets, it is also clear that a unique window of opportunity has opened to reconfigure the debate about what should constitute the boundaries of corporate governance. This requires, in turn, a restructuring of financial regulation.

IV   A NEW PARADIGM FOR FINANCIAL REGULATION

The very fact that the global financial crisis metastasized so quickly across regulatory systems is exceptionally revealing. To be sure, financial regulation can appear to be an unrewarding exercise of Sisyphean proportions. The strength of the Sisyphus myth rests on the fact that for a short period of time, order is restored.[61] Reform is either

---

[60] "Geithner, Summers Convene Offical Designees to Presidential Taskforce on the Auto Industry" (Press Release, Department of Treasury, Washington DC, 20 February 2009).

[61] Sisyphus is one of the great figures in Greek mythology, often associated with deception and hubris. A renowned trader and negotiator, he deceived the Queen of the Dead, Persephone, and escaped the Underworld. As a consequence, he was sentenced to an eternity of interminable labor for thinking that he could defy the Gods. This involved pushing a boulder to the top of a hill only for it to slip down, whereupon he was destined to repeat the process. The cruelty of the punishment was frustration.

introduced or repealed. It is the ephemeral nature of this order that constitutes the absurdity of the task: scandal leads to reform; gradual dissipation of public unease weakens the traction necessary to retain regulatory authority; the exercise of excessive discretion helps to transform the discourse; how to resolve the underlying problem is displaced by (real) concern about regulatory overreach; judicial criticism provides validation (of abuse); and depending on the stage of the electoral cycle, political pressure to weaken the restrictions comes to the fore. Despite two decades of corporate governance reform instituted, in the main, in the aftermath of scandal, we are no closer to finding moderating mechanisms. Instead, the deleterious effects of a dysfunctional system that allows for private profits and socialized risk have emerged into clear view.

The critical issue facing regulatory authorities across the world is how to deal with a model of capitalism based on technical compliance with narrowly defined legislation and a working assumption that unless a particular action is explicitly proscribed, it is deemed politically and socially acceptable. The absence of an ethical or cultural framework, rooted in personal experience and responsibility, lies at the heart of the current crisis of confidence. The unrelenting focus on the punishment of individual malefactors serves to obscure a much more fundamental problem. Corporate malfeasance and misfeasance on the scale witnessed cannot be readily explained by individual turpitude. Moreover, a retreat to rules will not necessarily guarantee better ethical practice or inculcate higher standards of probity. Indeed the passage of rules may itself constitute a serious problem. It creates the illusion of change. The spectacle resonates with the public through the parading in handcuffs of once deified executives but leave intact the structural defects. In this context, it was particularly striking in the United States that the policy debate in the aftermath of Sarbanes-Oxley centered on the need to repeal invasive oversight rather than reflecting on whether the reforms dealt with the structural and ethical defects exposed by the financial reporting scandals. Investors were encouraged to return to the marketplace on the basis of a Pauline conversion towards higher standards of integrity for which there was little or no empirical evidence.

The parameters of the global debate and its limitations have begun to emerge. In announcing his nominations for the chairmanship of the SEC (Mary Shapiro) and the Chicago-based Commodity Futures Trading Commission (Gary Gensler), Barack Obama commented that financial regulatory reform "will be one of the top legislative priorities of my Administration." He noted that the approach needed to be informed by "common-sense rules of the road that will protect investors, consumers, and our entire economy from fraud and manipulation by an irresponsible few. These rules will reward the industriousness and entrepreneurial spirit that's always been the engine of our prosperity, and crack down on the culture of greed and scheming that has led us to this day of reckoning. Instead of allowing interests to put their thumbs on the economic scales and CEOs run off with excessive golden parachutes, we'll ensure openness, accountability, and transparency in our markets so that people can trust the value of the financial product they're buying."[62]

The critical question is not whether the appointees have the experience to undertake the task, but rather whether they have a track record in aggressive enforcement, the necessary degree of independence and the willingness to accept that previously held positions were instrumental in exacerbating the crisis. Both nominees have significant track records and are firm supporters of self-regulation and the use of principles rather than invasive and prescriptive rules. Such an approach is clearly deficient in dealing with the global financial crisis in either the domestic US or the international dimension. Prior to her nomination, Shapiro was the head of the Financial Industry Regulatory Authority, which combines the enforcement arm of the National Association of Securities Dealers and the regulatory component of the New York Stock Exchange. It is the peak body responsible for monitoring self-policing. In confirmation hearings in January 2009, Shapiro quoted with approval the remarks made by the foundation chair, Joseph Kennedy, in 1934 that "the Commission will make war without quarter on any who sell securities by fraud or misrepresentation" and promised that she would "move aggressively to reinvigorate enforcement."[63] As the chair of the Senate confirmation panel put it, the Securities and Exchange Commission must address significant market and regulatory failures to oversee critical issues from "accounting to securitizations to credit default swaps to credit rating agencies and short-selling to the Madoff fraud." In such

---

[62] "President-elect Obama Names Key Regulatory Appointments" (Press Conference, Chicago, 18 December 2008).

[63] Prepared Statement by SEC Chairman Designate, Senate Banking, Housing and Urban Affairs, Washington DC, 15 January 2009 (M. Shapiro).

circumstances "it is absolutely critical that the Chairman and the Commissioners [of the SEC] make an extraordinary effort to pursue these issues fairly and independently—free from political considerations and from the industries which formerly employed them. That is always true—but particularly so today."[64]

The policy challenge ahead is to address incoherence in regulatory structures and purpose in both rules and enabling regimes. The US Treasury Secretary, Timothy Geithner, for example, has conceded that the regulatory system there "has evolved into a confusing mix of diffused accountability, regulatory competition, an enormously complex web of rules that create perverse incentives and leave huge opportunities for arbitrage and evasion, and creates the risk of large gaps in our knowledge and authority."[65] The lack of cohesion reinforces a reactive, piecemeal approach to functional regulation that is clearly unsustainable, particularly where innovation has left, by design or by default, large swathes of the financial services market either unregulated or under-regulated. The allegedly superior responsive principles-based regulatory regime in the United Kingdom proved equally defective in securing more than mechanistic (and ultimately valueless) compliance. Against this dismal reality, it is of debatable wisdom to strengthen mandatory rules or offer more specific guidance for enabling principles without addressing wider normative questions about the role of markets in contemporary society.

---

[64] Opening Statement, Hearing on Nominees for SEC, CEA, and Fed, Washington DC, 15 January 2009 (C. Dodd); see also, Editorial, "Starting the Regulatory Work," *New York Times*, 7 January 2009, A14 (noting that the nomination for the chair of the CFTC, Gary Gensler, a former Goldman Sachs banker who as Treasury Under Secretary in 2000 oversaw the legislation that exempted derivatives from regulation, was "troubling....It could be that the people whose actions contributed to the mess are best equipped to clean it up. That remains to be seen. But it would be tragic if Wall Street concludes from Mr. Obama's choices that it need not worry about the world changing in ways that would fundamentally alter its pursuit of profits.")

[65] T. Geithner, "The Current Financial Challenges: Policy and Regulatory Implications" (Speech delivered at Council on Foreign Relations, New York, 6 March 2008); H. Pitt, "Bringing Financial Services Regulation into the Twenty-First Century" (2008) 25 *Yale Journal on Regulation* 315; see also Evidence to House Committee on Financial Services, Washington DC, 21 October 2008 (S. Bartlett, President of Financial Services Roundtable). Bartlett complains, with cause, that federal and state financial regulators lack a common set of regulatory objectives. The new Treasury Secretary has promised a fundamental review; see Geithner, above n 46.

Sustainable progress cannot be achieved by focusing merely on what should be the optimum parameters of "smart regulation"—the reflexive and responsive counter-cyclical exercise of policy instruments and mechanisms, such as rules, principles, and norms to secure compliance with legal obligation and wider societal expectation.[66] To be effective, these instruments, principles, and mechanisms must be anchored within an overarching policy framework that articulates the rationale for regulatory intervention and delineates the duties and responsibilities required of corporate actors as well as their rights. Any attempt to instill values into the value proposition, however, will fail without first understanding and calibrating the drivers that animate current public and corporate behavior.[67]

Of equal importance is the need to design and implement systems of oversight that take into account the rising power of emerging markets, particularly China. As the global financial crisis has intensified Beijing has become increasingly vocal in its demands for fundamental reform. Managing China has become a major geopolitical as well as economic problem for policymakers across the globe but in particular for the United States and Australia. In the former, the issue centers on control of systemically important financial institutions. For Canberra the problem lies in whether ownership of supply threatens the national interest. How these issues are to be resolved will help determine whether there is substance beneath the rhetoric of change.

---

[66] N. Cunningham and P. Grabosky, *Smart Regulation: Designing Environmental Policy* (1998); see also S. Cohen, *Understanding Environmental Policy* (2006) 32-41.

[67] This has long informed environmental regulation; see for example, L. Milbrath, *Environmentalists* (1984); Cohen above n 57 ("every environmental problem we face is grounded in our value system and our view of how the world works....To develop effective environmental policy that reduces pollution and leads to sustainable development, we need to examine and understand the current political reality and the influence wielded by those with vested economic interests": at 133). See also S. Cohen and W. Eimicke, *The Effective Public Manager* (2002) 179–83.

Chapter 5

The New Mercantilism

On October 13, 2008, the British Prime Minister, Gordon Brown, traveled to the Reuters headquarters at Canary Wharf, the new heart of the City of London. The choice of location was deeply symbolic. Over the past twenty years, the center of gravity within the City had migrated to the once troubled precinct. Designed and opened in the 1990s without an adequate infrastructure, its initial problems typified the limitations of free market planning. Now Brown argued that these deficiencies applied to the products designed and marketed within the skyscrapers that still look out over one of the most deprived areas of the capital. Transparency, integrity, responsibility, and sound banking practice needed, he claimed, to be integrated into an overarching system of oversight. Brown was telegraphing to a changed world that London could—and should—play a central role in delivering sustainable social and economic growth.

> The global financial system, let's be honest, is too clouded with opacity, conflicts of interest, irresponsible risk-taking, and when problems occur countries have tended to look inwards and deal with them in isolation when it is clear that the only way forward is to look outwards and join in international cooperation....We are open, not sheltered economies, that we have international, not national capital markets, that we have global, not local competition, and we need an international financial system that captures the full benefit of global markets and capital flows, minimises the risk of disruption and maximises opportunities for all, lifting up the most vulnerable in different parts of the world.[1]

---

[1] G. Brown, "The Global Economy" (Speech delivered at Reuters Building, London, 13 October 2008).

While the United Kingdom has been at the forefront of calls for a New World Order, the rotation of the European presidency has given its cross channel arch-rival an even greater opportunity to reclaim a global standing not seen since the heyday of nineteenth century imperialism. The French president lost little time in advancing a fundamental critique of the Anglo-American model of financial capitalism. He claimed it had inculcated the "hateful practices" that led to the current crisis. Five days after Brown's Reuter's speech, President Sarkozy traveled to Washington with the president of the European Commission. Both made clear to their United States counterpart that a "new global financial order" was required, supported with a much more expansive regulatory dimension. The European visitors advanced a potentially far-reaching reform program. Innovation should, they argued, be subject to stringent and integrated oversight and those responsible for the crisis prosecuted. For the French president, it was no longer possible or politically acceptable for global society to be vulnerable to the vagaries of the market. "We can only go forward with a sense of responsibility and that those who have made the mistakes bear the brunt of their errors and shoulder that burden of responsibility." To do otherwise would be "a betrayal of the sort of capitalism we believe in."[2]

Cognizant of dimming credibility, the United States agreed to a series of summits to "seek agreement on principles of reform needed to avoid a repetition [of the current crisis] and assure global prosperity." Following an initial gathering in Washington, subsequent events would be convened to "implement agreement on specific steps to be taken to meet those principles."[3] President Bush demanded, without conviction, that the inevitable regulatory or institutional changes must safeguard innovation. "It is essential," he argued, "that we preserve the foundations of democratic capitalism—a commitment to free trade, free enterprise and free trade."[4] By the time world leaders gathered in Washington for the first summit, however, reality dulled such enthusiasm. The presence of the BRIC countries—Brazil, Russia, India, and China—reflected a subtle but profound shift in economic power. At the same time, the absence of concrete proposals demonstrated that having a seat at the table did not translate into discernible advantage Thus, while the search

---

[2] "US to Host Global Finance Summit," *BBC News*, 19 October 2008.
[3] Statement of the United States, France, and the European Commission (Washington DC, 18 October 2008).
[4] *BBC News*, above n 2.

for a credible solution could not proceed without the liquidity provided by emerging economies, their leverage capability to transform that into changes in trade and foreign direct investment policy remained weak. In such a vacuum, it was not surprising that rhetorical flourishes abounded as protectionist measures were debated and progressively introduced in both Europe and crucially the United States. The rhetoric became even more pronounced at a meeting of the Asia Pacific Economic Cooperation (APEC) held in Peru in late November. The meeting was convened just as Citigroup, one of the most powerful banks in the world and a symbol of once dominant North American hegemony, faced imminent collapse. The Chinese premier, Hu Jintao, caught the mood when he explained to his Russian counterpart, Dmitiri Medvedev, that "the global political and economic architecture is undergoing the deepest and most complicated changes since the Cold War."[5] Not least of these changes is the role played by state capitalism.

Sovereign Wealth Funds provide the most promising, if controversial, form of funding for under-capitalized banks. These state-backed asset management pools have become pivotal actors. The rising power of the asset class sparked an acrimonious debate on whether the "New Mercantilism" threatens legitimate national interests, or, more alarmingly, the capacity to maintain social cohesion in recipient countries.[6] Thus, while greater transparency and accountability of Sovereign Wealth Fund investment activity may limit the extent of formal political control over investment decisions, it is unlikely to address the geopolitical realities of what the Vice Chancellor of the Delaware Court of Chancery has, somewhat controversially, termed the rise of societies that "sink even deeper beneath the normative floor that the West sets for the ethically and socially responsible conduct of corporate affairs."[7] The policy challenge is to ensure that the normative benefits of greater transparency and accountability extend beyond the Sovereign Wealth Fund sector and are integrated with concomitant improvements in the

---

[5] T. Walker, "APEC Talks 'Confronting,'" *Australian Financial Review*, 25 November 2008, 10 (reporting attempts to advance an Asia Pacific Community to rival the European Community by 2010).

[6] See R. Gilson and C. Milhaupt, "Sovereign Wealth Funds and Corporate Governance: A Minimalist Response to the New Mercantilism" http://ssrn.com/abstract=1095023 at 27 January 2009.

[7] L. Strine, "Towards Common Sense and Common Ground: Reflections on the Shared Interests of Managers and Labor in a More Rational System of Corporate Governance" (2007) 33 *Journal of Corporation Law* 1 at 17.

governance of inward investment processes. To do otherwise preordains conflict at a time in which western leverage is severely compromised.

Sovereign Wealth Funds invested $24.8 billion in the first two months of 2008, just under half the total amount dispersed in 2007. Since January 2007, of a total of $72.9 billion, $60.7 billion has been invested in the financial sector. Despite the concentration of media coverage on investments from China and the Gulf, it has been the city-state of Singapore that has been the most aggressive, with portfolio enhancements of $41.7 billion.[8] Contestation centers on the perceived transparency and accountability deficit associated with their governance, particularly those from China and Russia. It is far from clear, however, whether the risks identified—financial contagion, the exercise of soft power, the need to protect legitimate national interests and governance deficiencies—represent pressing dangers or thinly veiled protectionism. Moreover, the clumsy shoehorning of explicit political desiderata into economic policy within recipient countries cuts against the open investment policy that informs the stated aims of financial globalization.[9]

This, in turn, poses profound legitimacy and authority risks for international organizations, including the IMF and the OECD, which are attempting to broker a compromise between competing trade and political imperatives. Agreement has been reached on a set of "Generally Accepted Principles and Practices for Sovereign Wealth Funds"—the Santiago Principles.[10] The principles are comprehensive and while voluntary, provide a cohesive framework for evaluating institutional, credit regulatory, and reputational risk. Moreover, the explicit endorsement of shareholder ownership rights, including board representation, reflects a determination by the funds that activism may be necessary to protect the value of their financial investments. The

[8] J. Burton, "Wealth Funds Exploit Credit Squeeze," *Financial Times*, 24 March 2008, 18.

[9] OECD, *Sovereign Wealth Funds and Recipient Country Policies* (Paris, 4 April 2008).

[10] It is indicative of the sensitivities involved that the principles themselves were not published when announced in September 2008. See comments made by Hamad Al Suwaidi and David Murray, Co-Chair of International Working Group Drafting Group and Under-Secretary of the Abu Dhabi Department of Finance on release of Santiago Principles http://www.iwg-swf.org/tr.htm 2 September 2008 (According to Al Suwaidi: "There was a very frank exchange....A lot of the discussion focused on the need to preserve the economic and financial interests of the sovereign wealth funds so as not to put them at a disadvantage when compared to the other types of investors such as hedge funds, insurance companies, and other institutional investors.")

publication of the Santiago Principles has done much to reduce the accountability deficit within the Sovereign Wealth Fund sector. There remain, however, significant problems on how these can be implemented and enforced. Consequently, this chapter identifies the potential risks associated with the injection of liquidity from sources not governed by western market mores. Second, it evaluates the efficacy of current regulatory approaches, with particular reference to foreign investment review processes. Finally, it assesses the impact of the debate on capital flows and financial globalization more generally.

I   WHITE KNIGHTS OR ERRANT KNAVES?

The combination of a commercial failure to exercise restraint and defective external oversight within the global investment banking community has offered an extraordinary commercial opportunity and risk to state-sponsored investment funds. The extent of the risk is made apparent by major paper losses on investments in Citigroup, Morgan Stanley and Blackstone, the private equity firm which partially listed at the height of the boom. Paradoxically, their capacity to take such large positions is linked to a deficit in direct and ongoing accountability, which partially shields them from short-term pressures. It also exacerbates perceptions that the funds may be used to further political objectives.

It must be stressed at the outset that there is no empirical evidence for this fear. Indeed, as the global financial crisis intensified throughout 2008, the degree of opposition weakened considerably, suggesting that protectionism was a much stronger driver. It is, perhaps, indicative that Barney Frank, the Democratic Chairman of the US House of Representatives Financial Services Committee, plaintively admitted: "we need the money....[W]e'd be worse off without it".[11] A similar view pertains in Brussels. The European Commissioner for Internal Markets has wryly noted the "irony that the entities that were being demonized [by vested interests in Europe]...have in recent months been the saviors rather than the demons."[12]

Sovereign Wealth Funds have been in existence without contestation for a number of years. The source of seed capital can derive

---

[11] D. Enrich, R. Sidel, and S. Craig, "World Rides to Wall Street Rescue," *Wall Street Journal*, 16 January 2008, A1.
[12] C. McCreevy, "The Credit Crisis and its Aftermath" (Speech delivered at Society of Business Economists, London, 6 February 2008).

from one-off windfalls, such as the proceeds from privatization.[13] Recurring foreign exchange receipts from natural resource exploitation provides a second revenue stream.[14] A third derives from the investment of profits accruing from adroit trading.[15] They form an increasingly important component of overarching macro-economic strategies to take advantage of a spike in commodity prices.[16] In part, this can be traced to a determination in emerging economies to reduce vulnerability to sudden capital outflows or commodity price declines. Individual funds, if mandated to be invested overseas, can also lower domestic demand or inflationary pressures by diverting excess liquidity.[17] Unlike traditional stabilization funds, which tend to invest in easily convertible treasury bonds to ensure immediate access in the event of a sudden deterioration in critical export markets, the larger Sovereign Wealth Funds tend to adopt longer-term investment horizons. Moreover, there is an increasing propensity to diversify into a much broader range of equities and alternative asset classes, including, for example, private equity and real estate as well as the US film industry and British soccer.

It is impossible, however, to characterize Sovereign Wealth Funds as a homogenous group. Moreover, it can be argued that it is conceptually incoherent to devise an overarching regulatory approach to deal with such diverse pools of capital. Despite this, the increased visibility of the sector inevitably raised political objections which, if left untreated, could have been exceptionally damaging to capital flows at precisely the same time as the Doha trade talks had collapsed. Governmental asset holdings have now eclipsed hedge funds and private equity in funds under management. It is estimated that the total investment pool (without leverage) could reach as such as $12 trillion by

---

[13] The Australian Future Fund, established in 2006, received seed capital from the proceeds of the federal government's stake in Telstra, which was privatized the previous year.
[14] Examples here include the Norwegian Government Pension Fund – Global, and the Abu Dhabi Investment Authority.
[15] The two Singaporean Sovereign Wealth Funds—the Government of Singapore Investment Corporation and Temasek Holdings—are paradigmatic examples.
[16] Brazil, for example, has announced plans to set up its own Sovereign Wealth Fund, which will have an initial capitalization of $10 billion; see M. Moffett, "Brazil Joins Front Rank of New Economic Powers," *Wall Street Journal*, 13 May 2008, A1.
[17] Australia's new government, for example, has diverted part of an AUS $22 billion surplus arising (in part) from mineral exports into three separate infrastructure funds. It is unclear, however, whether these funds will be time-limited and what the likely effect will be, if any, of liquidation timed to synchronize with the political calendar.

2015. The European Commission has recognized that Sovereign Wealth Funds now form an essential transmission belt within the engine of financial globalization.[18] Informal polling at the 2008 World Economic Forum characterized Sovereign Wealth Funds as both global powers and global power brokers.[19] The visibility has ensured that, like private equity and hedge funds before it, the sector has attracted the attention of policymakers. Critically, this concern was evident even before the implosion of the securitization market demonstrated serious flaws in the overarching regulatory systems of control.

> The experience of large corporations in the industrialized world demonstrates that potential for error and abuse exists even in apparently highly rated and well-managed organizations. From a systemic perspective, transparency will facilitate the maintenance of openness to investment. What may have been tenable in a world where Sovereign Wealth Funds manage only several hundred billion dollars may not be tenable in a world where Sovereign Wealth Funds manage several trillion dollars.[20]

Policymakers in both London and Brussels remark candidly, if privately, that the core dilemma is how to engage a resurgent Beijing. The chair of the influential Treasury Select Committee, John McFall, argues that "there is a paranoia, particularly in Washington, about China."[21] One of the most senior European regulators remarked to this researcher that it was important to be brutally frank: "This is not about Singapore or Norway or even the Gulf Sovereign Wealth Funds; this is about how to deal with the power of China."[22] The rhetoric was much more

---

[18] Commission of the European Communities, *A Common European Approach to Sovereign Wealth Funds* (27 February 2008); see also OECD, above n 9, 2.

[19] M. Useem, "Lessons From Davos, One of Globalization's Best Classrooms," *Knowledge@Wharton*, 6 February 2008.

[20] C. Lowery, "Sovereign Wealth Funds and the International Financial System" (Speech delivered at Asian Financial Crisis Revisited Conference, Federal Reserve Bank of San Francisco, San Francisco, 21 June 2007).

[21] Interview, Glasgow, 7 April 2008. For discussion of anti-Chinese sentiment in Congress and its impact on policy, see S. Lubman, "The Dragon as Demon: Images of China on Capitol Hill" (2004) 13 *Journal of Contemporary China* 541.

[22] Interview, Brussels, 15 April 2008. This is not to downplay concern in Europe about a resurgent Russia; see R. Kagan, *The Return of History* (2008); E. Lucas, *The New Cold War* (2008); see also media coverage of the dispute over BP's Russian subsidiary; C. Levy and S. Kishkovsky, "Fight Over TNK-BP Revives Worries About Kremlin,"

pronounced in US discourse, in part because of electoral exigencies. Echoes could be found, however, across the Atlantic. Influential countries within the European Union—such as Germany and France—have always been deeply skeptical about the benefits of financial capitalism, irrespective of the source.[23] The more muscular foreign policy adopted by Russia serves to heighten skittishness. The suspicions that Russia is prepared to deploy its energy reserves strategically in order to advance political objectives, for example, are reinforced by the revolving door between Gazprom and the Kremlin.[24] The interlinked governance and investment principles proposed to alleviate the risk of political imperatives trumping economic ones in the context of an invigorated state capitalism will be explored more fully below. First, however, it is necessary to evaluate the precise nature of the problems allegedly posed by Sovereign Wealth Funds. The risks associated with Sovereign Wealth Funds can be usefully broken into three core areas: the risk of financial contagion; the exercise of soft political power; and national security considerations. Each will be briefly outlined and the cogency of the regulatory approaches suggested by the United States, Europe, and Australia will be evaluated.

II   PROTECTING THE NATIONAL INTEREST

The US Federal Reserve and the European Union, along with the OECD, emphasize the stabilizing role of Sovereign Wealth Funds in ameliorating

---

International Herald Tribune, 17 June 2008, 13; R. Pagnamenta, "Harassed TNK-BP Chief Quits Russia," *The Australian*, 26 July 2008, 39.

[23] The acrimonious debates on the alleged deleterious implications of private equity last year testify to the strength of this ideational tension; see J. O'Brien, 'Charting an Icarian Flightpath: The Implications of the Qantas Deal Collapse' in J. O'Brien (ed), *Private Equity, Corporate Governance and the Dynamics of Capital Market Regulation* (2007) 295; J. Cioffi, "Corporate Governance Reform, Regulatory Politics, and the Foundations of Finance Capitalism in the United States and Germany" (2006) 7 *German Law Review* 533.

[24] A Kramer, "As Gazprom's Chairman Moves Up, So Does Russia's Most Powerful Company," *International Herald Tribune*, 11 May 2008 (Online Edition); see more generally, A. Aslund, "Russia Energy and the European Union: Perspective on Gazprom" (Speech delivered at the European People's Party, European Parliament, Brussels, 15 May 2008). See also, however, A. Goldthau, "Resurgent Russia: Russian Energy Inc" (2008) http://ssrn.com/abstract=1137616.

the current crisis.[25] The size, scale, and degree to which investment strategies are disclosed differ dramatically, however. Variable opacity makes it difficult to gauge whether inappropriate or misguided investment expansion could potentially generate economic distortions. An apparent increase in risk tolerance, for example, may not be politically sustainable. Sharp commodity price fluctuation, large losses arising from misguided investment decisions or further deteriorations in equity markets could test the faith of new market entrants. The publication of exact measures used to set performance is central to the argument that sudden capital outflows must be managed to prevent, or at the least ameliorate, wider contagion.[26] There is no evidence, however, that this risk is anything more than hypothetical.

Investment bankers in London and New York speak positively of their experiences with executives from the major funds. One research director for a major investment bank suggested that the funds have become a magnet for rising stars within the asset management firmament.[27] Moreover, the larger funds emphasize the quality of external advice and internal controls. The leading Singaporean fund, Temasek Holdings, recently sent its executive director to a congressional hearing to impress upon US lawmakers how the fund is insulated from political influence. Temasek, noted Simon Israel, has an eight-member majority-independent board structure, supplemented by an international advisory panel that includes William McDonough (Vice Chairman of Merrill Lynch) and David Bonderman (founding partner of Texas Pacific Group).[28] Similarly, the ranking civil servant responsible for the oversight of the Norwegian Government Pension Fund—Global, Europe's largest Sovereign Wealth Fund, emphasized to Congress its own well-developed controls and the need for regulatory restraint.[29]

---

[25] Evidence to House Committee on Financial Services, "Hearing on Foreign Government Investment in the US Economy and Financial Sector," Washington DC, 5 March 2008 (G Alvarez); Commission of European Communities, above n 18; OECD above n 9; see also M. Allen and J. Caruana, "Sovereign Wealth Funds: A Work Agenda" (International Monetary Fund, Washington DC, 29 February 2008) 13.
[26] Lowry, above n 20.
[27] Interview, London, 19 July 2008.
[28] Evidence to House Committee on Financial Services, "Hearing on Foreign Government Investment in the US Economy and Financial Sector," Washington DC, 5 March 2008 (S. Israel).
[29] Evidence to House Committee on Financial Services, "Hearing on Foreign Government Investment in the US Economy and Financial Sector,' Washington DC, 5 March 2008 (M. Skancke). The fund details all of its investments and conforms

Not surprisingly, the governance structure adopted by the
Norwegians is often presented as paradigmatic of best practice.[30] It
invests across an investment universe, with risk tolerance levels set and
monitored by the Ministry of Finance.[31] The portfolio is diversified across
geographic dimensions and 3% limits on individual holdings lower risk.[32]
As Thomas Ekeli, a senior official in the Department of Finance in Oslo
has pointed out, "this balance ensures the fund can ride out any short-
term market fluctuations."[33] While there has been much talk about
replicating the checks and balances adopted by the Norwegian
Government Pension Fund—Global, this is not without substantial short-
term destabilizing risks. A leading investment banker in New York
conceded in an interview, for example, that "those who advocate a
Norwegian solution clearly have not read the underpinning rules
governing its operation."[34] Many of the recent share acquisitions in
global financial investment banks are substantial. The scale of individual
contributions far exceeds the tolerance limits provided to Norwegian
fund managers. Disinvestment on the scale necessary to ensure
compliance with Norwegian norms could be exceptionally problematic.

A related problem centers on the activist approach taken by the
Norwegian fund in the exercise of its obligations as a shareholder.
Forcing Sovereign Wealth Funds to demonstrate independence from

---

to an ethical code of practice. The precise governance rules of the Norwegian
Government Pension Fund – Global are published online: http://www.norges-
bank.no/Pages/Article____68360.aspx at 17 March 2008.

[30] See S. Chesterman, "The Turn to Ethics: Disinvestment From Multinational
Corporations For Human Rights Violations: The Case of Norway's Sovereign Wealth
Fund," *American University International Law Review* (2008) forthcoming.

[31] Norwegian Ministry of Finance, *On the Management of the Government Pension Fund
in 2006* (Report No 24) 38–43.

[32] Ibid at 85–88.

[33] Interview, Oslo, 11 April 2008. The evidence of the risk of sudden capital outflows
derives from funds based in the South Pacific. A fund established in Nauru invested
solely in "lumpy" real estate. A second in Tonga consisted of three holdings in major US
corporations. In both cases, not surprisingly, the result was major losses, see E. Le
Borgne and P. Medas, "Sovereign Wealth Funds in the Pacific Island Countries: Macro-
Fiscal Linkages" (International Monetary Fund, Washington DC, WP/07/297, December
2007) 20. There is demonstrable difference in the quality of the fund managers brought in
to run the major operations in Russia, China, and the Gulf. Notwithstanding their
expertise and standing, however, there is no way of predicting whether these agents have
the capacity to moderate the behavior of their political masters in the event of an
escalating trade or diplomatic dispute.

[34] Interview, New York, 25 April 2008.

political considerations by adopting purely passive positions cuts against the trajectory of responsible corporate governance, a trajectory which has been taken very seriously by the Norwegian Pension Fund – Global.[35] Within the academy, this imperative has gone even further, with the suggestion that Sovereign Wealth Funds should be automatically stripped of ownership rights.[36] Two leading US academics have proposed what they term a minimalist solution. They argue that the political problem of how to "ensure that market-based capitalist regimes are protected against incursion by new mercantilist regimes" can be resolved by "a simple corporate governance fix" whereby "the equity of a US firm acquired by a foreign government controlled entity would lose its voting rights, but would regain them when transferred to non-state ownership."[37] The Santiago Principles reject such a reduction in power. Forcing Sovereign Wealth Funds to disengage from ownership responsibility is unlikely to solve one key dimension of the crisis. Indeed, as will be explored below, it would exacerbate it. A defining feature of the contemporary crisis was the failure of institutional investors to take their ownership responsibilities seriously enough.

A second wider source of concern centers on the complex relationship between Sovereign Wealth Funds and financial engineers. While the International Monetary Fund has broadly welcomed Sovereign Wealth Funds, it has expressed concern that any tie up in private equity, combined with the danger associated with "shorting" particular stocks or sectors, could prove exceptionally destabilizing. Its Director of Research

---

[35] Most controversially, the Ethics Council of the Norwegian Pension Fund – Global advocated that the Fund disinvest from Walmart. This centered on fears that Walmart's supply chain management was defective and could implicate the corporation, and therefore the fund, as the owner of its shares, in the violation of International Labor Organization working condition standards. See generally, Chesterman, above n 30. It has also divested its $500m stake in Rio Tinto because of concerns that the management of the world's biggest gold mine led to unacceptable and unethical environmental degradation; see Norwegian Ministry of Finance, "The Government Pension Fund Divests its Holding in Mining Firm' (Press Release, Oslo, 10 September, 2008). Significantly, Rio Tinto is not involved in the operational management of the mine, which is in Indonesia. On the same day, the Ministry of Finance rejected a request to divest from Monsanto because of concerns over child labor, citing improvements in corporate governance.

[36] Gilson and Milhaupt, above n 6 at 10; see also however, Skancke, above n 29 ('We see no cause for regulations that would restrict the present investment activities of our Fund, or any regulation imposing restrictions on SWF over and above those applying to non-SWF investors': at 6).

[37] Gilson and Malhuapt, above n 6 at 10.

has pointed out that "as sovereign funds grow in importance, they effectively become a significant unregulated set of intermediaries that may or may not invest with hedge funds in the future."[38] An inevitable consequence is the potential amplification of market manipulation.[39] Despite regulatory suspicion that hedge funds may have colluded to put financial stocks into play,[40] there is no evidence that Sovereign Wealth Funds have either funded or directly engaged in such short-term asset management strategies. As with state-controlled corporations seeking to make strategic acquisitions, one further issue surrounds the risk of insider trading because Sovereign Wealth Funds may have access to and take advantage of price-sensitive information. Again, it is essential to emphasize that this risk is purely hypothetical. There is no evidence that any Sovereign Wealth Fund has engaged in such activity.

Paradoxically, shrill rhetoric emanating from recipient countries reinforces the dynamic interplay between Sovereign Wealth Funds and private equity. Some funds have sought to head-off criticism of disguised motives by developing indirect conduits, most notably through a deepening of collaborative ventures. The Chinese Investment Corporation has contributed to a major fund established by JC Flowers. The Government Investment Corporation of Singapore has emerged as a key underwriter of a similar fund established by Texas Pacific Group. Investment in distressed financial stocks and the leveraged acquisition of committed senior debt at fire-sale prices provides both sets of institutional actors with a clear commercial opportunity. It is a thought

---

[38] S. Johnson, "The Rise of Sovereign Wealth Funds" (2007) *Finance and Development* (September) 1.

[39] The Securities and Exchange Commission has flagged the asymmetrical informational issue and its application to Sovereign Wealth Funds and, more problematically, state-controlled funds with privileged access to market sensitive information; see Evidence to House Committee on Financial Services, United States Congress, Washington DC, 5 March 2008 (E. Tafari).

[40] The dissemination of rumors in March 2008 destabilized one of Britain's leading lenders, HBOS. The "trash and cash" operation prompted the Financial Services Authority to release a terse statement castigating the market manipulation and promising a thorough investigation; see R. Sutherland et al, "Inside the Hunt for the City's Bank Raiders," *The Observer*, 23 March 2008, 22–23. As a consequence, the FSA introduced rules necessitating greater disclosure of shorting strategies; see FSA, "Financial Services Authority Introduces Disclosure Regime for Significant Short Positions in Companies Undertaking Rights Issues" (Press Release, London, 13 June 2008). The Securities and Exchange Commission went further, temporarily banning short selling in 19 major financial stocks; see SEC, Emergency Order (Release No. 58166, Washington DC, 15 July 2008).

that is captivating private equity mandarins. The Abu Dhabi Investment Authority will, in time, "effectively replace Wall Street," according to Guy Hands, the head of Terra Firma, a leading private equity provider.[41] Although that statement is tinged with hyperbole, it is indicative of growing interdependence.[42] The linkage magnifies, however, the opacity problems associated with the acquisition and divestiture of portfolio companies. If the aim of policymakers is to limit the short-term nature of contemporary market practice, it is surely counter-productive to force an arranged marriage between two largely unregulated sectors of the financial economy.

Sovereign Wealth Funds represent a fundamental shift in market dynamics precisely because of the (potential) fusion of political and commercial imperatives. Their growth provides confirming evidence that the claim that the triumph of liberalism and global diffusion of western economic policies would inevitably lead to the demise of the state is, at best, premature.[43] For the larger established funds, there is no evidence that investment strategies differ in substance from those of traditional pension funds. Indeed it is arguable that any short-term attempt to destabilize the market would be exceptionally counter-productive to longer-term interests precisely because the initial exit could be easily traced. The boom in commodity prices, in particular, however, compounds the perception that investment strategies could be used to advance the potential exercise of political "soft power."[44]

A number of plausible concerns arise in this regard. Corporate takeovers and the acquisition of strategic stakes (particularly if accompanied by board rights) give state actors potential access to proprietary intellectual capital. Without appropriate and enforceable checks and balances, misuse of this information could be disseminated to a wider range of "national champions." A related risk is that the investment could influence strategic imperatives (for example by skewing lending priorities towards projects favored by donor countries), thus

---

[41] M Arnold, "Wealth Funds Fill Bank Gap for Buy-Out Groups," *Financial Times*, 28 February 2008, 1.
[42] The involvement of a Texas Pacific Group founding partner on the international advisory panel set up by the Singaporean SWF, Temesek Holdings, indicates this. The governance procedures allows for Bonderman (or any other advisor) to be excused from deliberations in cases where a conflict of interest exists; see Israel, above n 28.
[43] For original formulation, see F Fukuyama, *The End of History and the Last Man* (1992).
[44] See J. Nye, *Soft Power: The Means to Success in World Politics* (2005).

undermining the efficacy of specific corporate governance controls.[45] The more aggressive investment strategies developed by China and Russia, in particular, but also from authoritarian governments in the Gulf, have exacerbated these concerns. While there is no evidence that any Sovereign Wealth Fund has ever been used to further political ambitions, ascertaining the motives of secretive or authoritarian governments is a notoriously imprecise exercise. Notwithstanding the advantages of increased disclosure in helping to divine intent, it is important to emphasize that Sovereign Wealth Funds is only one component of state economic influence.

The opacity level increases when strategic investments derive from state-controlled corporations and clouds over completely when the acquisition comes from business oligarchs with discernible but informal links with political power in authoritarian regimes. The point here is that restricting Sovereign Wealth Fund acquisitions or limiting voting rights to demonstrate passivity could lead to the expansion of even more opaque investment mechanisms. The governance debate and its implications will be further explored below. First it is necessary to evaluate how the national interest is defined, consider the impact of Sovereign Wealth Fund investment on that definition and the consequence for capital flows.

Many countries impose restrictions on foreign direct investment in parts of the critical infrastructure because of strategic and cultural factors. These can include restrictions in dual-use technologies or protection of core communication portals, such as media markets, from undue foreign influence.[46] The restrictions can be complete, partial or entail a review process, which, in turn, may or may not privilege investment (dependent on the salience of wider security concerns). The problem centers on a lack of agreement on what 'critical' means and the parameters that governments can use to define 'national security' interests.[47] The inevitable consequence is a lack of transparency in investment review processes. This makes the entire process susceptible to political and economic populism. Until the publication of the Santiago principles, the most frequently considered policy framework to address

---

[45] Allen and Caruana, above n 25 at 14.

[46] See GAO, *Foreign Investment: Laws ands Policies Regulating Foreign Investment in 10 Countries* (Washington DC, February 2008); OECD, *Protection of "Critical Infrastructure" and the Role of Investment Policies Relating to National Security* (Paris, May 2008), 6.

[47] OECD, *Transparency and Predictability for Investment Policies Addressing National Security Concerns: A Survey of Practices* (Paris, May 2008).

the symbiotic nature of the problem of SWF regulation has been the European Union.[48] Its proposed code of conduct had suggested the need for common disclosure standards in both host and recipient countries. This was designed, specifically, to ensure policy coherence within recipient nations (i.e. a common definition of what constitutes the public interest). There are sound policy reasons for advocating such an approach. The European Union President, Jose Manuel Barroso, has warned that support for open markets is waning across the community.[49] In this context, the absence of an overarching agreement on what constitutes the national interest risks the further politicization of foreign investment review processes across the European Union.[50] The fear is that any further advance of economic populism and protectionist rhetoric at national level may distort the authority and credibility of wider competition policy. This, argues the European Commission, is counter-productive to collective strategic interests. Such lofty aspiration is not, however, matched by realities on the ground. The frameworks and the extent to which inward investment is compromised by injudicious political rhetoric are now evaluated by way of two extended examples.

The United States

Concern over national security issues has become particularly acute in the United States. The imperatives governing the "war on terror" have sharpened the potential conflict between the benefits of global exchange and the impact on national security. The current legal framework dates from the 1988 "Exon-Florio" amendment to the *Defense Production Act*.[51] The amendment authorized presidential right of veto if a foreign investment risked the integrity of national defense. The investigative authority was delegated to the Committee on Foreign Investment in the

---

[48] Commission of the European Communities, above n 18.

[49] L. Barber and T. Walker, "Barroso Protectionism Alert," *Financial Times*, 3 March 2008, 1. This echoed earlier calls at a summit in London between the leaders of Britain, France, Germany, and Italy to reject "futile attempts to stem financial globalization"; see G. Parker, T. Barber, and B. Benoit, "Barroso Tells EU Leaders to Avoid Protectionism," *Financial Times*, 31 January 2008, 1. See, more generally, P. Stephens, "Uncomfortable Truths for a New World of Them and Us," *Financial Times*, 30 May 2008, 9.

[50] The chairman of China Investment Corporation, Lou Jiwei, has ruled out investment across parts of Europe because he "feels extremely unwelcome there"; see B Davis, "China Investment-Fund Head Says Focus is on Portfolios," *Wall Street Journal*, 1 February 2008, A13.

[51] 50 USC app. S 2170.

United States (CFIUS), an inter-agency agency established thirteen years earlier to further inward investment. From the start, two competing philosophical worldviews were in conflict.[52] As one of those involved in compiling the reports commented recently, "one side [representing Treasury and facilitative trade agencies] never saw a deal they didn't like, while the other [initially Defense but extended in 1988 to include Justice and Homeland Security in 2003] never saw a deal they did."[53] The problems are exacerbated by a failure to define what constitutes national security in either the supporting legislation or regulatory procedures.[54] There are of course sound policy reasons for such an approach. Most notably, it gives policymakers exceptional flexibility. Nevertheless, the abortive investment by state-owned Dubai Ports World in P&O's stevedore operations on the US eastern seaboard in 2005 demonstrates the unintended consequences. The failure to disentangle the national interest and how to order potentially incommensurable commercial and military imperatives severely compromised the integrity of the regulatory system.[55]

The controversy centered on the interpretation of an Executive Order. It had opined "certain national infrastructures are so vital that their incapacity or destruction would have a debilitating impact on the defense or economic security of the United States".[56] Despite the support of the Bush administration, political pressure convinced Dubai that it had, in reality, little choice but to divest. This political pressure demonstrates that the voluntary system of review could be short-circuited by policy entrepreneurs. The *Foreign Investment and National Security Act* (2007)

---

[52] The potential dysfunction was highlighted in two critical reports by the Government Accountability Office; see GAO, "Defense Trade: Mitigating National Security Concerns under Exon-Florio Could be Improved" (GAO-02-736, Washington DC, 12 September 2002); GAO, "Defense Trade: Enhancements to the Implementation of Exon-Florio Could Strengthen the Law's Effectiveness" (GAO-05-686, Washington DC, 28 September 2005).

[53] Interview, Washington DC, 28 May 2008. Moreover, the OECD has found no evidence or evaluation of how investment policy actually furthers or impedes national security; see OECD, above n 47, 7 (Rather, it acts as a mechanism of last resort.)

[54] The Department of Homeland Security, for example, defines as part of its mandate the need to protect "systems and assets, whether physical or virtual, so vital to the United States that the incapacity or destruction of such systems and assets would have a debilitating impact on national security"; cited in OECD, above n 48, 3.

[55] See generally, E. Graham and D. Marchick, *US National Security and Foreign Direct Investment* (2006).

[56] Executive Order 13010.

was designed to address this defect by codifying the entire foreign investment review process.[57] It reinforces earlier Executive Order imperatives in the definition of critical infrastructure. Significantly, the financial services industry is omitted from the list of controlled sectors in the primary legislation. Individual agencies have maintained that the sector is a component of critical infrastructure. As such, the Committee on Foreign Investment in the United States remains a politically charged arena. Moreover, the supporting legislation specifically calls on the Committee to take into consideration "the relationship of the acquiring country with the United States, specifically on its record of cooperating in counter-terrorism efforts."[58]

This degree of politicization is particularly problematic for Chinese domiciled investors. The scale of distrust was already evident in the blocking of the sale of a Californian-based oil company to the Chinese National Oil Corporation in 2006. This unease re-emerged in the machinations surrounding the recent attempted takeover of 3Com, a leading telecommunications firm. The deal was structured to give the Chinese conglomerate Huawei just 16.5% of the stock, with the remainder held by a US private equity group, Bain Capital. The deal was derailed, in part, because of fears expressed outside the committee process that the integrity of network security protocols could not be protected.

The alleged links between Huawei and the Chinese Peoples' Liberation Army represented an even more nebulous concern. Recognition that these concerns could not be readily dismissed—at least in the court of public opinion—led to the withdrawal of the US \$2.2 billion offer.[59] It is questionable, absent a fundamental overarching agreement on how to deal with expanded state reach, whether Chinese controlled investment vehicles, in particular, can gain ongoing political support in Washington.[60] Administration support appears conditional on adherence to a further generic set of principles that operate outside of the

---

[57] PL 110-49, 121 Stat 246.
[58] GAO, above n 46, 34.
[59] S. Kirchgaessner, "US Insiders Point to Bain Errors over 3Com," *Financial Times*, 4 March 2008, 30; S. Kirchgaessner, "Washington Obstacle Course Sees Chinese Companies Re-Examine Their US Ambitions," *Financial Times*, 4 March 2008, 30.
[60] The chairman of the Senate Banking Sub-Committee on Security and International Trade and Investment suggests that the current regulatory approach is "naïve," see E. Bayh, "Time for Sovereign Wealth Fund Rules," *Wall Street Journal*, 13 February 2008, A2.

formal legal and regulatory guidelines that underlie the CFIUS procedure. This requires an explicit commitment that "investment decisions should be based solely on commercial grounds rather than. . .advance, directly or indirectly, the geopolitical goals of the controlling government." According to the US Treasury, "greater information disclosure in areas such as purpose, investment objectives, institutional arrangements and financial information…can reduce uncertainty and build trust in recipient countries."[61] While national security has been deliberately framed to give "the broadest latitude" possible, reinstating the financial sector gives rise to understandable ire on the part of Sovereign Wealth Funds, who see in the current debate geo-political gamesmanship devoid of policy cohesion.[62] It is also important to note that there are significant structural and policy differences between the 3Com deal and those recently consummated within the financial sector.[63] The recent financial acquisitions have been scoped to ensure that they remain below mandatory government review thresholds. Under US law, if there are no accompanying voting rights (or the portfolio investment is below 10%), then the investment is automatically deemed passive and therefore not subject to formal review. Secondly, as noted above, the passage of the *Foreign Investment and National Security Act* explicitly deleted financial services from the list of prescribed sectors. This does not mean, however, that monetary policymakers lack the capacity to block financial investments. The *Bank Holding Company Act* requires Federal Reserve approval before direct or indirect investment of more than 25% of voting shares can be authorized. In addition, a controlling interest, which is defined as having 10% of voting shares, can trigger a formal review. The critical question is whether the Committee on Financial Investment can or should have the capacity to second-guess the Federal Reserve.

Australia
The global demand for resources has been central to Australia's relative insulation from the effects of the credit crisis. The country has significant

---

[61] Y. Otaiba, "Our Sovereign Wealth Plans," *Wall Street Journal*, 19 March 2008, A16.

[62] Oral comments provided to the author by a representative of a conglomerate of SWFs at a seminar given to the International Monetary Fund, Washington, DC, 27 May 2008.

[63] It is also important to emphasize that the main source of foreign investment in the United States comes from Europe, particularly the United Kingdom, France, and Germany. Despite the sharp spike in Sovereign Wealth activity, as a sector it remains relatively small provider of overall foreign direct investment in the United States; see GAO, above n 46, 8.

reserves of alumina, zircon, and tantalum as well as liquid natural gas, nickel and iron ore, much of these lying in Western Australia. The state is the world's leading producer of bauxite, rutile and zircon. Western Australia has the largest known reserves of nickel and the second largest supply of iron ore, gold, bauxite, and diamonds. The state has been a magnet for inward investment. Between 1998 and 2007, mining operations expanded from AUS \$5 billion to AUS \$15 billion.[64] China is now Western Australia's most significant trading partner, as consumer of its products and provider of inward investment, particularly the development of low metal content iron ore mines. Chinese concerns have become some of the most significant competitors to the dominant domestic holdings—BHP Billiton and Rio Tinto, which are dual-listed on the London market—and the increasingly important Fortescue Metals Group.

While the investments to date have generally been structured as joint ventures, the number of hostile bids for medium sized Australian operations has increased.[65] There are, of course, clear commercial grounds for such an approach. From the Chinese corporate perspective, synergies produce economies of scale, reduce dependency on the major Australian exporters and minimize the risk of reliance on volatile spot markets. Conversely, the facilitation of inward capital flows may also depress prices in cases where the same entity extracts and uses the resources. The fear expressed in Canberra centers on the fact that this linkage could benefit disproportionately the customers of Australian resources, namely the Chinese. Less focus is placed on the fact that Australia's share of the Asian market has reduced by as much as thirty per cent, a consequence, in part, of a lack of publicly available transport infrastructure. The policy implications have sharpened because of a strategic raid by Chinalco and its (junior) American partner, Alcoa, on the Rio Tinto share register in London, itself the then target of BHP Billiton's planned audacious attempt to consummate the largest takeover in history.[66] Under Australian law, foreign investment is evaluated under

---

[64] Data supplied by the Department of Industry and Resources, Western Australia.

[65] The most significant example in this regard was the hostile AUS \$1.36 billion bid for control of iron ore producer Midwest. Opposition to the deal related primarily to the price not the principle; see J. Freed, "Sinosteel Gets Control But Likely to Have Company at Midwest", *Sydney Morning Herald*, 8 July 2008 (Online edition).

[66] BHP abandoned the takeover attempt on 26 November 2008, citing deteriorating credit conditions and asserting that the debt exposure posed unacceptable risks to shareholder value. BHP is to write costs of \$450 m associated with the bid.

the *Foreign Acquisitions and Takeovers Act* (1975). The analytic function is delegated through policy to a Foreign Investment Review Board (FIRB), an advisory arm of the Department of Treasury. The Act requires investors to obtain a statement of no objections in advance of taking a voting or material interest in excess of 15% in a company with assets in excess of AU $100 million.[67] Under policy guidance, all investments by Sovereign Wealth Funds and state-owned enterprises "irrespective of size are required to be notified for prior approval." Legal advice to Chinalco held that neither Australian law nor policy covered the share raid on a component of a corporation listed in London, making it unnecessary to notify or seek prior federal approval.

Two weeks after the initial raid, the Australian federal government attempted to reconcile competing objectives by refining the principles used to evaluate potentially controversial commercial deals. The first principle covers the investor's independence from the relevant government (to monitor for actual foreign government control). It is unclear what degree of independence is deemed appropriate. Moreover, it is uncertain whether this provision could be enforced against a publicly listed entity in which a state or regional government held a formal but minority interest. Second, the Board will review the investor's litigation record and "common standards of business behavior" (i.e. the extent to which investor has clearly expressed commercial objectives and the quality of its corporate governance). It is equally uncertain whether this would apply to a newly listed corporation or one with no previous litigation history. Third, the FIRB will assess the impact of the investment on competition (to be determined in consultation with the Australian Consumer and Competition Commission). Such an approach may have value in the case of major acquisitions, such as BHP Billiton's proposed takeover of Rio Tinto. It is questionable what impact the transfer of a mid-tier company could have on competition policy, making the provision largely irrelevant unless invoked for short-term political reasons. Fourth, the FIRB will evaluate the impact of the proposed investment on government revenue or other policies, including tax and environmental protection. It is hard to see how this could be used only against state-owned investment vehicles without compromising equity of treatment principles. Fifth, it will evaluate national security considerations, which include undefined "strategic interests." Sixth, the

---

[67] Section 26.

board will determine the impact on the operation and direction of Australian business, "as well as its contribution to the Australian economy and broader community," which includes taking into consideration "the interests of employees, creditors and other stakeholders."

The effect, however, has been to introduce uncertainty into the marketplace. The principles make clear that the Foreign Investment Review Board retains an advisory role. Ultimate decision-making authority in determining whether a proposed investment violates the national interest remains with the Treasurer. The principles do little to provide clarity. As a leading corporate lawyer in Sydney has commented, "the key point to note in relation to these Guidelines is that no guidance has been given by the government as to how their consideration of the national interest would be impacted by each of these factors and the extent to which each factor is or is not satisfied or to what level the government will need to be satisfied of each factor."[68] Indeed, the clarification has politicized the issue and ratcheted up tension with Chinese conglomerates.

The Federal Treasurer, Wayne Swan, has sought to display his pro-inward investment credentials and displace concern by suggesting that his office is swamped by Chinese proposals. He has publicly stated that the government had approved a Chinese investment once every nine days since coming to office. He also intimated, however, that Chinese investment proved exceptionally complex; it required a more detailed examination, which in turn allowed for an expansion of the timeframe for approval beyond thirty days. Under Australian law, foreign investors can withdraw an application if it has not been accepted within the timeframe, thereby guaranteeing confidentiality. In one recent case involving Sinosteel, a Chinese-based corporation, the Australian government refused the request for withdrawal. According to a senior representative of the Chinese firm involved, this decision was contrary to its wishes and demonstrated "discriminatory practice."[69] The government eventually approved an application limiting the investment to 49.99%, on the

---

[68] G. Golding and R. Bassil, "Australian Regulation of Investments by Sovereign Wealth Funds and State Owned Enterprises" (Paper delivered at Sovereign Wealth funds in an Evolving Global Financial System Conference, Lowy Institute, Sydney, 25 September 2008) 7. Greg Golding was the principal legal advisor to Chinalco in the Rio transaction and had earlier advised the private equity consortium that bid for control of Qantas in 2007.
[69] Interview, Beijing, 5 September 2008.

grounds that a controlling interest would be contrary to competition policy. The proposals have generated considerable ire in Western Australia, where those involved in facilitating inward investment complain that it is important to "differentiate between stock market and real miners." They also suggest that linking the national interest to the need to separate supply and demand misunderstands the dynamics of the mining industry. This is precisely the message the Federal Treasurer promulgated in a recent speech in Melbourne.

> The key is that investments are consistent with Australia's aim of maintaining a market-based system in which companies are responsive to shareholders and in which investment and sales decisions are driven by market forces rather than external strategic or political considerations... Our predisposition is to more carefully consider proposals by consumers to control existing producing firms. We usually welcome and encourage some participation by the buyer...but we need to ensure that investment is consistent with Australia's aim of ensuring that decisions continue to be driven by commercial considerations and that Australia remains a reliable supplier in the future to all current and potential trading partners.[70]

The rationale for such an interventionist approach was explicitly justified by reference to the international debate on the regulation of Sovereign Wealth Funds. The empirical basis for such an assertion is hard to justify.[71] Not surprisingly, it is a theme also developed by Chinese and

[70] See W. Swan, "Australia, China, and This Asian Century" (Speech delivered at Australia-China Business Council, Melbourne, 4 July 2008).

[71] As with the United States, the rate of Chinese investment lags considerably behind that of international competitors. In 2006–2007, the United States was the single largest investor in Australia with US $45 billion. In total US $156.4 billion was invested, with China contributing only US $10 billion. According to one of Australia's leading political economists, Peter Drysdale, an emeritus political economy professor at the Australian National University, "the current ambiguities are damaging to Australia's economic and long-term political-strategy interests', see M Stutchbury, "Swan's Line in the Sand Risks Turning Chinese Investors Away", *The Australian*, 5 September 2008 (Online Edition). In a recent academic paper the political economist went even further; see P. Drysdale and C. Findlay, "Chinese Foreign Direct Investment in Australia: Policy Issues for the Resource Sector" (Paper delivered at East Asia Forum, Australian National University, Canberra, 4 September 2008) in which the researchers argue that "unnecessary regulation of capital from this source into the Australian market will not only be detrimental to Australian economic interests by driving it to other markets, possibly less supportive of reform of corporate structures and corporate behavior, but is likely to encourage a retreat

Chinese-linked mining concerns. Interviews conducted by this researcher in Beijing in recent months make it clear that both components are both puzzled and annoyed at what they perceive to be an admixture of discriminatory practices, bad faith, and policy incoherence. One of the most significant investments in Western Australia, for example, has come from a subsidiary of CITIC Pacific, a listed Hong Kong corporation, in which, at the time, the Chinese government retained a 30% passive stake. The director of CITIC Pacific's Australian operation is scathing about what he sees as the apparent lack of knowledge in Canberra of either Chinese realities or the economics of iron ore extraction. Wang Gongcheng maintained that the Australian government mindset remains wedded to outmoded conceptions of Chinese management:

> Things are very different now to when I first negotiated the agreement for China's first substantial foreign investment [with Hammersley Mines in Chennar, now a joint venture with Rio Tinto]. Economic decision-making is now devolved totally to the enterprises themselves, which have responsibility for sourcing the necessary financing. In such circumstances, it is understandable that enterprises are seeking to secure supply. It is in their commercial interests to do so.[72]

While it is arguable that CITIC Pacific could be construed as a private company, it cannot be vouchsafed because an accounting scandal has substantially increased CITIC Beijing's ownership stake. For mainland-based corporations, navigating the foreign investment review process in Australia has become exceptionally problematic. The General Manager of the International Cooperation Department at Sinosteel, for example, argues "that on the surface the Australian government guidelines have not changed" but its treatment indicates, to him, a profound change in policy has occurred.[73] In a scathing aside, the Sinosteel manager wonders, with reason, whether current policy "can be consistent with Australia's conception of itself as a market economy." The decision to limit Sinosteel's acquisition in a neighboring mining corporation is inconsistent with OECD guidelines and with Australia's

---

to appeals to the power of the state in ways that are likely to be damaging to both our long-term economic and political interests."

[72] Wang Gongcheng, CP Mining Management Pty Ltd (Interview, Beijing, 5 September 2008).

[73] Jiang Baocai, Sinosteel (Interview, Beijing, 5 September 2008),

own corporation law, which mandates a takeover offer if holdings increase beyond 19.99%. Not only does such an arrangement severely limit Sinosteel's capacity to deliver clear commercial objectives; it also curtails the systematic development of the infrastructure and the emergence of competition.

The problems for the Australian government sharpened significantly in late February 2009, when Rio Tinto announced that it had secured a potential $19.5 billion capital injection from Chinalco in the form of convertible warrants. The complex deal prompted the Federal Treasurer to amend the Foreign Acquisition and Takeovers Act to cover complex financial instruments that have the effect of providing control. The decision comes at a time when China is ramping up its planned investment in Australia. Fortescue Metals Group disclosed it has had preliminary negotiations with the China Investment Corporation head, Lou Jinwei, who traveled to Australia at the invitation of David Murray, head of the Future Fund and a pivotal figure in the negotiations that led to the publication of the Santiago principles. While the Treasurer is keen to protect the national interest, the worsening economic conditions mean that China may be the only institutional actor capable of ensuring ongoing employment across swathes of Western Australia. Never has competing policy requirements appeared so intractable.

III   THE LIMITS OF TRANSPARENCY

Transparency has long been offered as a panacea to regulatory failure and as a proxy for the integrity of public policy systems. As the OECD has commented, transparency, "involves offering concerned parties the opportunity to comment on new laws and regulations, communicating the policy objectives of proposed changes, allowing time for public review and providing a means to communicate with relevant authorities."[74] Moreover the OECD maintains the need for international cooperation. This is necessary "to ensure policy transparency by defining common standards [procedural fairness] and providing support for multilateral peer review and capacity building."[75] The OECD's table of procedural transparency and predictability speaks volumes about serious wider deficiencies in the accountability regime at the national recipient level. The lack of formal requirements to publicly announce outcomes, give

[74] OECD, above n 47, 2.
[75] Ibid.

reports to legislative bodies or publish an annual report with sufficient information to ascertain review patterns is the norm in all countries surveyed, with the exception of the United States and (partially) Australia.[76]

Introducing policy changes in an incremental manner through bilateral agreements, as in the United States, runs counter to OECD principles. In Australia, the articulation of Foreign Investment Review Board principles was not subject to external debate or validation. Rather, the initiative was presented as a bureaucratic clarification. As such, it did not require prior notification to or consultation with interested parties. In both cases, the introduction of new criteria to adjudication state-owned or controlled investment entities reflect discriminatory impulses.

It is entirely appropriate for national governments to protect legitimate national interests. If the process is opaque, however, there may be a concomitant undermining of legitimacy. Authority requires clearly defined parameters. In addition, the rationale must be explained and the rules applied in a proportionate impartial manner. To do otherwise obviates longstanding principles of equity in international investment. As such, proposals to regulate Sovereign Wealth Funds must be linked to foreign direct investment processes and to a wider recalibration of what is expected of institutional shareholders in the control of major corporations. At the same time, it is also clear that the generation of new norms or principles of best practice need to take account of changing power relations. The transfer of capital from south to north and east to west partially rebalances the centre of political and economic power, and reveals, in the process, glaring deficiencies in western conceptions of what constitutes—or should constitute—regulatory best practice.[77]

While Sovereign Wealth Funds have traditionally shunned the media spotlight, there are already clear signs of bristling at what is seen as a partial and self-serving rewriting of the rules governing financial globalization. This is most notable in the case of the Abu Dhabi Investment Authority. The emirate remains deeply suspicious of the benefits of disclosure; its website consists of five sparsely populated pages. Nonetheless a clear message has been transmitted to Washington.

---

[76] Ibid, 9.

[77] Recently announced plans to change the governance structure of the IMF reflect and reinforce this broader shift; see IMF, *Report of the Executive Board to the Board of Governors, Reform of Quota and Voice in the International Monetary Fund* (Washington DC, 28 March 2009).

The investment authority has stated explicitly that the Abu Dhabi "government has never and will never use its investment organizations or individual investments as a foreign policy tool."[78] It emphasizes that financial experts manage 80% of its investments. ADIA, it is stated, has "operated predominantly as a passive investor, with the overwhelming share of its portfolio consisting of minority stakes in companies that have included no control rights, no board seats, and no involvement in the management or direction of the receiving companies."[79]

The phrasing is instructive in its ambiguity. The passivity is predominant but not exclusive. It is unclear whether the portfolio balance is based on size or value. Furthermore, the lack of control, board representation, and directional guidance may not necessarily be used in all cases. More generally, it is mistaken to believe that the absence of voting rights precludes the exertion of influence. No entrenched management team is likely to ignore the voice of (perceived) interests of significant shareholders. The problem is that the current lack of disclosure means that there is no way of knowing what advice, if any, has been dispensed. Likewise there is no ongoing mechanism to hold the fund to account. Along with mollification has come an unsubtle warning. The ADIA cautions that "in a world thirsty for liquidity, receiving nations should be mindful of the signals sent through protectionist rhetoric and rash regulation."[80] The chairman of Dubai World has argued that the introduction of formal regulatory oversight is unwarranted and contrary to the interests of recipient states.[81] Similarly, the chief executive of Dubai International Capital, which holds strategic stakes in both Standard Chartered and HSBC, has bluntly stated that leading investment banks may not be able to survive without Sovereign Wealth Fund financing. He told a conference that "it would take a lot more money [than already secured from Abu Dhabi, Singapore, and Kuwait] to rescue Citigroup,"[82]

---

[78]Otaiba, above n 61.

[79] Ibid.

[80] Ibid.

[81] Sultan Ahmed Bin Sulayem argued that "If somebody comes with regulations that make it difficult for someone from certain geographical locations to invest in Europe or the west, people will take their investment somewhere else." He also claimed however that political interference was a red herring. "If you put a politician in charge of an investment, believe me, that investment fund will not last for a very long time." See "Dubai Fund Hits Back at Criticism", *BBC News*, 29 February 2008.

[82] M Sleiman and A. Critchlow, "Dubai Firm's Chief Says Citigroup Needs More Cash," *Wall Street Journal*, 4 March 2008 (Online edition).

one of the most over-extended investment houses and the first to seek recapitalization.

Similar sentiment is evident in Beijing. The vice president of the China Investment Corporation, Jesse Wang, has expressed irritation at the calls for a code of conduct, saying it was "unfair" and that "the claims that Sovereign Wealth Funds are causing threats to state security and economic security are groundless. We don't need outsiders to come tell us how we should act."[83] The International Monetary Fund is exceptionally cognizant of the sensitivities involved in brokering a solution. It has signalled that a heavy-handed one-sided approach could backfire. The IMF Deputy Managing Director, John Lipsky, has argued that "if there were a sense that somehow "best practices" were decided by someone else and dictated [to the funds], that could be extremely counter-productive."[84] It was against this volatile background that the International Monetary Fund and representatives of twenty-six Sovereign Wealth Funds agreed a voluntary set of guidelines in Santiago this September.

The Santiago principles set out the legal, institutional, and macroeconomic strategies adopted by each fund, including information about the risk appetite. According to the co-chair of the International Working Group drafting committee, the "governance and accountability arrangements give considerable comfort especially in the area of the separation of operations of the sovereign wealth fund from its owner, and the investment policies and risk management together with the other things are intended to make it clear that sovereign wealth funds act from a commercial motive and not other motives."[85] Although no formal surveillance mechanism is envisaged, the co-chair of the International Working Group, the Under-Secretary at the Abu Dhabi Department of Finance, Hamid Al Suwaidi, gave explicit assurance that compliance could be achieved: "This is a voluntary set of practices. The sovereign wealth funds will publicly announce their adoption of the GAPP once it's approved. And then it's for the public really to see where the respective

---

[83] V. Ruan, "China's Investment Fund Pushes Back, *Wall Street Journal*, 7 March 2008, A6; E. Wong, "An Emboldened China Scolds US Over Economy," *International Herald Tribune*, 17 June 2008, 1; see more generally, S. Schwartzman, "Reject Sovereign Wealth Funds at Your Peril", *Financial Times*, 20 June 2008, 13.

[84] B. Davies, "US Pushes Sovereign Funds to Open to Outside Scrutiny," *Wall Street Journal*, 26 February 2008, A1.

[85] D. Murray (Press Conference, International Working Group on Sovereign Wealth Fund Regulation, Santiago, 2 September 2008).

funds are adhering to these principals and practices."[86] What that means in practice is exceptionally difficult to determine.

The governance procedures followed by the Norwegian Government Pension Fund – Global provides one potential way forward. Its terms of reference necessitate that detailed information is provided about where it invests and how it exercises its ownership obligations.[87] While there are corporations in which the fund simply will not invest (for example those involved in the arms trade), the fund also adopts a pragmatic teleological or consequential approach to ownership. It "aims to be a leader in active ownership and develop strategies and priorities that can win the support of others."[88] As its most recent annual report makes clear, "there is an expectation...[by]...the Norwegian people and their political representatives that the fund managers should act responsibly and look after their financial assets in an ethically acceptable way."[89] Given that the current financial crisis stems primarily (if not exclusively) from ethical failure, then it necessarily follows that it is only through responsible ownership that effective oversight can return. As noted above, proposals to curtail voting rights risk delivering a suite of unintended consequences, not least of which is a reversal of the work

---

[86] H Al Suwaidi (Press Conference, International Working Group on Sovereign Wealth Fund Regulation, Santiago, 2 September 2008).At the same time, distinct limits on disclosure are envisaged. The Australian representative noted: "Sovereign Wealth Funds have to compete in the market, and there are two implications of that, one in terms of the confidentiality of arrangements that other people make with sovereign wealth funds and the protection of that confidentiality, and the confidentiality of their day-to-day transacting, but also the notion that if other parties in the market believe that a sovereign wealth fund can be forced to disclose certain information, then that would close down the range of people who would be prepared to deal with Sovereign Wealth Funds. So disclosure is important, but as with an other institutional investor, there must be a limit which protects confidentiality of dealings for sovereign wealth funds and their counter parties." See D. Murray (Press Conference, International Working Group on Sovereign Wealth Fund Regulation, Santiago, 2 September 2008).
[87] *Norges Bank Investment Management Annual Report* (2007) 4.1. This process is buttressed by an external Council on Ethics. The Council has the power to exclude a specific corporation in the event that investment is deemed to carry a significant risk of complicity. This message has been exported in recent weeks by the Governor of the Norges Bank; see S. Gjedrem, "Ethics and the Government Pension Fund – Global" (Speech delivered at Investing for the Future Conference, Oslo, 16 January 2008); K. Halvorsen, "Sovereign Wealth Funds as Serious Financial Investors," *Financial Times*, 15 February 2008.
[88] Ibid.
[89] *Norges Bank Investment Management Annual Report* (2007) 4.1.

done by the Norwegian Pension Fund – Global to embed integrity in its operating model. Moreover, forcing Sovereign Wealth Funds to abdicate responsibility exacerbates the problem of the separation of ownership and control within individual corporations and undermines the salience of regulatory theory.

A more appropriate and integrated response is to enhance the narrative basis of accountability based on an agonistic understanding of what business integrity means in practice. To be effective, this needs to transcend the desultory reality of the much vaunted but now partially discredited "comply or explain" model of financial reporting advanced by the United Kingdom. This is not the impossible task it may appear. A useful precedent can be found in the indirect ways in which private equity was persuaded to enhance its accountability. The transformative potential (and risk) of private equity occurs at a number of levels. The involvement of existing management in private equity bids creates intractable conflicts of interest. The processes through which initial exit is managed raise difficult questions about the efficacy of existing rules governing control transactions. The narrow focus on financial performance, alongside the shortened timeframes in which ownership is exercised, may produce short-term gains but negatively impact on the longer-term sustainability of the enterprise and its relationship with key internal and external stakeholders. Paradoxically, the primary virtue associated with private equity, namely its capacity to evade the public disclosure regime, ultimately became its Achilles Heel. It made the industry particularly vulnerable to critiques based on transparency and accountability deficiencies.

While opacity is common to many alternative investment vehicles, private equity has a very public face. Moreover, the extent to which iconic (and profitable) corporations were being de-listed and restructured had an immediate market as well as socio-political impact. In such circumstances, stonewalling by the industry was simply untenable. As the industry-sponsored review into its operations in the United Kingdom acknowledged: "The context for this enquiry is that a position that full disclosures and reporting to limited partners, the ultimate owners of private equity, are alone sufficient is no longer politically and otherwise sustainable, at least in respect of the largest portfolio companies."[90] According to the review, the only way to reduce

---

[90] Walker Working Group, *Guidelines for Disclosure and Transparency in Private Equity* (2007), 40.

contestation was to attend to the interlocking needs of legitimacy and authority. In order to achieve this, the Walker Guidelines maintain that attention to integrity dimension is crucial.

> What is meant by decency and integrity is more substantive than conformity with contractual provision or the law: it relates to a set of principles and values that cannot be encapsulated in a detailed set of rules. Second, standards of conduct are contagious, and malpractice in a particular business situation can have a powerful negative effect on general expectations of what is and what is not normal business conduct and weaken the legitimacy of corporate structures as a whole.[91]

A similar dynamic is now facing the Sovereign Wealth Funds. Indeed it is in the sector's interest to take a much more active approach in overseeing portfolio corporations, if only to safeguard their investment. Misguided reliance on the bureaucratic, legal and political domains in developed markets has demonstrated that need all too clearly. The critical question is how to generate the leverage to ensure that the codes of conduct gain widespread adoption. Here the omens are not auspicious. Despite a communiqué from the OECD to accompany a ministerial meeting in June highlighting support for the IMF discussions and the need for recipient countries to implement a code of practice governing investment principles, there has been little formal coordination between the working groups in Washington and Paris. Such an approach is not only misguided; it is likely to preordain conflict.

There are a number of sound policy reasons to request greater disclosure from Sovereign Wealth Funds. Greater disclosure could provide an early warning system of volatile build-ups of capital within particular sectors. Greater oversight reduces the potential of sudden capital withdrawals causing or amplifying financial crises. Thirdly, it serves broader public aims, including a hoped for increase in the transparency of overarching domestic fiscal policy. Fourthly, requiring Sovereign Wealth Funds to render explicit their investment strategies reduces perception that foreign policy objectives trump commercial ones. The critical but as yet unresolved policy question remains, therefore, how to ensure compliance to a substantive code that has the potential to deliver meaningful transparency and accountability.

---

[91] Ibid.

Success in this endeavor can only be vouchsafed if clarification extends to foreign investment review processes that guarantee commitment to long-standing principles governing equity of treatment. Notwithstanding agreement in Santiago, resolution of political contestation requires that adequate attention is placed on this dimension of the equation. There is, however, an unacceptable degree of ambiguity in the proposals emanating from Brussels, Washington and Canberra. Each maintains political discretion over ill-defined "strategic interests." The search for accountability is therefore a symbiotic process that requires careful sequencing. If proposals to regulate Sovereign Wealth Funds are used merely as a cover for a nascent protectionism, the cause of financial liberalization will be set back. In such a scenario, both lender and recipient will be egregiously impoverished.

Chapter 6

Enhancing Integrity Through Design

In order to avoid a repetition of past failure, it is necessary to combine an assertive prosecutorial stance with informal approaches to guide behavioral change. The necessary first step is to articulate a common standard of corporate accountability. Benchmarking absolute and relative performance against this standard makes self-regulation more credible and effective. It reduces the space and justification for contestation at each stage of the enforcement pyramid by resolving incommensurability between differing conceptions of compliance form and function. The competition in muscularity is one that regulators will (almost) inevitably lose. Building from this insight, it seems reasonable to conclude that effective oversight requires the deployment of multiple regulatory instruments and strategies, including rules and principles that emphasize pre-emptive restraint. Crucially, it also involves simultaneously leveraging with greater sophistication the restraining power of self-regarding norms.

Emergent evidence from Australia suggests a possible way forward. In line with its counterparts across the globe, the Australian Securities and Investments Commission (ASIC) faces competing pressures. Alongside constant industry derived demands to reduce the regulatory burden has come a politically sanctioned emphasis on the need to submit internal agency decision-making processes to greater public scrutiny. This interlinked agenda has, in turn, been framed by the importation of market-based accountability mechanisms, such as the design and implementation of key performance indicators (KPI). For example, ASIC has completed an overarching strategic review. This review was not only informed by extensive consultation with key external stakeholders. Much more significantly, the review was determined, in part, by stakeholder validation.

The most visible manifestation of this consensus-based approach to regulation is to be found on the agency's website homepage.[1] Prior emphasis on enforcement has been replaced by a formal announcement that ASIC is committed to "better regulation." The goal of securing market integrity is explicitly understood in the context of the agency, financial intermediaries, and market participants working together to develop "fair and efficient" markets. This acknowledgment of interdependence offers both a threat and an opportunity. If the regime emphasizes measures that focus solely on the cost-reduction dimension of regulation, there is a danger that institutional integrity will fail. Much more problematically, effective oversight could be fatally compromised. Conversely, however, careful alignment has the potential to reconfigure the way in which capital market regulation is implemented.

Opportunity and risk pivot on the capacity of the regime—as understood by the totality of actors within it—to align competing but at times conflating interests. This multi-faceted dynamic interplay of interests has been nicely captured as "the complex of institutional [physical and social] geography, rules, practice and animating ideas that are associated with the regulation of a particular risk or hazard."[2] Importantly, within a specific regime the advancement of a particular sector's self-interest depends on its capacity to translate narrow terms of reference into operational imperatives that generate broader societal support. The extent and direction of possible change may be further determined by the salience of professional norms and behavioral mores. Effective reform requires an integrated suite of measures that reinforces these restraining norms and reduces the capacity to engage in technical compliance. Consequently, the remainder of the chapter is structured as follows. First, the rationale for (and risk associated with) importing market-based performance measurements to the public regulatory sphere is examined. This allows for a deeper understanding of the dynamics of regulatory action, i.e. how conceptions of "best-practice" are arrived at and legitimated. Second, features of the proposed ASIC approach to embedding desired values within the regulatory matrix are outlined and some suggestions are offered for improving both internal agency processes and external engagement in this context. Finally, the efficacy of the approach is evaluated.

---

[1] http:www.asic.gov.au [accessed 11 February 2009].
[2] C. Hood, H. Rothstein and R. Baldwin, *The Government of Risk*, (2004) 8.

I   POLICY RATIONALES FOR FINANCIAL REGULATION

At the heart of the contemporary debate on regulation lies a paradox. The goal of reducing and simplifying red tape has been accompanied by an exponential increase in both regulatory domain and form.[3] Across the globe, cross cutting agencies have been established to manage the resulting conflict in both practices of, and perspectives on, regulation. This has, arguably, gone furthest in the United Kingdom, where the problem of ascertaining the limits of regulatory reach is now placed under the purview of an eponymous cabinet department.[4] Notwithstanding stated preferences for regulatory initiatives to be subject to stringent and ongoing cost-benefit analyses, the conflict between the logic of governance and the political need for short-term solutions influences the degree to which any given polity is truly wedded to policy coherence.

The tension is essentially one of determining opportunity costs. One of the simplest ways to resolve a pressing political problem, for example, is to introduce or enhance regulatory oversight. Conflicting political imperatives make it exceptionally difficult, however, to dislodge ceded regulatory authority. This is particularly the case if subsequent associated debates feed perceptions that any reduction in command and control oversight leaves target communities vulnerable. In practice, therefore, this often necessitates the political establishment granting a preservation order that mandates maintenance of the external architecture (albeit within specified time-frames). While external appearances remain unchanged, incremental change can, however, reduce overarching effectiveness. This was particularly evident in the progressive dismantling of the securities regulation architecture in the United States during the 1990s. Opposition to the Sarbanes-Oxley legislation, introduced in the aftermath of the financial reporting scandals associated with Enron and WorldCom, followed this dismal trajectory, with an

---

[3] See M. Marinetto, "Governing Beyond the Centre: Critique of the Anglo-Governance School," (2003) 51 *Political Studies* 592 (finding that regulatory intervention has expanded exponentially); for application to the financial sector, see M. Moran, *The British Regulatory State* (2003); see more generally, P. May, "Regulatory Regimes and Accountability," (2007) 1 *Regulation & Governance* 8.

[4] The Department for Business, Enterprise and Regulatory Reform, established when Gordon Brown took over as Prime Minister in June 2007, incorporates the Better Regulation Executive, previously a Cabinet Office initiative.

emergent (and now partially discredited) orthodoxy linking regulatory robustness to increased costs, reduced choice, and capital flight.[5]

Key performance indicators represent one mechanism by which a regulatory agency can inoculate itself from such political pressures. The problem is that simplistic metrics can be misleading. This is most notable in the case of enforcement. On one level, it is not surprising that enforcement remains a widely used indicator in measuring regulatory performance. Prosecutorial records provide a highly visible and easily quantifiable metric, particularly when individual agency performance is benchmarked against international practice (adjusted appropriately for market differences). Stark variance in regulatory styles between the United States and the United Kingdom—the most liquid capital markets—demonstrate, however, the critical importance of allowing for cultural differences, legal frameworks, and the political environment in regulatory approaches.[6]

At a more fundamental level, different regulatory approaches to enforcement point to competing (and potentially conflicting) interpretations of what constitutes risk. Viewed in isolation, enforcement proclivity can skew policy direction, budgetary priorities, operational capacity, and overarching effectiveness. If, for example, the offences prosecuted are trivial, the unweighted data becomes misleading. Much more problematically, an active but misaligned enforcement strategy may also evidence a dysfunctional accountability regime within the regulatory agency. A much more specific picture of the socio-economic environment must be presented if the data is to be interpreted accurately.

One highly influential approach is to transplant from the corporate sector the multi-dimensional "balanced scorecard" for reporting.[7] This suite of measurements includes financial and non-

---

[5] See D. Langevoort, "The Social Construction of Sarbanes-Oxley," (2007) 105 *Michigan Law Review* 1817.

[6] See R. Kagan, "Understanding Regulatory Enforcement," (1989) 11 *Law & Policy* 89; for wider discussion of diverse regulatory styles in capital market oversight, see I. MacNeil, "Enforcement of Capital Markets Regulation: The United Kingdom and Its International Markets," in J. O'Brien (ed), *Private Equity, Corporate Governance and the Dynamics of Capital Market Regulation* (2007), 143 (noting a preference for "supervisory action, theme work and public consultation" over enforcement and noting financial penalties have been imposed on only 49 occasions since the *Financial Services and Markets Act 2000* (UK) came into operation on 1 December 2001: at 147–48).

[7] See D. Bryde, "Methods for Managing Different Perspectives of Project Success," (2005) 16 *British Journal of Management*, 119; J. Allen, "Performance Measurement for Securities Supervisors: Report on the Findings of a Workshop on the Balanced

financial indicators. It undoubtedly improves the quality of internal intelligence. If appropriately packaged, it can also indicate responsiveness to demands of core external stakeholders. But even within the corporate sector itself, explanatory value is clouded by lack of clarity over methodological rigor and the extent to which results are replicable (i.e. the rationale governing indicator choice, specific ranking or interpretation etc.). The extent to which the balanced scorecard reflects actual practice or engenders cultural change is also far from certain. These problems are magnified in the transition to regulatory agencies.

Market participants may distort the baseline chosen for analysis. Regulated entities, for example, tend to overestimate direct costs, a process driven, in part, by those who seek opportunistic rents by exaggerating the threat.[8] Moreover, while certain aspects of regulatory mission can be monetized (e.g. the time it takes to process routine regulatory filing), setting time-management or cost reduction targets as the critical indicator of performance in other areas can be problematic. Reducing the length of time it takes to conduct an investigation may, for example, result in sub-optimal oversight, which in turn lowers the effectiveness of a randomized inspection regime. How, for example, does one rank progress in cost reduction against the risk that such a process may embed mechanistic compliance? If the reduction of the latter is a legitimate goal, how does one ascribe value to the resulting trade-off? In addition, benchmarking against international practice is problematic. Given the small number of comparable agencies, differing statutory objectives, and the indirect nature of regulatory goals, benchmarking against international best practice is exceptionally problematic.

Properly designed and explicitly linked to public articulation of strategy, however, key performance indicators can resolve disparities in the form and substance of market oversight. Periodic weeding of the regulatory code, associated guidance notes, and practice imperatives can—and should—ameliorate unnecessary duplication and provide for a more certain legal framework. Greater consultation over the cost implications of compliance can—and should—improve both the framing and implementation of regulation. Clearer internal governance and

---

Scorecard" (Speech delivered at Toronto Centre for Leadership in Financial Supervision, 8–14 July 2007).

[8] See B. Hutter and C. Jones, "From Government to Governance: External Influences on Business Risk Management," (2007) 1 *Regulation & Governance* 27.

accountability structures can—and should—place the exercise of regulatory discretion within accepted parameters. Adaptive and responsive design can—and should—minimize the risk of choosing indicators designed for administrative convenience. Finally, reconstituting regulatory "purpose" can reduce inconsistencies in approach and provide a clearer conceptual foundation. It is important in this regard to articulate what constitutes good performance and differentiate it from what does not. As the twentieth century's most celebrated mathematician recognized, "not everything that counts can be counted, and not everything that can be counted counts."[9]

The policy problem is that perception of what constitutes value differs among institutional actors in the regulatory matrix. Moreover, market participants may agree on key normative imperatives but differ profoundly on what constitutes a breach of those stated values.[10] Relative ranking of value and values inevitably impact on the design and authority of deployed indicators and indeed the approach that the overarching regime takes to risk management. In this regard, it is unhelpful simply to advocate calibrating the regime towards a principles-based approach. Rules, after all, are merely the clarification of principles. Corporate advisory firms, for example, have long adopted a range of "perfectly-legal" strategies to transact around both rules and underlying principles governing compliance obligations, including justified—if not necessarily ethically justifiable—deviance from internally devised and policed codes of conduct.

This is not to suggest that corporate practice is inherently ethically challenged; rather, law and legal obligation are inherently indeterminate. The interaction of these core conflicts raises a fundamental but often neglected question of regulatory design. What is the purpose of regulation? The appropriate first order question is not how to regulate but why. If new rules, principles or standards are to be introduced—each altering the appropriate mix of regulatory strategies—what should the benchmark be? Who should set it and on what basis? When core values conflict, which approach or approaches should be preferred and why? Should interpretation of (non)compliance and censure rest with the corporation itself, the market, the regulator or wider

---

[9] The quotation was appended to a sign outside Albert Einstein's office at Princeton University.

[10] T. Prosser, "Regulation and Social Solidarity," (2006) 33 *Journal of Law and Society* 364.

society (through legislative reinterpretation of the core responsibilities owed by the corporation)? Can this be done in a piecemeal manner? Ultimate resolution of these issues requires articulation of a common standard of what constitutes responsibility and concomitant clarification of requisite accountability structures. This is not to suggest that the normative value of the key performance indicator is irredeemably lost in translation. It does mean, however, that regulatory agencies must be cognizant of how the chosen indicators affect both the costs and integrity of supervision. Ultimately, performance needs to be measured against the goals, not just the processes of regulation. This is crucial and cannot be achieved without recognizing the impact of the specific socio-economic, legal, and political environment in which the agency is nested.

II   REGULATING THE AUSTRALIAN CAPITAL MARKET

The capital markets in Australia are regulated through a "twin peaks" model of oversight, established in conjunction with a wide-ranging Corporate Law Economic Reform Program. Within this framework, the Australian Prudential Regulation Authority has responsibility for ensuring capital adequacy, banking and insurance regulation, and the superannuation industry. Market integrity issues, including continuous disclosure, regulation of director conduct and fiduciary obligations imposed on intermediating professions fall within the ambit of the Australian Securities and Investments Commission.[11] The peak regulatory agencies interact with Treasury and specialist organizations, including the Reserve Bank of Australia (on macro-economic stability and payments system matters), the Australian Taxation Office (on the impact of financial engineering on corporate revenue), the Australian

---

[11] The objects (or mission) of ASIC are set out in the primary legislation constituting the regulator, *Australian Securities and Investments Commission Act 2001* (Cth). Under section 1 "(2), ASIC must strive to (a) maintain, facilitate and improve the performance of the financial system and the entities within that system in the interests of commercial certainty, reducing business costs, and the efficiency and development of the economy; and (b) promote the confident and informed participation of investors and consumers in the financial system; and (d) administer the laws that confer functions and powers on it effectively and with a minimum of procedural requirements; and (e) receive, process and store, efficiently and quickly, the information given to ASIC under the laws that confer functions and powers on it; and (f) ensure that information is available as soon as practicable for access by the public; and (g) take whatever action it can take, and is necessary, order to enforce and give effect to the laws of the Commonwealth that confer functions and powers on it."

Consumer and Competition Commission (on trade practices), and the Takeovers Panel (as the primary adjudicator of contractual disputes during corporate mergers and acquisitions).

This hybrid architecture contrasts with the unitary approach to market governance adopted by the United Kingdom's Financial Services Authority. In contrast to the multiplicity of organizational forms given authority in the United States,[12] the formal separation of prudential and disclosure regulation is conceptually neat and intellectually cogent. The separation allows for the simultaneous adoption of both coercive and of less intrusive forms of market surveillance within an integrated framework.[13] Unlike its major counterparts in London and Washington, ASIC does not have the capacity to set rules.[14] Independence is further circumscribed by specific policy guidelines, which are framed within a legislative requirement that explicitly requires the reduction of transactional costs.[15]

All major policy revisions require an accompanying Regulatory Impact Statement (RIS). Following standard public policy formulations, the RIS defines the problem, sets out objectives, delineates options, evaluates cost and benefit, includes a consultation and recommendation statement, and outlines the strategy for implementation. Despite these restrictions, an independent taskforce charged with evaluating effectiveness has identified signs of "regulatory creep" across the institutional framework. According to its final report, "risk aversion" imperatives were particularly present in the financial sector.[16] The taskforce ruminated that enforcement strategies were in part to blame,

---

[12] The Securities and Exchange Commission has oversight for the capital markets, but regulation of banks fall to the Federal Reserve and the Office of the Comptroller of the Currency. In addition, state regulators have formal delegated authority and State Attorney Generals have emerged as increasingly important autonomous actors.

[13] The formal separation has not been trouble-free. An independent commission found gaping holes in the regulatory apparatus (HIH Royal Commission, 2003, 24.1.6–24.1.12).

[14] While discretion is limited to interpretation of legislative intent, this is a substantial power.

[15] *Australian Securities and Investments Commission Act 2001* (Cth) s 1 (2) (a).

[16] *Rethinking Regulation (2006) Report of the Taskforce on Reducing the Regulatory Burden on Business* (Canberra: Commonwealth of Australia) 14–15. This apocalyptic vision stands in contrast to cross-country comparisons, which suggest that Australia has one of the least burdensome regulatory regimes. The *Heritage/Wall Street Journal Index of Economic Freedom* (2007) ranks Australia the third freest (after Hong Kong and Singapore). The OECD also commended Australia are having the least regulated product markets and a system of oversight that minimized impact on economic decision making.

thus having a detrimental impact on the "overall efficiency and dynamism of the economy."[17]

This conception of regulatory purpose privileges a minimalist *ex post* approach to intervention, with a focus only on cases in which there has been a demonstrable "market failure." This is further underscored by the emphasis on direct costs rather than social value associated with regulatory action. This approach pervades Australian regulatory practice and political discourse. There are, of course, strong benefits associated with this approach, not least of which is the curtailing of regulatory adventurism. But setting the overarching objective as the reduction of business costs generates opportunity for a range of participants to dispute and block various regulatory initiatives. What remains unclear, therefore, is how the regulator should mediate potential conflict between market promotion and market integrity. Moreover, how does the agency generate sufficient political consensus to support both its preferred resolution and the measurements used to determine success?

The focus on business integrity within ASIC's strategic review presents a profound challenge to the agency, market participants, and indeed the conceptual foundation of the wider Australian regulatory regime. Integrity represents a much more finely grained concept than can be encompassed within a legal definition. Securing general agreement on its definition and application in the business context reduces the space and justification for contestation. Benchmarking the absolute and relative performance of each component of the regulatory matrix against these more exacting standards strengthens the interaction between legal and non-legal norms. Furthermore, it provides legitimacy and authority for the agency's use of enforcement mechanisms against those whose actions threaten public confidence in how well professional and informal associational norms work. How to achieve this goal is examined further below.

III   ADDING SUBSTANCE TO NEGOTIATED REGULATION

As noted above, the transformative exercise begun by the Australian Securities and Investments Commission has the potential to profoundly change the regulation of the Australian capital markets. The changed focus was formally articulated in a presentation to the Senate Standing Committee on Economics in May 2007 at which the new chairman

---

[17] *Rethinking Regulation*, above n 16, 90.

unveiled five priorities. These commit ASIC to focus on outcomes with performance measured against stakeholder feedback; to develop initiatives to help retail investors manage and protect wealth through enhanced disclosure and better surveillance; to introduce new investigative and other techniques to reduce insider trading and market manipulation; to reduce red-tape in delivery of administrative function; to facilitate inward and outward investment in capital markets with minimum roadblocks to investment flows, commensurate with adequate protection. The ordering is instructive.

Conscious of the need to counter negative perception, linked to his career trajectory as a corporate lawyer and former chief executive of the Australian bourse, the new chairman has not foreclosed the (threatened) deployment of enforcement. Indeed, he endorses its use to the fullest possible extent in cases involving insider trading or market manipulation. The increased focus on investigative techniques is designed to alert potential participants in insider trading schemes that there is an increased risk of detection. Just as significantly, the priorities also indicate that the use of enforcement needs to be integrated more closely with wider "whole of agency" objectives. This represents a profound cultural and organizational shift for the agency.

Enforcement action, or its threatened use, is to be contemplated only "where it can make a positive impact to lift business integrity." This narrows significantly the definition of what constitutes "regulatory impact." Moreover, it also suggests that previous ambiguity marred effectiveness. According to an internal briefing, the operational definition as presently understood with the agency and communicated to the market by its actions "seems to be too vague—it gives enforcement enormous discretion to decide whether to do something or not."[18] The potential for dysfunction is exacerbated by what are signaled to be sub-optimal organizational dynamics. "Where other directorates [within ASIC] are involved, they are the client and, as such, they should be the decision-makers with the assistance of enforcement. That is not always the case at the moment where enforcement have (sic) the final decision on whether to take something on."[19]

The need for this change in direction was underscored by the Federal Court's judgment in the Citigroup insider trading and conflicts management case, handed down four weeks later. At its heart were what,

[18] Internal ASIC Communication, 4 May 2007.
[19] Internal ASIC Communication.

on the facts pleaded, were unfounded allegations of a lack of business integrity. The regulator claimed that Citigroup had engaged in unconscionable conduct by trading on its own account while performing corporate advisory services for Toll Holdings in its—eventually successful—bid for Patrick Corporation. Justice Jacobson ruled that insider trading did not take place and that the "law does not prevent an investment bank from contracting out of or modifying any fiduciary obligation."[20] The judge opined that the imposition of fiduciary responsibilities was "a matter for the legislature, not the courts."[21] Judicial resolution does not solve the underlying problems identified in the litigation. Indeed, it is arguably the case that the range and intractability of potential conflicts have deepened.

The dynamics of financial capitalism reconfigure, in profound manner, institutional timeframes, conceptions of corporate duty, the efficacy of the shareholder-dominated corporate governance paradigm, and throw into stark relief the roles and responsibilities of financial intermediaries. What the Citigroup case also demonstrated, however, is how blunt and ineffective the enforcement instrument can be in dealing with this complex reality. The relief sought by ASIC on the conflicts case could arguably have been better secured by less intrusive means. The address to Senate and internal briefings to staff explicitly tie enforcement strategies to outcomes. They implicitly suggest that the pursuit of a high-profile defendant through the courts, no matter how well-intentioned, to clarify an underlying principle is not necessarily the most appropriate mechanism to secure general understanding of how that principle should be applied in daily business practice. Thus while enforcement is not precluded, it has to pass a more stringent cost-benefit analytic.

Any credible assessment of control mechanisms requires that attention be paid to the critical interaction between how a regulatory agency gathers information; its degree of emphasis on the setting of minimum standards and its propensity or reluctance to advance strategies based on modifying behavior.[22] The strategic priorities announced by ASIC make clear that its objectives are to be understood within the context of improving market integrity. Interviews with senior ASIC staff suggest that this broader normative goal can only be achieved if an

---

[20] NSD 651 (28 June 2006) [601].

[21] Ibid [602].

[22] See Hood, Rothstein and Baldwin, above n 2, 180.

alignment of interests can be effected between the agency and market participants. The strategic review provides a roadmap to a more informed, less polarized regulatory environment. The first stage in this process has begun with the commissioning of an independently administered climate survey. The survey is designed to set a benchmark from which to measure subsequent progress, or lack thereof. This is to be welcomed. However, a survey, in itself, is insufficient.

Proactive communication strategies are required to disseminate much more widely regulatory aims and objectives. This needs to be accompanied by the creation of specific working groups to tease out the implications from the aggregated data. Consultation and engagement in national and international forums serve a dual function. First, they provide invaluable intelligence about latent and emergent problems. Second, this proactive approach acts as a transmission belt for dissemination of regulatory values. In this regard, it is useful to conceptualize the relationship as a constitutive stakeholder dialogue. Regular reports give both structure and depth to the consultation process.[23] This is, of course, not without risk, particularly when accountability for maintenance of market probity requires ongoing credible commitments from those given responsibility for delegated oversight within "de-centered" processes of self-regulation and co-regulation. However, as will be explored in the following section, these risks can be offset through the leveraging power of reputation.

It is axiomatic that when a complex trading model disintegrates, the calls for action inevitably target the regulator. ASIC has been particularly vulnerable following three high profile property collapses: Fincorp, Westpoint, and Australian Capital Reserve. In each case, investors loaned money to the investment vehicle in return for a debenture (or promissory note), periodic but higher interest repayments than provided in the mainstream banking sector and a return on initial capital at the end of the term. The market in unrated, unlisted bonds accounts for AUS$8 billion and involves 92 vehicles. ASIC has been careful to note that risk-levels vary considerably within this grouping. Its decision to publish the full list of providers in a consultation paper adds significantly to the demonstration power of reputation. As such investment vehicles seek to retain or grow market share, they are much more likely to provide the enhanced disclosure. These include

---

[23] See M. Kaptein and R. van Tulder, "Towards Effective Stakeholder Dialogue," (2003) 108 *Business and Strategy Review* 203.

benchmarked articulation of risk-benefit across credit rating, equity capital, liquidity, lending principles, portfolio diversification, valuation of stock, related party transactions and rollovers, and early redemption possibilities and penalties. There is a risk that enhanced levels of disclosure can obfuscate as well as illuminate, making the sector potentially more resistant to transparency. To counter this possibility, ASIC has suggested that attention must also be placed on, and accountability demanded from, those providing corporate advisory services and the creation and dissemination of technically legal but misleading advertising. These include not just trustees and auditors but also copywriters, production teams, publishers, and broadcasters who sell the print, audio-visual and online space.

On one reading, this could be construed as a further example of regulatory creep. On the other, it is recognition that the regulator lacks the resources to resolve the problem on its own. Rather, it requires professional groups to acknowledge their own responsibility and be accountable for their actions, meaning in this narrow sense acquiescing to external scrutiny of what codes of conduct mean in practice. None of this, however, is going to be of any use to those bewitched by the potential returns. While investment guides can and should be simplified by their very nature, these products are exceptionally complex. Investor education programs are to be encouraged, particularly when couched in terms that highlight the investors' own personal responsibilities. Behavioral change, however, needs to be inculcated at a higher level within the product market and it is for this reason alone that the consultation paper provided by ASIC is to be warmly welcomed and endorsed. Harnessing the power of greater awareness and acceptance of appropriate professional norms has enormous benefits, particularly as one seeks to address broader questions of insider trading and market manipulation.

Regulators and those providing intermediating services are repeat players, whose interests are substantially harmed by spillovers from those who flout market convention. While the introduction of advanced training and investigative techniques are to be welcomed, in the absence of a catastrophic failure, it is unrealistic to expect a regulator to understand the dynamics and, therefore, design the optimal form of compliance for any given organization. Even in such a case, it is arguable that the measures introduced may fail to deal with the substantive underlying problem. This partly accounts for the controversy over the role and function of enforceable undertakings and other innovative mechanisms to embed compliance, such as pre-trial diversion in the United States.

This is not to suggest that the corporate probation that the enforceable undertaking permits is indefensible on legal, ethical or public policy grounds, as some scholars have argued.[24] Rather, it is to argue that efficacy is likely to be improved as a result of understandings reached from a robust dialogue and that this is unlikely to occur in circumstances in which the regulator imposes solutions. It is, therefore, necessary that the design and implementation of enforceable undertakings be the product of cross-cutting internal agency taskforces which are, in turn, advised by high-level working groups that are informed (if not determined) by external compacts.

This requires a much more sustained dialogue than has been evidenced to date in Australia. The climate survey commissioned by ASIC has gone some way towards identifying the key areas of distrust and the confrontation that currently exist within the marketplace. Its longer-term effectiveness, however, is predicated on ASIC recognizing its own limitations. This does not mean ceding regulatory authority. Rather it requires that the agency establish mechanisms that build informal trust networks. This not only enhances the quality of market intelligence; it also reinforces the restraining power of articulated norms. By adopting a less intrusive approach to the construction of organizational frameworks—in return for access to the organizational blueprints, as required for wider demonstration effect—the regulator also fulfills a statutory objective to reduce regulatory burden without necessarily sacrificing effectiveness.

One of ASIC's key objectives is to reduce the administrative burden on regulated entities. While capacity to fulfill that objective is framed by legislative requirements set down in the Corporations Act, ASIC has considerable discretion to interpret both the meaning of the specific provisions and to allocate resources across intra-agency directorates. In this context, while there is considerable merit in the call to ASIC staff to be more responsive to indicators of client satisfaction, care must be taken to ensure that any reduction in informational flows does not compromise overarching surveillance capacity. This caveat aside, a reduction in administrative filing requirements can pay

---

[24] See J. Hasnas, "The Politics of Crime: Ethics and the Problems of White Collar Crime," (2007) 54 *American University Law Review* 579.

significant dividends. Not only is progress easily measurable, the wider impact is of significant value. It can help change negative perceptions of an unaccountable regulator, aloof from the compliance burden imposed by inappropriate and out-of-date legal requirements. Moreover, further administrative reform can help secure the final objective, that of facilitating inward investment.

Identifying and repositioning the precise intersection between law and ethics requires the design and implementation of an integrated set of carefully nuanced strategies. To be effective, the set must align the interests of institutional actors to the overarching regulatory "mission" or "purpose." In this regard, the motivational rationale of specific actors is irrelevant. By building on a foundation of common **stated** values, a general understanding of what constitutes acceptable practices is generated, from which deviation lowers reputational standing and access. This framework is sustained through an interlocking dissemination network comprising and reinforcing formal and informal nodes.

The resulting synthesis has three key practical and normative advantages. First, it reduces real and artificial incommensurability problems between participants in the regulatory conversation (irrespective of whether or not they have been accorded formal surveillance authority). Second, it reduces the retreat to legal formalism, de-escalates confrontation and contributes to behavioral modification across the regulatory matrix. Third, by clarifying accountability responsibilities, it offers greater certainty for corporations and the markets in which they operate, thus facilitating investment flows. It provides a more meaningful baseline from which to measure and evaluate subsequent regulatory performance.

As with the social and political systems in which they are nested, financial centers depend on integrity. Disclosure, transparency and accountability mean little if the polity understands these in formal mechanistic fashion, rather than as socially appropriate modes of behavior. The problems now apparent in the global securitization market demonstrate the consequences of such an approach to governance. The credit freeze symbolizes a profound climate change in global markets. The impact of all of this on the real economy is profound. Embedding restraint has become a policy priority for the entire regulatory community, not just in the United States but in every major securities market. The problem cannot be resolved by recourse to legal means. Securitization is, after all, perfectly legal. What is also clear, however, is that the exponential growth was facilitated by the conceptual and practical bifurcation of capability and opportunity from accountability and responsibility. The securitization crisis offers an opportunity for a realignment, which can only be achieved by strengthening informal nodes of control. The opportunity exists now for reinvigorated conversation about the purpose of regulation, articulation of common goals, and alignment of interests. The strategy offered by ASIC offers an opportunity for Australia to take the lead in this process. It is in its own interests, the interests of domestic participants, and the interests of wider markets that the opportunity is grasped.

Conclusion

The art of street hustling is a dynamic if deeply disconcerting business on Union Square in central San Francisco. It is a burgeoning industry. The homeless, the mentally ill and the drug addicts compete outside high end galleries and empty department stores with gaily dressed college students. The outsized garishly painted papier-mâché costumes worn by the students provide a veil of anonymity for an act of humiliation. The shame matters less to the more seasoned practitioners, much to the consternation of the neophyte outsiders. Walk just three blocks east from the theatre district and the contrast between rich and poor becomes much starker and bleaker. An ambitious and now stalled attempt at gentrification, the South of Market District (SOMA) sees five star hotels and luxury condominiums nestled next to pockets of urban decay. The district is a microcosm of much broader social currents as the country comes to terms with rising unemployment and worsening rates of foreclosure. The social safety net, already of dubious utility in the United States has become threadbare. The failing economy has forced stringent budgetary cuts, particularly here in California, which is facing a fiscal crisis. While the Obama administration talks increasingly of evidence of green shoots of recovery, the plight of the multitudinous homeless and dispossessed in San Francisco, one the country's most sophisticated and tolerant cities, reflects the true human cost of the global financial crisis.

Policymakers at the stunning new headquarters of the Federal Reverse Bank of San Francisco, which towers over SOMA, have a birds-eye view of an increasingly desperate cityscape. Whether the policy options contemplated will ameliorate the problems remains an open question. As with the architecture of SOMA, innovation, renewal and stagnation conflict and conflate. This is most apparent in the thorny issue of how to wean the banking sector off its addiction to irresponsible and unsustainable lending and trading practices. Treatment options were clarified with the release on 7 May 2009 of stress tests conducted by the

Federal Reserve in conjunction with the Department of Treasury into 19 of the most important banks. Not surprisingly, given the extensive media management that preceded publication, prognosis was favorable.

As widely reported, the Charlotte-based Bank of America is the most exposed. The bank is required to enhance capital reserves by $34 billion. Citigroup, by contrast, one of the weakest major banks, requires only $5.5 billion. The former investment banks, Morgan Stanley and Goldman Sachs, have fared much better. Morgan Stanley has been cautioned to raise just $1.5 billion. Goldman is regarded as adequately capitalized as is JP Morgan Chase, which has managed the integration of Bear Stearns much more successfully than the hapless management at Bank of America, where empire building led to the disastrous acquisition of Merrill Lynch and Countrywide at the peak of the crisis. Remarkably, this exercise in regulatory oversight did not identify the need to change senior management. Indeed, the overall picture presented was of relative strength not weakness. In total only $75 billion was deemed necessary to insulate the banking sector. For Timothy Geithner, the US Treasury Secretary, investors should now be reassured that all losses were accounted for and that entrenched management was credible. 'With the clarity today's announcement will bring, we hope banks are going to get back to the business of lending,' he said in a news conference. The suggestion overstates the case.

The content and conduct of the tests and the way in which the results were disseminated leave huge questions about the ultimate purpose and who will stand to gain most of all from this exercise in managing expectations. There are a number of profound methodological flaws. The tests used worst-case scenario baselines that have already been proved optimistic. More problematically, the banks were able to negotiate privately with the Government over how the latter interpreted the results. None of this gives confidence in the veracity of claims that the banking sector, as a whole, is adequately capitalized or would remain so if explicit and implicit guarantees were removed. What is clear, however, is that a process of differentiation has begun, which is likely to intensify in coming months.

The perceived stronger banks will seek to extricate themselves from congressionally imposed remuneration caps and trading restrictions. JP Morgan Chase and Goldman Sachs have already sought to repay mandatory loans advanced under the Troubled Asset Relief Program (TARP). Weaker banks will now have to raise new sources of capital from markets in which the true state of individual bank counter-party risk remains hideously opaque. The total recapitalization of $75 billion may persuade some investors to plunge back into the financial sector. Already there is evidence that this is working with successful capital raising conducted by some of the leading banks. Moreover, the vote of confidence spurred a short-term rally in financial stocks around the world that was particularly pronounced in the United States. There are a number of reasons for caution. Weaker entities face unpalatable options. They can off-load prize assets at bargain-basement prices or convert government stakes, which take the form of preferred stock, into common equity. This raises a profoundly difficult policy option that the Treasury is, for now, evading.

Preferred stock provides the Government with the privileges of repayment over holders of common equity. It also attracts a guaranteed interest premium and a lower risk profile. Common equity, on the other hand, forces the Government to articulate a vision of how it will exercise its ownership rights and for what purpose. For the moment, economic policymakers appear to favor creative ambiguity. This involves the creation of the Mandatory Convertible Preferred Share. The MCPS is designed for conversion into common equity only when required. Crucially, it does not dilute further existing shareholders. It also delays the need for an articulation of what kind of banking sector the federal government would like to see established. This has clear short-term benefits. First, it staves off the immediate need for partial or total nationalization, a policy option that is anathema to leading economic advisors, including Timothy Geithner himself. Second, it quells, partially, investor fear of expropriation just as the Government suggested a pragmatic revoking of decades of precedent in bankruptcy law. Its controversial support for the Chrysler re-organization sees the UAW trades union retirement fund privileged over bondholders, who were pressured to accept a payment of just 30 cents in the dollar.

Crucially the plan gained the support of major banks. Many had a vested interest in not being seen to contradict the government. It was not a good idea to alienate the body that is to decide your viability just days before adjudication. Bondholders outside this US version of a tarnished golden circle rejected the deal on the grounds that liquidation would generate a fairer outcome. President Obama dismissed their understandable concerns as the greed of speculators who failed to put America first. The Obama administration is playing a very dangerous game here. Any suggestion that the banks acted under duress or colluded in the Chrysler deal for political not corporate motives raises the potential for class actions. The discovery process alone could prove exceptionally embarrassing for an administration that prides itself on the need to inculcate a new ethics of responsibility. Already the Treasury and Federal Reserve stand accused of attempting to coerce Bank of America into its ill-starred acquisition of Merrill Lynch. The Obama administration clearly thrives on its can do attitude. This approach to politics was memorably captured by the White House Chief of Staff, who famously declared before the inauguration that it was essential never to waste a crisis. Such strategies risk tarnishing the administration with the oxidization of Chicago-style politics, a messy and morally bankrupt brand of compromise inconsistent with the mantra that we can and should expect change we can believe in. The potential saving of a single American institution, even one as storied as Chrysler, is an enormous price to pay if it reduces capacity to engineer broader change in the operation of the banking sector.

There can be no doubt that the presentation of policy has improved significantly since the debacle that accompanied the announcement of what was billed, rather grandiloquently, a comprehensive plan for economic reform in February. The lack of detail undermined already weak confidence. A reformulated plan to kick-start lending by offloading "legacy assets" to public-private partnerships in which the downside risk was disproportionately held by the taxpayer proved more palatable to the market than an increasingly irate populace. Despite the remarkably generous terms the program remained stalled. This can be traced to the failure until now to resolve two intractable issues. First, the banks were not prepared to relinquish "legacy assets" at prices the markets are prepared to offer. Note here the subtle but deliberate change in terminology. The lexicological illusion is to transform what remain exceptionally suspect financial products of questionable value into something of intrinsic value. Alchemy, it appears, is not confined to the securitization process itself. Second, the stated policy position that no major bank would be allowed to fail reduced the pressure to disinvest. Washington, scared and scarred by the Lehman debacle, was mindful of the unintended consequences of addressing questions of moral hazard, if only from an economic perspective.

The release of the stress tests only partially changes this dynamic. At the same time, dismissing bondholders as amoral speculators risks undermining the stated policy goal of engaging in public-private partnerships. Creative ambiguity may well be an effective short-term strategy but unless the entire enterprise is underpinned by a practical, ethical framework the opportunity to transform in a fundamental manner the operation of the capital markets will be lost. While much has been made of plans to regulate the over the counter derivatives market and impose more stringent caps on executive pay, neither initiative offers fundamental change. The first will provide more transparency but does not necessarily deliver on more effective risk management. Securitization was and remains perfectly legal. Used in moderation and as part of a integrated investment strategy geared toward the long-term, the mechanism does have value. The problem is not the products but the way in which they were deployed. A marketplace in which ideological considerations trump security may be acceptable to private actors, but when such views are promoted with abandon by the political establishment, on both the left and the right, the social risks are magnified. We are all paying the price for that miscalculation. Suggesting that the marketplace is somehow cleansed and chastened by the experience is naïve. There is simply no evidence of the Pauline conversion that the Obama administration is suggesting has occurred. The second focus on executive remuneration, while laudable, derives from imperatives imposed by Congress rather than the White House, which had initially argued that such policies were too invasive. What makes matters even more problematic is the conditions to allow banks to exit Congressional oversight are remarkably lax.

Securing partial Wall Street approval for industrial policy, which may yet be deemed unacceptable by the bankruptcy courts, could allow the banks to get away with what, in financial and moral terms amounts to the crime of the century. Sadly, the stage is now set for one of the largest transfers of wealth in US banking history. Those with the highest rating, including Goldman Sachs, Morgan Stanley and JP Morgan Chase are best placed to take advantage. This occurs precisely because differentiation flatters disproportionately. Far from controlling Wall Street, the Government's policy is likely to increase its capacity at precisely the same time as the economic crisis hits Main Street with increasing force. The unfortunate reality is that corporate beggars have a lot to teach the individual ones forced to inhabit the streets of San Francisco and beyond and who are likely to do so for some time to come.

Bibliography

ARTICLES AND CONTRIBUTIONS TO BOOKS

Allen, M. and J. Caruana. "Sovereign Wealth Funds: A Work Agenda." International Monetary Fund, Washington, DC, 29 February 2008.

Aviram, A. "Counter-Cyclical Enforcement of Corporate Law." 25 *Yale Journal on Regulation* (2008): 1.

Baker, J. "Reforming Corporations Through Threats of Federal Prosecution." 89 *Cornell Law Review* (2004): 310.

Bottomley, S. "From Contractualism to Constitutionalism: A Framework for Corporate Governance." 19 *Sydney Law Review* (1997): 277.

Bovens, M. "Two Concepts of Accountability." Paper presented at the Kettering Foundation, Dayton, Ohio, 23 May 2008.

Braithwaite, J. and V. Braithwaite. "Democratic Sentiment and Cyclical Markets in Vice." 46 *British Journal of Criminology* (2006): 1110.

Bryde, D. "Methods for Managing Different Perspectives of Project Success." 16 *British Journal of Management* (2005): 119.

Chesterman, S. "The Turn To Ethics: Disinvestment From Multinational Corporations For Human Rights Violations: The Case of Norway's Sovereign Wealth Fund." 23 *American University International Law Review* (2008): 577.

Christie, C. and R. Hanna. "A Push Down the Road of Good Corporate Citizenship: The Deferred Prosecution Agreement Between the US Attorney for the District of New Jersey and Bristol-Meyers Squibb Co." 43 *American Criminal Law Review* (2006): 1043.

Cioffi, J. "Corporate Governance Reform, Regulatory Politics and the Foundations of Finance Capitalism in the United States and Germany." 7 *German Law Review* (2006): 533.

---. "Revenge of the Law: Securities Litigation Reform and Sarbanes-Oxley's Structural Regulation of Corporate Governance." In *Creating Competitive Markets: The Politics and Economics of Regulatory Reform* eds. M. Landy, M. Levin, and M. Shapiro, p. 60. Washington, DC: Brookings Institution Press, 2007.

Corporate Crime Reporter. "Crime Without Conviction: The Rise of Deferred and Non-Prosecution Agreements." *Corporate Crime Reporter* 28 December 2005.

---. "Interview with Mary Jo White." 19 *Corporate Crime Reporter*, 48 12 December 2005.

Dell'Ariccia, G, D. Igan and L. Laeven. "Credit Booms and Lending Standards: Evidence from the Sub-Prime Mortgage Market." Washington, DC: International Monetary Fund, 2008.

Drysdale, P. and C. Findlay. "Chinese Foreign Direct Investment in Australia: Policy Issues for the Resource Sector." Paper delivered at East Asia Forum, Australian National University, Canberra, 4 September 2008.

Dubnick, M. "Sarbanes-Oxley and the Search for Accountable Corporate Governance." In *Private Equity, Corporate Governance and the Dynamics of Capital Market Governance*, ed. J O'Brien, pp. 284–88. London: Imperial College Press, 2007.

Easterbrook, F. and D. Dischel. "The Corporate Contract." 89 *Columbia Law Review* (1989): 1416.

Gilson, R. and C. Milhaupt. "Sovereign Wealth Funds and Corporate Governance: A Minimalist Response to the New Mercantilism" available at http://ssrn.com/abstract=1095023 at 27 January 2009.

Golding, G. and R. Bassil. "Australian Regulation of Investments by Sovereign Wealth Funds and State Owned Enterprises." Paper delivered at Sovereign Wealth Funds in an Evolving Global Financial System Conference, Lowy Institute, Sydney, 25 September 2008) 7.

Goldthau, A. "Resurgent Russia: Russian Energy Inc." (2008) available at: http://ssrn.com/abstract=1137616.

Gorton, G. "The Sub-Prime Panic." 15 (1) *European Financial Management* (2009): 10.

Greenblum, B. "What Happens to a Prosecution Deferred? Judicial Oversight of Corporate Deferred Prosecution Agreements." 105 *Columbia Law Review* (2005): 1863.

Hanrahan, P. "ASIC v Citigroup: Investment Banks, Conflicts of Interest, and Chinese Wall." In *Private Equity, Corporate Governance and the Dynamics of Capital Market Governance*, ed. J. O'Brien pp. 117. London: Imperial College Press, 2007.

Hasnas, J. "The Politics of Crime: Ethics and the Problems of White Collar Crime." 54 *American University Law Review* (2007): 579.

Hill, J. "Evolving Rules of the Game." In *Private Equity, Corporate Governance and the Dynamics of Capital Market Governance*, ed. J. O'Brien p. 29. London: Imperial College Press, 2007.

Hutter, B. and C. Jones. "From Government to Governance: External Influences on Business Risk Management." 1 *Regulation & Governance* (2007): 27.

Ireland, P. "The Myth of Shareholder Ownership." 62 *Modern Law Review* (1999): 32.

Johnson, S. "The Rise of Sovereign Wealth Funds." *Finance and Development* (2007): 1.

Kagan, R. "Understanding Regulatory Enforcement." 11 *Law & Policy* (1989): 89.

Kaptein, M. and R. van Tulder. "Towards Effective Stakeholder Dialogue." 108 *Business and Strategy Review* (2003): 203.

Langevoort, D. "The Social Construction of Sarbanes Oxley." 107 *Michigan Law Review* (2007): 1817.

Laufer, W. "Corporate Prosecution, Cooperation, and the Trading of Favors." 87 *Iowa Law Review* (2002): 643.

Le Borgne, E. and P. Medas. "Sovereign Wealth Funds in the Pacific Island Countries: Macro-Fiscal Linkages" International Monetary Fund, Washington, DC, WP/07/297, December 2007.

Lerner, J. and A. Schoar. "Does Legal Enforcement Affect Financial Transactions? The Contractual Channel in Private Equity" 120 *Quarterly Journal of Economics* (2005): 223.

Levi, M. "Suite Revenge? The Shaping of Folk Devils and Moral Panics about White Collar Crimes." 49 *British Journal of Criminology* (2009): 48.

Lopez, J. "Disclosure as a Supervisory Tool." 22 *Federal Reserve Bank of San Francisco Economic Letter* (2003): 1.

Lubman, S. "The Dragon as Demon: Images of China on Capitol Hill." 13 *Journal of Contemporary China* (2004): 541.

MacNeil, I. "Enforcement of Capital Markets Regulation: The United Kingdom and Its International Markets." In *Private Equity, Corporate Governance and the Dynamics of Capital Market Regulation*, ed. J. O'Brien, pp. 143. London: Imperial College Press, (2007).

Marinetto, M. "Governing Beyond the Centre: Critique of the Anglo-Governance School." 51 *Political Studies* (2003): 592.

Mason, E. "The Apologetics of Managerialism." 31 *Journal of Business* (1958): 1.

May, P. "Regulatory Regimes and Accountability." 1 *Regulation & Governance* (2007): 8.

McNulty, P. "Memorandum on Principles of Business Organizations to the Heads of Department Components, US Attorneys." Department of Justice, Washington, DC, 12 December 2006.

Moohr, G. S. "Prosecutorial Power in an Adversarial System: Lessons from Current White Collar Cases." 8 *Buffalo Criminal Law Review* (2004): 165.

O'Brien, J. "Charting an Icarian Flightpath: The Implications of the Qantas Deal Collapse." In *Private Equity, Corporate Governance and the Dynamics of Capital Market Regulation*, ed. J. O'Brien, p, 295. London: Imperial College Press, 2007.

Orts, E. "The Complexity and Legitimacy of Corporate Law." 50 *Washington and Lee Law Review* (1993): 1565.

Parkinson, J. "Legitimacy Problems in Deliberative Democracy." 51 *Political Studies* (2003): 180.

Pitt, H. "Bringing Financial Services Regulation into the Twenty-First Century." 25 *Yale Journal on Regulation* (2008): 315.

Pound, J. 'The Promise of the Governed Corporation' in *Harvard Business Review on Corporate Governance* (2000): 89.

Prosser, T. "Regulation and Social Solidarity." 33 *Journal of Law and Society* (2006): 364.

Quinn, D. and T. Jones. "An Agent Morality View of Business Policy." 20 *Academy of Management Review* (1995): 22

Romano, R. "The Sarbanes-Oxley Act and the Making of Quack Corporate Governance." 114 *Yale Law Journal* (2005): 1521.

Romsek, B. and M. Dubnick. "Accountability in the Public Sector: Lessons from the Challenger Tragedy." 47 *Public Administration Review* (1987): 227.

Schwartz, S. "The Alchemy of Securitization." 1 *Stanford Journal of Law, Business and Finance* (1994): 133.

Stiglitz, J. "Principles of Financial Regulation: A Dynamic Portfolio Approach." 16 (1) *World Bank Research Observer* (2001): 1.

Stone, C. "Corporate Vices and Corporate Virtues: Do Public/Private Distinctions Matter?" 130 *University of Pennsylvania Law Review* (1981): 1441.

Strine, L. "Towards Common Sense and Common Ground: Reflections on the Shared Interests of Managers and Labor in a More Rational System of Corporate Governance." 33 *Journal of Corporation Law* (2007): 1.

Strine, L. and W. Chandler. "The New Federalism of the American Corporate Governance System: Preliminary Reflections of Two Residents of One Small State." 152 *University of Pennsylvania Law Review* (2003): 953.

Thompson, L. "Principles for Prosecution of Business Organizations." Department of Justice, Washington, DC, 20 January 2003.

Tsoukas, H. "The Tyranny of Light: The Temptations and Paradoxes of the Information Society." 29 *Futures* (1997): 827.

Useem, M. "Lessons From Davos, One of Globalization's Best Classrooms." *Knowledge@Wharton*, 6 February 2008, available at: http://knowledge.wharton.upenn.edu/article.cfm?articleid=1893 (14 February 2009).

Warin, F. and A. Boutros. "Deferred Prosecution Agreements: A View From the Trenches and a Proposal for Reform." 93 *Virginia Law Review* (2007): 107.

Wray, C. and R. Hur. "Corporate Criminal Prosecution in a Post-Enron World." 43 *American Criminal Law Review* (2006): 95.

Williamson, O. "Corporate Boards of Directors: In Principle and In Practice." 24 *Journal of Law, Economics, & Organization* (2008): 247.

BOOKS

Berenson, A. *The Number: How the Drive for Quarterly Earnings Corrupted Wall Street and Corporate America.* New York: Random House, 2003.

Bitner, R. *Confessions of a Sub-Prime Lender.* Hoboken, NJ: John Wiley and Sons, 2008.

Bottomley, S. *The Constitutional Corporation, Rethinking Corporate Governance.* Aldershot: Ashgate Publishing, 2007.

Calomiris, C. W. *US Bank Deregulation in Historical Perspective.* Cambridge, MA: Cambridge University Press, 2006.

Coffee, J. C. Jnr. *Gatekeepers, The Professions and Corporate Governance.* Oxford: Oxford University Press, 2006.

Cohen, S. *Understanding Environmental Policy.* New York: Columbia University Press, 2006.

Cohen, S. and W. Eimicke. *The Effective Public Manager.* San Francisco: Josey Bass, 2002

Collins, H. *Regulating Contracts.* Oxford: Oxford University Press, 1999.

Cunningham, N. and P. Grabosky. *Smart Regulation: Designing Environmental Policy* New York: Oxford University Press, 1998.

Easterbrook, F. and D. Fischel, *The Economic Structure of Corporate Law.* Cambridge Mass: Harvard University Press, 1991.

Edelman, M. *The Symbolic Uses of Politics.* Illinois: University of Illinois Press, 1964.

Fraser, S. *Wall Street, A Cultural History.* London: Faber and Faber, 2007.

Fukuyama, F. *The End of History and the Last Man.* London: Penguin Books, 1992.

Galbraith, J. K. *The Affluent Society.* New York: Houghton Mifflin, 1998.

---. *The Economics of Innocent Fraud.* New York: Houghton Mifflin Co., 2004.

---. *The Great Crash.* London: Penguin Business, 1954, 1975 edition.

Galbraith, J. K. (Jnr). *The Predator State*. New York: Free Press, 2008.

Geisst, C. *Wall Street: A History*. Oxford: Oxford University Press, 1999.

Gourevitch, P. A. and J. Shinn. *Political Power and Corporate Control: The New Global Politics of Corporate Governance*. Princeton N.J: Princeton University Press, 2005.

Graham, E. and D. Marchick. *US National Security and Foreign Direct Investment*. Washington, DC: Institute for International Economics, 2006.

Green, S. *Lying, Cheating and Stealing: A Moral Theory of White Collar Crime*. Oxford: Oxford University Press, 2006.

Hessen, R. *In Defense of the Corporation*. Washington, DC: Hoover Institution, 1979.

Hood, C., H. Rothstein, and R. Baldwin. *The Government of Risk*. Oxford: Oxford University Press, 2004.

Kagan, R. *The Return of History and the End of Dreams*. New York: Random House, 2008.

Kendall, L. and M. Freeman. *A Primer on Securitization*. Cambridge, MA: MIT Press, 1996.

Kraakman, R., P. Davies, H. Hansmann, and G. Hertig, *The Anatomy of Corporate Law: A Comparative and Functional Approach*. New York: Oxford University Press, (2004).

Kuttner, R. *The Squandering of America: How the Failure of Our Politics is Squandering Our Prosperity*. New York: Vintage Books, 2008.

Lowenstein, R. *When Genius Failed*. New York: Random House, 2000.

Levitt, A. *Take on the Street: What Wall Street and Corporate America Don't Want You to Know*. New York: Pantheon Books, 2002.

Lewis, M. "How the Eggheads Cracked." *New York Times Magazine*, 24 January 1999, reprinted in M Lewis (ed), *Panic: The Story of Modern Financial Insanity*. London: Penguin Books, 2008.

Lucas, E. *The New Cold War*. New York: Palgrave Macmillan, 2008.
    Penguin Books Ltd, 2007.

Mace, M. L. *Directors: Myth and Reality*. Cambridge, MA: Harvard Business School Classics, 1971.

Marglin, S. *The Dismal Science: How Thinking Like an Economist Undermines Community*. Cambridge, MA: Harvard University Press, 2008.

Milbrath, L. *Environmentalists: Vanguards for a New Society*. New York: State University of New York Press, 1984.

Miller, T. and R. Holmes. *Heritage/Wall Street Journal Index of Economic Freedom*. New York: Heritage Foundation and Dow Jones and Company Inc., 2007.

Milhaupt, C. and K. Pistor. *Law and Capitalism: What Corporate Crises Reveal about Legal Systems and Economic Development around the World*. Chicago: University of Chicago Press, 2008.

Moran, M. *The British Regulatory State*. Oxford: Oxford University Press, 2003.

Morris, C. *The Trillion Dollar Meltdown*. Philadelphia PA: Perseus Books Group, 2007.

Muolo, P. and M. Padilla. *Chain of Blame: How Wall Street Caused the Mortgage and Credit Crisis*. Hoboken, NJ: John Wiley and Sons, 2008.

Nye, J. *Soft Power: The Means to Success in World Politics*. New York: Perseus Group, 2005.

O'Brien, J. *Wall Street on Trial*. Hoboken, NJ: John Wiley and Sons , 2003.

---. *Redesigning Financial Regulation*. England: John Wiley & Sons Ltd, 2007.

Rubin, R. *In An Uncertain World*. Jacob Weisberg Books, 2003.
Scott, R. *Organizations, Rational, Natural and Open Systems*. NJ: Prentice- Hall Incorporated, 2003.
Schumpeter, J. *Capitalism, Socialism, and Democracy*. Harper Collins Publishers, 1943.
Sennett, R. *The Culture of the New Capitalism*. New Haven: Yale University Press, 2006.
Shiller, R. *The Sub-Prime Solution*. Princeton, NJ: Princeton University Press, 2008.
Sinclair, T. *The New Masters of Capital*. Ithaca, NY: Cornell University Press, 2005. 61–9
Soros, G. *The New Paradigm of Financial Regulation*. Public Affairs, 2008.
Stiglitz, J. *The Roaring Nineties*. London: Penguin Books Ltd, 2003.
Stone, C. *Where The Law Ends: The Social Control of Corporate Behavior*. New York: Harper and Row, 1975.
Taleb, N. *The Black Swan: The Impact of the Highly Improbable*. London:

MEDIA REPORTS

"A Conspiracy Theory Debunked." (Editorial.) *Wall Street Journal*, 20 December 2008, A14.
Abrams, P. "Loopholes v Earmarks." *Huffington Post* (Washington), 6 October 2008 (Online Edition).
Al Suwaidi, H. and D. Murray. Co-Chairs of International Working Group Drafting Group and Under Secretary of the Abu Dhabi Department of Finance on release of Santiago Principles, http://www.iwg-swf.org/tr.htm 2 September 2008.
Arnold, M. "Wealth Funds Fill Bank Gap for Buy-Out Groups." *Financial Times*, 28 February 2008, 1.
Barber, L. and T. Walker. "Barroso Protectionism Alert." *Financial Times*, 3 March 2008, 1.
Barnett, M. "An Einhorn in Her Side." *Portfolio*, 23 May 2008 (Online Edition).
---. "I Am Short-Seller, Hear Me Roar." *Portfolio*, 12 June 2008 (Online Edition).
Bayh, E. "Time for Sovereign Wealth Fund Rules." *Wall Street Journal*, 13 February 2008, A2.
Bear Stearns. "Press Release." New York, 14 March 2008.
BBC News. "Brown to Announce Bank Bailout Plan." 18 January 2009.
---. "Dubai Fund Hits Back at Criticism." 29 February 2008.
---. "UK Banking Plan Faces Criticism." 19 January 2009.
---. "US Law Makers Publish Rescue Plan." 28 September 2008.
---. "US to Host Global Finance Summit." 19 October 2008.
Berkshire Hathaway, *Letter to Shareholders*. 2003.
Berman, D. "On the Street, Disbelief and Resignation." *Wall Street Journal*, 9 December 2008, C3.
Blankfein, L. "Do Not Destroy the Essential Catalyst of Risk." *Financial Times*, 9 February 2009, 13.
Boyer, P. "Eviction." *The New Yorker*, 24 November 2008, 48.
Brennan, J. "Quinn Admits He Was Too Greedy as Losses Hit Euro 1 billion." *Irish Independent*, 31 January 2009, 2.
Brennan, N. "Quinn Says He Did No Wrong in Anglo Share Deal. For the Moment I Am Sceptical." *Irish Independent*, 31 January 2009, 25.
Bull, A. "Lehman Failure Seen as Straw Which Broke Credit Market." *The Guardian*, 9 October 2008 (Online Edition).

Burton, J. "Wealth Funds Exploit Credit Squeeze." *Financial Times*, 24 March 2008, 18.

Cassidy, J. "Anatomy of a Meltdown." *New Yorker*, 1 December 2008, 49.

Chan, C. "Citic Pacific Bail-Out Is Best Option, Says Chairman." *South China Morning Post*, 20 December 2008, A2.

Coorey, P. and P. Hartchner. "Rudd Snubs Reserve Bank." *Sydney Morning Herald*, 28 January 2009, 1.

Cox, C. "We Need a Bailout Strategy." *Wall Street Journal*, 11 December 2008, A16.

Chung, J. "Systemic Failure Turns More Ire on SEC." *Financial Times*, 15 December 2008, 18.

Chung, J. "Senator Probes SEC Role in Bear Rescue." *Financial Times*, 23 October 2008, 2.

Connors, E. "Future Fund Chief Sees Day Of Reckoning For Banks." *Australian Financial Review*, 14 January 2008, 1, 38.

Cornell, A. "Smith Calm as Others Lose Heads." *Australian Financial Review*, 19 February 2008, 52.

Craig, S. "Lehman's Straight Shooter." *Wall Street Journal*, 17 May 2008 (Online Edition).

Crittenden, M. and D. Solomon. "Watchdog Says US Overpaid For Troubled Assets." *Wall Street Journal*, 6 February 2009, C3.

Daneshkhu, S. "Latest Controversial Trading Bet Brings French Banks Into Question." *Financial Times*, 18 October 2008, 9.

Dash, E. and J. Creswell. "Citigroup Saw No Red Flags Even As It Made Bolder Bets." *New York Times*, 23 November 2008, A1.

Davis, B. "China Investment-Fund Head Says Focus is on Portfolios." *Wall Street Journal*, 1 February 2008, A13.

Doyle, D. "Irish Outlook 'Appropriate' After Cuts Moody's Says", *Bloomberg*, 4 May.

Duhigg, C. "Pressured to Take More Risk, Fannie Reached Tipping Point." *New York Times*, 5 October 2008, A1.

Efrati, A. "Former Enron Prosecutor Speaks Out: Criminal Charges Shouldn't Be So Easy." *Wall Street Journal*, 21 November 2008 (Online Edition).

---. "Are Borrowers Free to Lie." *Wall Street Journal*, 31 May 2008, B2.

Eisinger, J. "Diary of a Short Seller." *Portfolio*, 12 May 2008 (Online Edition).

Enrich, D., R. Sidel and S. Craig. "World Rides to Wall Street Rescue." *Wall Street Journal*, 16 January 2008, A1.

Farrell, G. "Goldman Hit By Quarterly Loss." *Financial Times*, 17 December 2008, 13.

Financial Services Authority. "Financial Services Authority Introduces Disclosure Regime for Significant Short Positions in Companies Undertaking Rights Issues." Press Release, London, 13 June 2008.

Fitzpatrick, D., S. Craig and C. Mollenkamp. "Thain Ousted in Clash at Bank of America." *Wall Street Journal*, 26 January 2009, A1.

Frank, B. "Statement on GAO TARP Report." Press Release, Washington, DC, 3 December 2008.

Freed, J. "Sinosteel Gets Control But Likely to Have Company at Midwest." *Sydney Morning Herald*, 8 July 2008 (Online edition).

Gapper, J. "Wall Street Insiders and Fools Gold." *Financial Times*, 18 December 2008, 9.

Gongcheng, W. CP Mining Management Pty Ltd. Interview, Beijing, 5 September 2008.

Government Statement on Financial Support, Department of Treasury. Press Release, London, 8 October 2008.

Gow, D. "Mandelson Calls for IMF Reform and a Voice for New Champions." *The Guardian*, 29 September 2008 (Online Edition).

Greenspan, A. "We Will Never Have a Perfect Model of Risk." *Financial Times*, 17 March 2008, 13.

Greider, W. "Economic Free Fall." *The Nation*, 18 August 2008, 18.

Guerrera, F., B. White and K. Guha. "Wall Street Rescues Bear Stearns." *Financial Times*, 15 March 2008.

Guerrera, F. "Morgan Stanley Hit by 'Savage' Downturn." *Financial Times*, 18 December 2008, 16.

Guha, K. and A. Beattie. "Pressure Builds For Action On Bank Crisis." *Financial Times*, 22 January 2009, 3.

Halvorsen, K. "Sovereign Wealth Funds as Serious Financial Investors." *Financial Times*, 15 February 2008.

Henriques, D. "Anger and Drama at a House Hearing on Madoff." *New York Times*, 5 February 2009.

Holm, E. and H. Son. "AIG Host with Most to Explain." *Sydney Morning Herald*, 11 October 2008, 42.

Hughes, J. "Mortgage Fraud Crackdown on Brokers." *Financial Times*, 19 July 2008, 1.

Ibison, D. "Citigroup Promises to Compensate Japanese Clients." *Financial Times*, 30 November 2004 (Online Edition).

Jolly, D. "Belgium to Fight Ruling on Plan to Sell Fortis." *International Herald Tribune*, 17 December 2008, 11.

JP Morgan and Bear Stearns. "Revised JPM-BSC Deal." Press Release, New York City, 2 March 2008.

Kelly, O. "Dunne Denied Permission For Ballsbridge Project." *Irish Times*, 31 January 2009, 8.

Kelly, K., S. Ng, and J. Strasburg. "In Dealing with Bear Stearns Wall Street Plays Guardedly." *Wall Street Journal*, 13 March 2008, C1.

Kelly, G., G. Ip and R. Sidel. "Fed Races to Save Bear Stearns In Bid to Steady Financial System." *Wall Street Journal*, 15 March 2008, A1.

Kenna, C. "Financial Regulator Believes It Was Misled By Anglo," *Irish Times*, 20 February 2009, 1.

Kirchgaessner, S. "Profligacy of AIG's Executives Draws Fire." *Financial Times*, 8 October 2008, 3.

---. "US Insiders Point to Bain Errors over 3Com." *Financial Times*, 4 March 2008, 30

---. "Washington Obstacle Course Sees Chinese Companies Re-Examine Their US Ambitions." *Financial Times*, 4 March 2008, 30.

Kolhatkar, S. "Wall Street's Most Powerful Woman." *Portfolio*, April 2008 (Online Edition).

Kramer, A. "As Gazprom's Chairman Moves Up, So Does Russia's Most Powerful Company." *International Herald Tribune*, 11 May 2008 (Online Edition).

Kristol, W. "A Fine Mess." *New York Times*, 22 September 2008, A29.

Krugman, P. "Cash for Trash." *New York Times*, 22 September 2008, A29.

Labaton, S. "Agency's '04 Rule Let Banks Pile Up New Debt." *New York Times*, 3 October 2008, A1.

---. "Yet Another Blow to SEC's Reputation." *International Herald Tribune*, 17 December 2008, 11.

Landler, M. and E. Dash. "Drama Behind a $250 Billion Banking Deal." *New York Times*, 15 October 2008 (Online Edition).

Lee, Y. and L. Santini. "CITIC Pacific May Face Big Hit on Currency Wagers Gone Bad." *Wall Street Journal*, 21 October 2008, C2.

Levy, C. and S. Kishkovsky. "Fight Over TNK-BP Revives Worries About Kremlin." *International Herald Tribune*, 17 June 2008, 13.

Lewis, M. "The End of Wall Street's Boom." *Portfolio*, November 2008 (Online Edition).

Lewis, M. and D. Einhorn. "The End of the Financial World as We Know It." *New York Times*, 4 January 2009, B1.

MacKensie, M., N. Bullock, and D. Brewster. "Investors Reel From Punishing Month." *Financial Times*, 1 November 2008, 1.

Madden, C. "Quinn Admits His Family Lost 1 Billion in Anglo." *Irish Times*, 31 January 2009, 19.

Maley, K. "Life on the Margin: How Green Blew Up Babcock," *Australian Financial Review*, 20 February 2009, 1.

Maley, P. "Car Dealers Saved by $2 Billion Financing Package." *The Australian*, 5 December 2008, 1.

McDonald, F. "How An Board Pleanala Shot Down Dunne Plan and Buried Celtic Tiger." *Irish Times*, 31 January 2009, 8.

McDonald, D. "Crisis Caused By Negligence and Incredible Stupidity." (Letter to Editor), *Financial Times*, 24 October 2008, 10.

McDonald, A. and C. Bryan-Low. "Turmoil Batters London's Status as Financial Center." *Wall Street Journal*, 22 October 2008, A1.

McGee, H. "Cowen Says Recession to Cut Living Standards by Over 10%." *Irish Times*, 6 February 2009, 1.

McKinnon, J. and J. Stoll. "US Throws Lifeline to Detroit." *Wall Street Journal*, 20 December 2008, A1.

Miller, J. "Belgium's Government Offers to Resign Over Fortis." *Wall Street Journal*, 20 December 2008, A8.

Moffett, M. "Brazil Joins Front Rank of New Economic Powers." *Wall Street Journal*, 13 May 2008, A1.

Mollenkamp, C., D. Solomon, R. Sidel, and V. Bauerlein. "How London Created a Snarl in Global Markets." *Wall Street Journal*, 18 October 2007, A1.

Morgenson, G. "Bear Stearns Says Battered Hedge Funds Are Worth Little." *New York Times*, 18 July 2007, A1.

---. "Behind Insurers Crisis, Blind Eye to a Web of Risk." *New York Times*, 27 September 2008, B1.

---. "House Panel Scrutinizes Rating Firms," *New York Times,* 23 October 2008, B1.

---. "How the Thundering Herd Faltered and Fell." *New York Times*, 9 November 2008, A1.

Munter, P. "Citigroup Says Bond Traders Miscalculated." *Financial Times*, 2 February 2005 (Online Edition).

Murdoch, S. "Macquarie's Woes Deepen." *The Australian*, 9 January 2009, 15.

Nakamoto, M. and D. Wighton. "Bullish Citigroup is 'Still Dancing' to the Beat of the Private Equity Boom." *Financial Times*, 10 July 2007.

Neil, A. "Why It's Looking Black For Conrad." *The Scotsman*, 25 November 2006 (Online Edition).

Nocera, J. "Diary of a Monumental Nightmare." *Australian Financial Review*, 3 October 2007, 64.

---. "As Credit Crisis Spiralled, Alarm Led to Action." *New York Times*, 2 October 2008, A1.

Nocera, J. and E. Andrews. "Struggling to Keep Up as the Crisis Raced On." *New York Times*, 23 October 2008, A1.

Norris, F. "A New Kind of Bank Run Tests Old Safeguards." *New York Times*, 10 August 2007 (Online Edition).

Norwegian Ministry of Finance. "The Government Pension Fund Divests its Holding in Mining Firm." Press Release, Oslo, 10 September, 2008.

Otaiba, Y. "Our Sovereign Wealth Plans." *Wall Street Journal*, 19 March 2008, A16.

Pagnamenta, R. "Harassed TNK-BP Chief Quits Russia." *The Australian*, 26 July 2008, 39.

Paletta, D., J. Hilsenrath, and D. Solomon. "At Moment of Truth, US Forced Big Bankers to Blink." *Wall Street Journal*, 15 October 2008 (Online Edition).

Parker, G., L. Barber, and J. Eaglesham. "Brown Orders British Banks to Come Clean." *Financial Times*, 17 January 2009, 1.

Parker, G. and J. Pickard. "Brown Goes on the Road to Sell Rescue Plan to Skeptical Voters." *Financial Times*, 10 October, 2008, 3.

Parker, G., T. Barber, and B. Benoit. "Barroso Tells EU Leaders to Avoid Protectionism." *Financial Times*, 31 January 2008, 1.

Politi, J. "Senators Question Bank Oversight Plan." *Financial Times*, 24 October 2008, 6.

Politi, J. "US Grapples With Shift of Mood in Jobs Markets." *Financial Times*, 24 October 2008, 6.

Prepared Statement by SEC Chairman Designate, Senate Banking, Housing, and Urban Affairs. Washington, DC: 15 January 2009 (M Shapiro).

President's Working Group on Financial Markets. *Policy Statement on Financial Market Developments*. Washington, DC, March 2008.

"President Bush Discusses Administration's Plans to Assist Automakers." Press Conference, Washington, DC, 19 December 2008.

"President-Elect Obama Names Key Regulatory Appointments." Chicago: Press Conference, 18 December 2008.

Quinn, E. "Developers Lost E6 Billion Gambling on Stocks with Controversial Wagers." *Sunday Tribune* (Dublin), 1 February 2009, B1.

---. "The Power of One." *Sunday Tribune*, 1 February 2009, B5.

Randall, J. "When the Going Gets Tough, Banks Yell for Nanny." *Daily Telegraph* (London), 26 March 2008 (Online edition).

Reed, J. "Crisis Has Resulted From Honest Misjudgments by Finance Sector." (Letter to Editor), *Financial Times*, 21 October 2008, 14.

Reilly, D. "Citigroup to Take $25 Million Hit in Dr Evil Case." *Wall Street Journal*, 29 June 2005, C3.

Rogers, J. "View of the Day." *Financial Times*, 22 January 2009, 25.

Ruan, V. "China's Investment Fund Pushes Back." *Wall Street Journal*, 7 March 2008, A6.

Rudd, K. "The Children of Gordon Gekko." *The Australian*, 6 October 2008, 12.

Scannell, K. "SEC Watchdog Faults Agency in a Bear Case." *Wall Street Journal*, 11 October 2008, B6.

Schwartzman, S. "Reject Sovereign Wealth Funds at Your Peril." *Financial Times*, 20 June 2008, 13.

Securities and Exchange Commission. "Broker-Dealer and Affiliate Supervision on Consolidated Basis." Washington, DC: Press Release, 28 April 2004.

Securities and Exchange Commission. "Chairman Cox Announces End of Consolidated Entity Program." Washington, DC: Press Release, 28 September 2008.

Securities and Exchange Commission, Emergency Order. Release No. 58166, Washington, DC: 15 July 2008.

Senate Committee on Banking, Housing, and Urban Affairs. "Dodd Commends Administration's Announcement on Executive Pay." Washington, DC: Press Release, 4 February 2009.

Shear, M. "With Bailout Vote, McCain Voted For Earmarks." *Washington Post*, 3 October 2008 (Online Edition).

Sleiman, M. and A. Critchlow. "Dubai Firm's Chief Says Citigroup Needs More Cash" *Wall Street Journal*, 4 March 2008 (Online edition).

Smith, R. "Citigroup CEO Pursues Culture of Ethics." *Wall Street Journal*, 2 March 2005 (Online Edition).

"Son of Tarp Follows in Father's Footsteps." (Editorial.) *Financial Times*, 11 February 2009, 12.

"Starting the Regulatory Work." (Editorial.) *New York Times*, 7 January 2009, A14.

"Statement of the 27 European Heads of State and Government on the Stability of the Financial System." Brussels: Press Release, 6 October 2008.

Stephens, P. "Uncomfortable Truths for a New World of Them and Us." *Financial Times*, 30 May 2008, 9.

Strauss-Kahn, D. Press Conference, International Monetary Fund, Washington, DC, 11 October 2008.

Stutchbury, M. "Swan's Line in the Sand Risks Turning Chinese Investors Away." *The Australian*, 5 September 2008 (Online Edition).

Sutherland R, et al. "Inside the Hunt for the City's Bank Raiders." *The Observer*, 23 March 2008, 22–3.

Thain, J. "Memo to Merrill Lynch Staff." *Wall Street Journal* 26 January 2009.

Thal Larsen, P., C. Hughes, and D. Shellock. "Banks' Cash Calls Shunned." *Financial Times*, 19 July 2008, 1.

Toobin, J. "Barney's Great Adventure." *The New Yorker*, 12 January 2009, 37.

United States Sentencing Commission, Guidelines Manual Section 8C2.5, Commentary Note 12, November 2004.

Uren, D. and S. Parnell. "Banks Turn to Future Fund." *The Australian*, 7 October 2008, 1.

Wachman, R. "HBOS 4bn Rights Issue is Massive Flop." *The Observer*, 20 July 2008, 1.

Walker, T. "APEC Talks 'Confronting.'" *Australian Financial Review*, 25 November 2008, 10.

Ward, A. "Republicans Face Battle for Party's Ideological Soul." *Financial Times*, 18 December 2008, 4.

Warren, E. and A. Warren Tyagi. "Protect Financial Consumers." *Harpers*, November 2008, 39.

White House. "Citation for 2005 Presidential Medal of Freedom." Washington, DC: Press Release, 9 November 2005.

---. "President Appoints Dr. Ben Bernanke for Chairman of the Federal Reserve." Washington, DC: Press Release, 24 October 2005.

---. "Presidential Medal of Freedom Recipients." Washington, DC: Press Release, 3 November 2005.

Wilson, P. "Europe Wants US Power Shift". *The Australian*, 1 October 2008, 36.

Wolf, M. "Why Obama's New Tarp Will Fail to Rescue the Banks." *Financial Times*, 11 February 2009, 13.

Wong, E. "An Emboldened China Scolds US Over Economy." *International Herald Tribune*, 17 June 2008, 1.

REPORTS
Anglo Irish Bank Annual Report (2008).

Basel Committee on Banking Supervision, *International Convergence on Capital Measurement and Capital Standards*. June 2006.

Berkshire Hathaway Annual Report. 2008.

Breeden, R. "Restoring Trust": Report to The Hon. Jed S. Rakoff The United States District Court For the Southern District of New York On Corporate Governance For The Future of MCI, Inc." New York, 2003.

---. "Report of Special Investigation by the Special Committee of the Board of Directors of Hollinger International." Washington, DC, 30 August 2004.

Commission of the European Communities. *A Common European Approach to Sovereign Wealth Funds*. 27 February 2008.

Committee on Capital Markets Regulation. *Interim Report*. 2006.

Congressional Oversight Panel. "Accountability for the Troubled Asset Relief Program." Second Report, Washington, DC, 9 January 2009.

Dell'Ariccia, G., D. Igan, and L. Laeven. "Credit Booms and Lending Standards: Evidence from the Sub-Prime Mortgage Market." Washington, DC: International Monetary Fund, DC, WP/08/06, April 2008.

Financial Services Authority (UK). *Annual Report* (2007/8).

Financial Stability Forum. "Observations on Risk Management Practices during the Recent Market Turbulence." Basel, 6 March 2008.

---. *Report of Financial Stability Forum on Enhancing Market and Institutional Resilience*. Basel, 12 April 2008.

Government Accountability Office. "Defense Trade: Mitigating National Security Concerns under Exon-Florio Could Be Improved." GAO-02-736, Washington, DC, 12 September 2002.

---. "Investment Banks: The Role of Firms and Their Analysts with Enron and Global Crossing." Washington, DC, March 2003, 39.

---. "Defense Trade: Enhancements to the Implementation of Exon-Florio Could Strengthen the Law's Effectiveness." GAO-05-686, Washington, DC, 28 September 2005.

---. "Foreign Investment: Laws and Policies Regulating Foreign Investment in 10 Countries." Washington, DC, February 2008.

---. "Troubled Asset Relief Program." GAO-09-61, Washington, DC, December 2008.

International Monetary Fund. *Report of the Executive Board to the Board of Governors, Reform of Quota and Voice in the International Monetary Fund.* Washington, DC, 28 March 2008.

---. *Europe: Dealing with Shocks.* Washington, DC, October 2008.

Joint Committee on Taxation. "Report of Investigation of Enron Corporation and Related Entities Regarding Federal Tax and Compensation Issues and Policy Recommendations." Washington, DC, February 2003.

McKinsey Report. *Sustaining New York's and the US' Global Financial Services Leadership.* 2007.

Norges Bank Investment Management Annual Report. 2007.

Norwegian Ministry of Finance. *On the Management of the Government Pension Fund in 2006.* Report No 24.

OECD. *Sovereign Wealth Funds and Recipient Country Policies.* Paris, 4 April 2008.

---. *Protection of "Critical Infrastructure" and the Role of Investment Policies Relating to National Security.* Paris, May 2008.

---. *Transparency and Predictability for Investment Policies Addressing National Security Concerns: A Survey of Practices.* Paris, May 2008.

Office of Inspector General. *SEC's Oversight of Bear Stearns and Related Entities: The CSE Program.* Report No 446-A. Washington, DC, 25 September 2008.

Powers, W. "Report of Investigation by the Special Investigative Committee of the Board of Directors of Enron Corporation." Houston, 1 December 2002.

PriceWaterhouseCoopers, "Project Atlas: Anglo Irish Bank" (Edited Extracts). Dublin, 20 February 2009.

Rethinking Regulation. Report of the Taskforce on Reducing the Regulatory Burden on Business. Canberra: Commonwealth of Australia, 2006.

Staff Report to Senate Committee on Government Affairs. "Financial Oversight of Enron: The SEC and Private Sector Watchdogs." Washington, DC, 8 October 2002.

Walker Working Group, *Guidelines for Disclosure and Transparency in Private Equity* 2007.

EVIDENCE BEFORE COMMITTEES

Congressional Oversight Panel for Economic Stabilization. "Questions About the $700 Billion Emergency Economic Stabilization Funds." Washington, DC, 10 December 2008.

Evidence to House Committee on Financial Services. Washington, DC, 21 October 2008 (S. Bartlett).

---. "Hearing on Foreign Government Investment in the US Economy and Financial Sector." Washington, DC, 5 March 2008 (G. Alvarez).

---. "Hearing on Foreign Government Investment in the US Economy and Financial Sector." Washington, DC, 5 March 2008 (S. Israel).

---. "Hearing on Foreign Government Investment in the US Economy and Financial Sector." Washington, DC, 5 March 2008 (M. Skancke).

---. "Regulatory Restructuring and the Reform of the Financial System." Washington, DC, 21 October 2008 (J. Stiglitz).

---. "Hearing on Foreign Government Investment in the US Economy and Financial Sector." Washington, DC, 5 March 2008 (E. Tafari).

---. "Hearing on Assessing the Madoff Ponzi Scheme and Regulatory Failures." Washington, DC, 11 February 2009 (H. Markopolos).

---. "Hearing on Assessing the Madoff Ponzi Scheme and Regulatory Failures." Washington, DC, 11 February 2009 (A. Donohue, L. Richards, E. Sirri, L. Chatman Thomsen, A. Vollmer).

---. "Hearing on Systemic Risk: Examining Regulators Ability to React to Threats in the Financial System." Washington, DC, 2 October, 2007 (R. Kuttner).

Evidence to House Committee on Oversight and Government Reform. "Hearing on the Causes and Effects of the AIG Bailout." Washington, DC, 7 October 2008 (E. Dinallo) 4.

---. "Hearing on the Role of Federal Regulators in the Financial Crisis." Washington, DC, 23 October 2008 (A. Greenspan).

---. "Hearing on the Credit Rating Agencies and the Financial Crisis." Washington, DC 22 October 2008 (F. Raiter).

---. "Hearing on Collapse of Fannie Mae and Freddie Mac." Washington, DC, 9 December 2008 (T. Stanton).

---. "Hearing on the Role of Federal Regulators in the Financial Crisis." Washington, DC, 23 October 2008 (J. Snow).

---. "Hearing on the Causes and Effects of the Lehman Brothers Bankruptcy." Washington, DC, 6 October 2008 (R. Fuld).

---. "Hearing on the Collapse of Fannie Mae and Freddie Mac." Washington, DC, 9 December 2008 (C. Calomiris).

Evidence to US Senate Committee on Banking, Housing, and Urban Affairs. Washington, DC, 3 April 2008 (C. Cox).

---. Washington, DC, 23 September 2008 (C. Cox).

---. Washington DC, 23 September 2008 (B. Bernanke and H. Paulson).

Evidence to "Hearing on Banking Crisis." Treasury Select Committee, Westminster, 10 February 2009 (A. Hornby).

House of Commons Treasury Committee. "The Run on the Rock." London: The Stationery Office, 2008.

Hornby, A. and Lord Stevenson. "Memo to Treasury Select Committee." Westminster, 10 February 2009.

"Memorandum from Lloyds Banking Group, Treasury Select Committee." Westminster, 10 February 2009, 42.

Moore, P. "Memo to Treasury Select Committee" Westminster, 10 February 2009.

Opening Statement. "Hearing on Mortgage Market Turmoil: Causes and Consequences." Senate Committee on Banking, Housing and Urban Affairs, Washington, DC, 22 March 2007 (C. Dodd).

Opening Statement. "Hearing on the Causes and Effects of the Lehman Brothers Bankruptcy." House Committee on Oversight and Government Reform, Washington, DC, 6 October (H. Waxman).

Opening Statement. "Hearing on the Causes and Effects of the Lehman Brothers Bankruptcy." House Committee on Oversight and Government Reform. Washington, DC, 6 October (T. Davis).

Opening Statement. "Hearing on the Causes and Effects of the AIG Bailout." House Committee on Oversight and Government Reform, Washington, DC, 7 October 2008 (H. Waxman).

Opening Statement. "Hearing on the Credit Rating Agencies and the Financial Crisis." House Committee on Oversight and Government Reform, Washington, DC, 22 October 2008 (H. Waxman).

Opening Statement. "Hearing on Collapse of Fannie Mae and Freddie Mac." House Committee on Oversight and Government Reform, Washington, DC, 9 December 2008 (H. Waxman).

Opening Statement. Hearing on Nominees for SEC, CEA and Fed, Washington, DC, 15 January 2009 (C. Dodd).

SPEECHES

Al Suwaidi, H. Press Conference, International Working Group on Sovereign Wealth Fund Regulation, Santiago, 2 September 2008.

Allen, J. "Performance Measurement for Securities Supervisors: Report on the Findings of a Workshop on the Balanced Scorecard." Speech delivered at Toronto Centre for Leadership in Financial Supervision, 8–14 July 2007.

Aslund, A. "Russia Energy and the European Union: Perspective on Gazprom." Speech delivered at the European Peoples' Party, European Parliament, Brussels, 15 May 2008.

Bernanke, B. "Risk Management in Financial Institutions." Speech delivered at Federal Reserve Bank of Chicago, Chicago, 15 May 2008.

---. "Stabilizing the Financial Markets and the Economy." Speech delivered at the Economic Club of New York, New York City, 15 October 2008.

Brown, G. "The Global Economy." Speech delivered at Reuters Building, London, 13 October 2008.

Cowen, B. Speech delivered at the Chamber of Commerce Annual Dinner, Dublin, 5 February 2009.

Donaldson, W. Speech delivered at Business Roundtable, Washington, DC, 14 October 2004.

Glassman, C. "Sarbanes-Oxley and the Idea of Good Governance." Speech delivered at American Society of Corporate Secretaries, Washington, DC, 27 September 2002.

Geithner, T. "The Current Financial Challenges: Policy and Regulatory Implications." Speech delivered at Council on Foreign Relations, New York, 6 March 2008.

---. "Reducing Systemic Risk in a Dynamic Financial System." Speech at Economic Club of New York, 9 June 2008.

---. "Remarks Introducing the Financial Stability Plan." Speech delivered at US Department of the Treasury, Washington, DC, 10 February 2009.

Gjedrem, S. "Ethics and the Government Pension Fund – Global." Speech delivered at "Investing for the Future Conference," Oslo, 16 January 2008.

Goldschmid, H. "A Lawyer's Role in Corporate Governance: The Myth of Absolute Confidentiality and the Complexity of the Counselling Task." Speech delivered at the Association of the Bar of the City of New York, New York City, 17 November 2003.

Greenspan, A. "Understanding Household Debt Obligations." Speech delivered at Credit Union National Association Annual Conference, Washington, DC, 23 February 2004.

---. "Banking." Speech delivered at American Bankers' Association, New York City, 5 October 2004.

---. "The Mortgage Market and Consumer Debt." Speech delivered at America's Community Bankers Annual Convention, Washington, DC, 19 October 2004.

Levitt, A. "The Numbers Game." Speech delivered at Center for Law and Business, New York University, 28 September 1998.

Lipsky, J. "Dealing with the Financial Turmoil: Contingent Risks, Policy Challenges and the Role of the IMF." Speech delivered to the Peterson Institute, Washington, DC, 12 March 2008.

Lomax, R. "'The State of the Economy." Speech delivered at the Institute of Economic Affairs, London, 26 February 2008.

Lowery, C. "Sovereign Wealth Funds and the International Financial System." Speech delivered at Asian Financial Crisis Revisited Conference, Federal Reserve Bank of San Francisco, San Francisco, 21 June 2007.

McCreevy, C. "The Credit Crisis and its Aftermath." Speech delivered at Society of Business Economists, London, 6 February 2008.

---. "International Financial Crisis: Its Causes and What to Do About It." Speech delivered at Alliance of Liberals and Democrats for Europe, Brussels, 27 February 2008.

Murray, D. Press Conference, International Working Group on Sovereign Wealth Fund Regulation, Santiago, 2 September 2008.

Obama, B. "Inaugural Address." Washington, DC, 19 January 2009.

Philip, M. "Remarks Announcing Results of Operation Malicious Mortgage." Press Conference, Department of Justice, Washington, DC, 19 June 2008.

Paulson, H. "Remarks on the Competitiveness of US Capital Markets." Speech delivered at National Economic Club of New York, 20 November 2006.

Strauss-Kahn, D. "The IMF and its Future." Speech delivered at Banco de España, Madrid, 15 December 2008.

Swan, W. "Australia, China and This Asian Century." Speech delivered at Australia-China Business Council, Melbourne, 4 July 2008.

Wray, C. "Remarks to the ABA White Collar Crime Luncheon Club." Speech delivered at American Bar Association, Washington, DC, 25 February 2005.

Index